CNC Machining Handbook

**Basic Theory, Production Data,
and Machining Procedures**

CNC Machining Handbook

Basic Theory, Production Data,
and Machining Procedures

James Madison

Industrial Press Inc.
200 Madison Avenue
New York, NY 10016

Library of Congress Cataloging in Publication Data

Madison, James G., 1957–
    CNC machining handbook : basic theory, production data, and
machining procedures / James G. Madison. — 1st ed.
    400 p., 17.8 x 25.4 cm.
    ISBN 0-8311-3064-4
    1. Machine-tools—Numerical Control—Handbooks, manuals, etc.
I. Title
TJ1189.M236   1996
671.3'5 —dc20   96-11226
                                                CIP

INDUSTRIAL PRESS INC.
200 Madison Avenue
New York, New York 10016-4078

First Edition, 1996

CNC Machining Handbook

Contents

Part II   Programming CNC Machine Motions

Chapter 6 Milling- and Boring-Center Machine
                        Motions   **103**

Chapter 8 Subroutines and Compensation   **187**

PREFACE

This *CNC Handbook* is the most comprehensive and authoritative reference available today on CNC Machining Centers and their capabilities, commonly used CNC Commands, and CNC-related Tooling for the production of precision machined components. *The Handbook* is written for a broad range of users: programmers, engineers, operators, and management personnel. It provides a ready reference for CNC basic theory, production data, and machining procedures.

The up-to-date text is an overview of the CNC automated production process in the modern industrial environment. It presents a complete systems approach in both content and organization. Covered are the major areas of Milling, Boring, Turning, Grinding, and related CNC Tooling proven successful in these areas. The entire machining systems are analyzed from setup/tool-force dynamics to economic analysis of potential programming procedures.

Unique to this *Handbook* is the organization and reference method for Programming Commands. Individual CNC Commands are listed/referenced by graphical representation of the toolpaths and surfaces produced. Every generic command is cross-referenced by industry-standard CNC machine formats and illustrated by the surface, machine movement, or toolpath that results from using the individual commands.

Engineers, programmers, and operators will find this reference method especially useful when writing programs, editing programs, and searching for commands required by the machine movements and toolpaths in workpiece geometry. The programming formats are generally selected to encompass all of the popular Control manufacturer formats in use today.

This new comprehensive *Handbook* covers the powerful new generation of graphical user interface Controls that bring revolutionary capabilities into the machining world, as well as features that will be introduced to CNC technology in the near future. This state-of-the-art text is a helpful tool to allow the user of precision machining centers and high-rate material removal systems that are especially designed to increase productivity and decrease machining costs of complex components, to become better programmers and more successful in general.

Throughout, examples are given to help the user's understanding of the subject matter. The examples given will work verbatim for several popular CNC

Controls and may vary slightly for others. Specific words throughout the text are capitalized (*M*anual, *M*ode, *M*ill, *T*urn, *E*dit), to indicate machine commands, switch positions, or selected functions on the Control. Although specific machine functions may vary from machine to machine, the *Handbook* provides an invaluable guide for any user of Computer Numerical Control. This seminal reference work is the most comprehensive of its kind, and will prove invaluable to working professionals and students.

CNC Machining Handbook

**Basic Theory, Production Data,
and Machining Procedures**

Controlling Machines by CNC

Being cognizant of the types and uses of CNC machines, the preparation that goes into programming, the forms of machine motion, and the different types of compensation is essential to your success in the CNC field.

Part I explains and illustrates how CNC works, its objectives, the types of CNC systems, movements of axes, axes configurations, and relevant Control variations. The precision measuring and positioning of CNC are covered, as well as the major components of CNC, operating principles, and axis drives.

Programming languages, formats, types of positioning methods, and Control geometry capabilities all play important roles in the thorough understanding of the application of CNC to the machining world. Also covered are programming tool moves in absolute and incremental modes of positioning. Designing ideal toolpaths and the execution of ultraclose-tolerance machining operations by CNC and the proper procedure for each are documented.

CNC operation selection by choosing the best subroutines and Control features are topics covered, as well as interpreting complex print features and the accurate translation to Control capabilities, the application of Control features for machining Arcs, Curves, Elliptical Toolpaths, complex Contours and feature-to-feature machining are all well-documented and illustrated topics.

There are various ways to format CNC programs, some more productive for certain applications. The fact that there are varying codes used to accomplish the same purpose from one Control builder to the next means that the formatting of CNC programs for every type of Control is not possible. Format information is the data a CNC machine requires in a certain order to function properly. Program formatting also allows a high level of consistency from one program to the next. Methods shown in Part I demonstrate the most common way to format tne CNC program for the particular machine type being covered. Every significant format is presented in accurate, up-to-date conventions.

CHAPTER 1

CNC SYSTEMS

HOW CNC WORKS

Computer Numerical Control (CNC) is a computer-assisted process to control general-purpose machines from instructions generated by a processor and stored in a memory system or storage media (tape, disk, chip, etc.) for present use as well as future use. Numerical Control means precisely what the term implies—control by numbers. Controlling machines by numerical command has brought about a revolution in manufacturing. CNC can be adapted to any kind of machine or process that requires direction by human intelligence. This text deals directly with CNC Milling Centers, Turning Centers, Boring Machines, and Grinding Machines.

CNC is a specific form of control system where *position* is the principal controlled variable. Numerical values, representing desired positions of tools and symbolic information corresponding to secondary functions, are recorded in some form (tape, disk, network, etc.) where the information can be stored and revised indefinitely. Hard Drives, Tape Readers, and other converters transform this information into signals that ultimately operate servo-mechanisms on each axis of the machine whose motions are to be controlled.

CNC was originally applied to metalworking machinery: Mills, Drills, Boring Machines, and Punch Presses. It has expanded to other areas of metalworking including applications in Robotics, on cutoff machines, tube benders, grinders of many types, gear cutters, broaching machines, electromechanical machining, flame cutting, and welding. CNC is also used for inspection, drafting systems, electronics assembly machines, laser cutting and bonding processes, automatic testing systems, printing machinery, woodworking machinery, step-and-repeat photography, and garment-cutting equipment. Today, 32- and 64-bit-bus microprocessors directly coupled with production machine control systems are expanding both the application and the basic definition of numerical control.

Objectives

The primary basic objective for the application of CNC to metalworking operations was to reduce the cost for the production of machined parts. This objective has been achieved by CNC reducing programming time, increasing operational capability of the NC systems in place, and making the entire machining process more user-friendly. CNC also achieved this objective by reducing machining time, fixturing costs and tooling storage, increasing cutter life, and lowering the skills required to automatically produce precision machined components. Other advantages include substantially reduced setup time, increased product uniformity, and an overall reduction of other costs. CNC has enabled the accurate estimation of the production process. Historically, CNC permitted more efficient shop scheduling, exact cost prediction, higher facilities utilization, and a more rapid return on equipment investment compared with less sophisticated machine control techniques or manual operations.

Types of CNC Systems

CNC systems range from very simple to quite complex systems. Point-to-Point Control systems and Open-Loop Control systems provide no feedback to the control console and are almost nonexistent in CNC machining today.

Continuous-Path Control systems contain computing elements (interpolators) that permit computation of successive points on desired line segments or curves, starting with minimal input data, such as end points, radii, and center coordinates. Interpolation may be Linear, Circular, or Parabolic. Continuous-Path Controls are also referred to as Contouring Controls.

Closed-Loop Control systems use position and velocity feedback. To control the dynamic behavior and final position of machine slides, a variety of position transducers of both the analog and digital types are employed. Synchros, Resolvers, and Linear Inductive Scales are some analog types. Binary Encoders, Rotary Pulsers, Linear Optical Scales, and Laser Interferometers are included among the digital devices.

The majority of CNC systems operate on the servo-mechanism, closed-loop principle. A closed-loop system incorporates a sensing device on the moving component of the machine to indicate the component's exact position as it moves. If a discrepancy is revealed between where the machine element should be and where it actually is, the sensing device signals the driving unit to make an adjustment, bringing the movable component to the exact location required.

In the closed-loop system, the taped instruction fed to the numerical control console can be compared to the file location command sent to the reading head in a disk drive of a computer. The feedback device of the closed-loop system indicates the actual position of the movable machine element, just as the reading head signals the computer it has located a file on the hard drive. And the machine tool's drive motor and worktable correspond to the components of the hard disk itself. The feedback circuit and the field of electronics have perhaps made the most significant contribution to the successful development of Numerical Control, and recent strides in computer speed and storage have tied everything together in the process, making possible the high rate of information exchange required.

Figure 1.1 illustrates the basic components of one common and popular electronic Closed-Loop Control System. The coded information contained on the storage medium (disk, tape) is converted in the Control to electronic pulses, where it is evaluated by the computer and the instructions are ultimately translated to electrical pulses that are sent directly to the machine-movement element. Each pulse is measured, controlled, and equivalent to a small incremental movement of the machine element (i.e., equaling revolution increments of

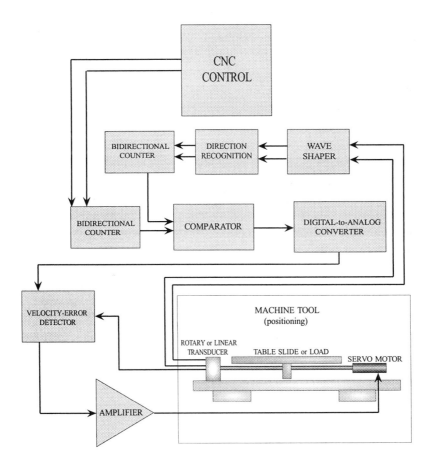

Figure 1.1 *CNC Closed-Loop Control System*

.0002", .0001", and .00004"). It is possible that pulses can be "lost" during the servo process, so they are converted to electric currents having a waveform similar to the common AC waveform.

A comparison is then done between the input wave pattern and an identical pattern generated by the feedback device. A phase *difference* between the two wave patterns, which indicates a positioning discrepancy, results in an adjusting current that activates the drive motor. As the motor adjusts the table or slide position, the "command" and feedback wave patterns move closer together until the table reaches the correct position, the phases of the two wave patterns coincide, and the current to the drive motor caused by the phase difference stops. The sequential move or machining operation then begins.

Machine tools such as milling machines that are used for contour milling and turning centers that remove material continuously from the surface of the workpiece use the continuous-path system. The objective is to continuously control a cutting tool that requires frequent changes in movement with respect to two or more machine axes simultaneously and that is in constant contact with the workpiece. The continuous-path system is more complex and requires a far greater input of detailed instructional information than point-to-point positioning systems. Therefore, the use of microcomputer controls has become indispensable for the programmer preparing instructions for machine tools controlled by a continuous-path system.

MOVEMENTS and MEASUREMENTS of CNC AXIS SYSTEMS

A system of rectangular coordinates, also called the "Cartesian Coordinate System," is the basis for measuring CNC machine-axis movement. All point positions are described in terms of distances from a common point called the Origin (X 0.000, Y 0.000, Z 0.000) and measured along certain mutually perpendicular dimension lines called Axes (two or more Axes). It is only necessary when describing the geometry of a part to locate every point of the part within a framework of three such major axes, called the X, Y, and Z axes. See Figure 1.2.

From an eye-level perspective centered on the Origin, the horizontal plane of a machining center is customarily represented as containing the X and Y axes. Measurements taken right on the Origin along the X axis in this plane are considered to be in a "plus X" direction (+X), and measurements taken to the left are in a "minus X" direction (−X). In the same plane (Z = 0), the Y axis with its "plus Y" and "minus Y" directions are established exactly 90° from the X axis. Perpendicular to both the X and Y axes is the third, or Z, axis, with its "plus Z" (+Z) and "minus Z" (−Z) directions.

The decimal inch system is commonly used in machine work throughout the United States, whereas the units of measurement along each of these three axes

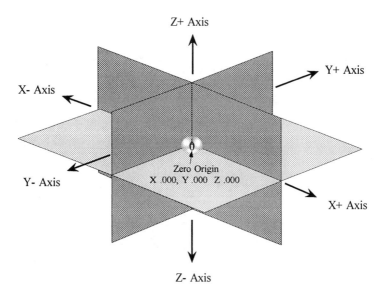

Figure 1.2 *The Cartesian Coordinate System of Measurement Used in CNC Machining*

can be chosen arbitrarily. This coordinate system is used to designate machine axes, and all programming for Numerical Control is based upon it. A *Metric Conversion Table*, for easy conversion of all values in this text, is shown on page 239.

Designation of the Machine Axis

The designation of the machine axis for each individualized type of machine tool is based on a rectangular coordinate system associated with the machine. The directions of motion indicated in Figure 1.3 are typical of the normal motions of milling machine travel. The longest motion that the machine axis is capable of traveling is generally designated as along, or parallel to, the X axis. Movement of the cutting tool in a single direction (normally to the right from a frontal viewpoint) is considered as "positive X" (+X), and movement in the opposite direction (left) is considered as "negative X" (–X). Lying horizontally from the point on the X axis (X = 0), and at an angle of exactly 90° to the X axis, is the Y axis with its positive and negative directions of motion in relation to the cutting tool, (+Y) (away from the frontal viewpoint) and (–Y) (back toward

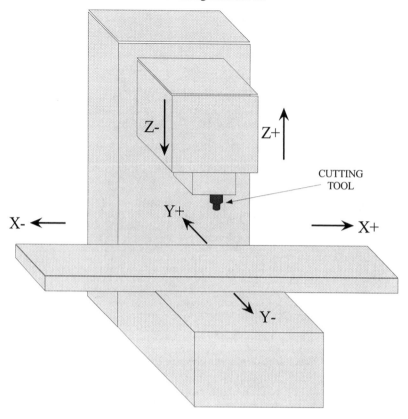

Figure 1.3 *Vertical Milling Machine CNC Axis Orientation*

the viewer), respectively. The motion of the table or head up or down (change in depth or Z level) is designated as along, or parallel, to the Z axis.

A typical configuration of axes for a CNC Turning Machine, or lathe, is shown in Figure 1.4. The X axis moves in a direction perpendicular to the "spindle plane." The X+ (positive) direction normally moves the cross-slide away from the operator/programmer's viewpoint, and the X– (negative) direction moves the cross-slide back toward the viewer. The Z+ (positive) direction of movement causes the carriage/turret/cross-slide to move away from the headstock spindle or workpiece, and the Z– (negative) direction in toward the workpiece.

Typically, spindle rotation is determined from a viewpoint centered from the X 0.0000 (Zero) position toward the center of the spindle. A Clockwise rotation is the C+ (positive) direction. A Counterclockwise rotation is the C– (negative) direction. Many new CNC Turning Machines are designed using a "Slant X Axis" feeding the cross-slide into the workpiece from a reverse position, requiring C+ *and* C– spindle rotation commands to be used in the program.

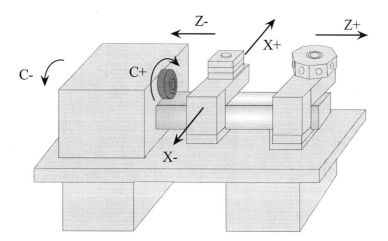

Figure 1.4 *CNC Turning Machine-Axis Orientation*

CNC CONTROL VARIATIONS

Three-Axis Controls

Three-axis CNC Controls are capable of two- and three-axis simultaneous machining. This is accomplished in two-axis combinations by feeding the table or cross-slide in the XY, XZ, or YZ planes in a predetermined path and distance from the machine spindle or headstock. See Figures 1.5(a) and 1.5(b).

In three-axis combinations, more complex surfaces can be machined. By moving the X, Y, and Z axes simultaneously, a precision controlled path can combine linear and circular geometry to form seamless workpiece features that previously required multioperation setups. See Figure 1.6.

Four- and Five-Axis Controls

Four- and five-axis CNC Controls provide multiple-axis machining capabilities beyond the standard three-axis CNC toolpath movements. Typically, the simultaneous contouring axes of a five-axis milling center include the three X, Y, and Z axes; the A axis, which is a rotary tilting of the spindle, or Z axis, parallel to the A axis; and the B axis, which can be a rotary index table or an additional tilting of the spindle parallel to the X axis. See Figure 1.7.

Five-axis turning capability is accomplished by the addition of other machin-

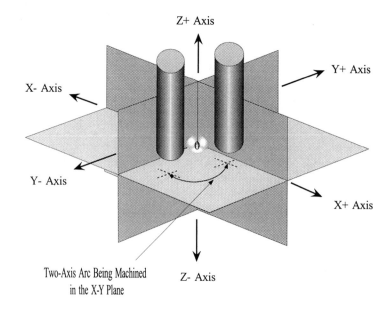

Figure 1.5(a) *Two-Axis Simultaneous Machining*

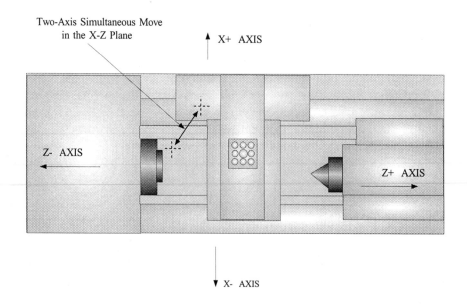

Figure 1.5(b) *Two-Axis Simultaneous Machining (Turning Machine)*

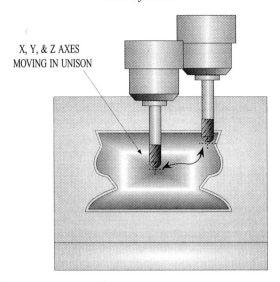

X, Y, & Z AXES
MOVING IN UNISON

Figure 1.6 *Milling Using a Three-Axis Combination Simultaneously*

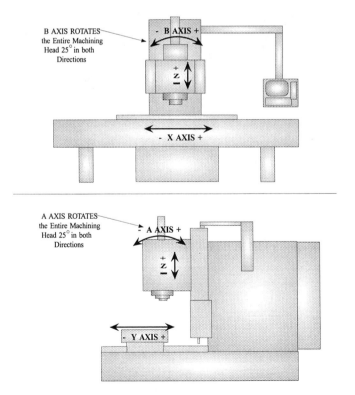

B AXIS ROTATES
the Entire Machining
Head 25° in both
Directions

- B AXIS +

+
Z
-

- X AXIS +

A AXIS ROTATES
the Entire Machining
Head 25° in both
Directions

- A AXIS +

+
Z
-

- Y AXIS +

Figure 1.7 *Four- and Five-Axle Orientation on a Milling Center*

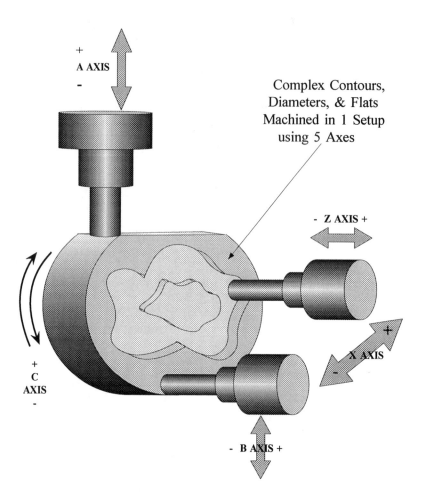

Figure 1.8 *Five-Axis Orientation of a CNC Turning Center*

ing axes and spindles to finish multiple machining operations while the workpiece is still clamped in the machine's headstock. Consider all of the machining
capabilities using every machining axis on the turning center in Figure 1.8.

CHAPTER 2

THE PRECISION MEASURING AND POSITIONING OF CNC

COMPONENTS of a CNC SYSTEM

In general, CNC systems can offer many advantages over conventional Numerical Control systems (traditionally built with hard-wire logic), including the elimination of (punched-) tape handling, the capability for on-line program revision, automatic correction of machine inaccuracies, the control of several machines from a single control center, and the capability for integration into a sophisticated total manufacturing control system.

Operating Principles

Many Closed-Loop Controls use velocity feedback as well as position feedback for two reasons: (1) to permit precise control of cutting feedrates and (2) to permit use of low-grain servos that reduce end-point overshoot, hunting, and other undesirable effects of high-gain servos.

The main components of a system are the Control, the Positioning mechanisms/devices, and the mechanical drive elements. The Control is responsible for managing the program data, reading them from media, computing any mathematical requirements of the processed commands, and sending output to the Positioning devices while reading and cross-checking feedback for accuracy. The Positioning devices are responsible for processing the signals sent from the Control, measuring the machine's movement to correspond to the commands sent, and sending feedback to the Control to verify moves made by the axis. The mechanical drive elements are the motors, positioning screws, and nuts and hardware that cause the particular axis to physically achieve the desired move sent from the Control.

The CNC Control includes a processor that completes all the mathematical calculations that a software application requires. The program is inputted through various media such as tape, disk, and network links, or for shorter programs, manual entry at the machine. The variable parameters of the program cause the software application to execute simple axis movements or complex subroutines, in turn, causing the machine axis to move.

The data is viewed through a conventional CRT, which displays the Program Blocks: individual command blocks that contain the instructional commands; positioning coordinates [0.0000"] for all the axes; axis feedrates for all axes (0.00 IPM) (0.00 °) for rotary tables and index positioners; and other machining parameters such as part #, job #, and machining time in the Program Data mode.

Low-voltage components such as the computer's processor and input keypad are coupled with higher-voltage components such as direct machine controls: feedrate overrides, cycle selections, start–stop controls, coolant controls, axis-control buttons. A typical Control is displayed in Figure 2.1, which shows individual components with their respective functions.

The Positioning devices include all of the components that ensure machine accuracy is achieved when an axis-move signal has been sent to the axis-drive servo-motors. The original signal for an axis to move is transmitted by counted pulses that actuate stepping motors. A specific number of pulses is known to move a drive motor (servo) in the clockwise or counterclockwise direction a known number of degrees. The servo-motor is hard-mounted on the end of a ground screw that is coupled with a recirculating ball-nut assembly. The recirculating ball-screw and nut assemblies allow zero screw backlash and corresponding error to enter the positioning process from screw reversal, wear, and mating-part differences.

The signal to move the X axis a required distance, such as +6.2000", for example, is converted to a number of pulses that is matched to the armature windings of the step motor. One typical revolution on a ground ball-screw is .200." The distance required for the move, therefore, is calculated by the control's computer and sent to the drive servo-motor for the X axis. Usually, if the smallest resolution of a machine move is .0002", one pulse will move the axis that amount. To index the stepping motor one revolution, or .200" of travel on the machine axis, 1000 pulses would have to be delivered to the motor. The required distance of a +6.2000 move, therefore, would need 30,000 individual pulses sent to the motor. (Reduction gearing on many stepping motors and pulse splitting [by powers of 10] reduce the number of actual pulses required.) See Figure 2.2.

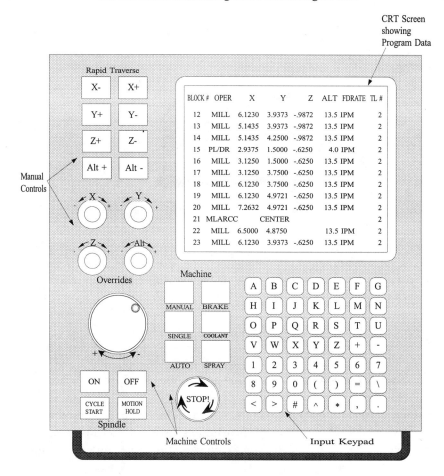

Figure 2.1 *CNC Control*

Once the pulses have been delivered to the servo, and the screw has been turned the desired number of rotations through counted pulses, the linear machine move must be cross-checked for error and possible adjustment. This is accomplished in most machine assemblies by Position Transducers. Rotary Encoders mounted on the end of axis screws are circular in shape. Linear Encoders that are mounted directly on machine axes span the length of the machine's travel for that axis and are the more accurate of the two types. Other types include laser-measured positioning systems that are the most accurate but not used on many cutting machines because of their delicacy and expense. Rotary Encoders or Position Transducers are used on lower-cost machines, but on larger precision machines, Linear Transducers must be used. Essentially incre-

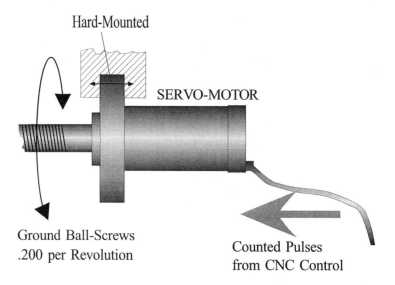

Hard-Mounted

SERVO-MOTOR

Ground Ball-Screws
.200 per Revolution

Counted Pulses
from CNC Control

Figure 2.2 *Pulses Sent to a Servo*

mental, Rotary Transducers can be changed to "absolute" by cascading several transducers through gear trains on a single axis.

Position Transducers operate on the sensing principle of passing objects. On the Rotary Encoder, an electric-eye proximity sensor, or laser-operated switch, is actuated or interrupted by divisions etched on the rotary disk hard-mounted to the machine screw. As the screw turns, the glass disk passes its divisions through the optical beam. On the glass disk are precision-etched divisions that trip the optical switch as the machine move is made. The computer counts the divisions and compares them to the required distance of the machine move made by the servo-motor. If they do not match the requirement, an adjustment is made. The move is cross-checked again until the desired comparison is reached. Problems can arise with the Rotary Transducer system because the reliance for linear accuracy is totally dependent upon the machine's positioning screws. Because every screw and nut has its inaccuracies, and wear over time, Rotary Encoders are usually found on inexpensive machines.

Linear Transducer Systems use sections of linear glass scales that span the entire length of each axis. The sensor, which is mounted on a component perpendicular to the linear scale, gives an actual position measurement in this configuration. The glass scales have precise etchings or demarcations that are inspected and traceable to the National Institute of Standards and Technology (formerly the National Bureau of Standards). They are normally assembled in 6" or 12" sections to the desired axis lengths, which make replacement of certain

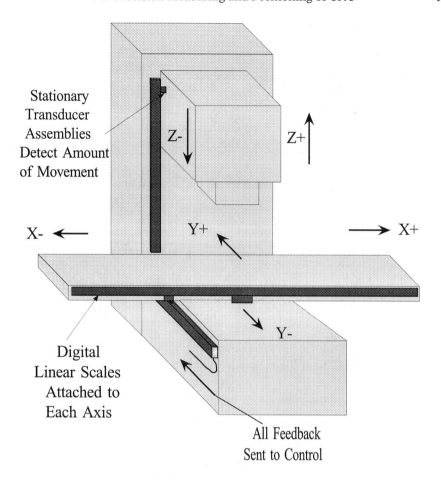

Stationary
Transducer
Assemblies
Detect Amount
of Movement

Z-

Z+

X-

Y+

X+

Y-

Digital
Linear Scales
Attached to
Each Axis

All Feedback
Sent to Control

Figure 2.3 *Vertical Milling Machine Linear Transducer System*

sections possible, instead of replacing long lengths of expensive scales. Sensors checking a long length of in-line (linear) measuring gages that are parallel to the actual workpiece plane result in a much more accurate indication of the machine move, and corresponding workpiece reproduction of that dimension. See Figure 2.3.

The Mechanical Drive Elements include the servo-motors, or drive stepping motors; the recirculating ball-screws and nuts; and the corresponding hardware for these components. The recirculating ball-screws and nuts are the most important mechanical components of the positioning system. The hardened and ground screw mates to accept hardened ball bearings that revolve in the spherically ground "threads" and fit the brass/bronze "nut" internally. The nut is mounted as a stationary component to the machine table/carriage. The balls

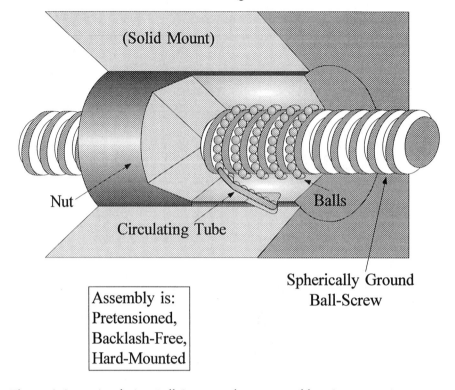

Figure 2.4 *Recirculating Ball-Screw and Nut Assembly—Cutaway View*

are pressure-loaded against each other and their path is recirculating by way of a linking tube that feeds the balls that have turned out of the nut back to the in-feed side. See Figure 2.4.

All drive components are mounted rigidly onto their respective machine parts with locator pins and secured with lock-screws and wired safety-nuts. Ball-screws revolve through precision bearings that allow zero end-float, and rigid brackets support the assembly. This ensures that positioning speeds up to 720 IPM with .0002" accuracy over long distances can be achieved without overtravel or system failure from braking inertia. The mass of milling machine tables and lathe carriages holding large workpieces during rapid traverse movements can place tremendous pressures on all drive components. Their design strength should be engineered with maximum rigidity to control this load and maintain .0002" or closer accuracy.

Servos or Stepping Motors

Stepping motors are electromechanical devices that rotate a discrete step angle when energized electrically. The increment usually is fixed for a particular

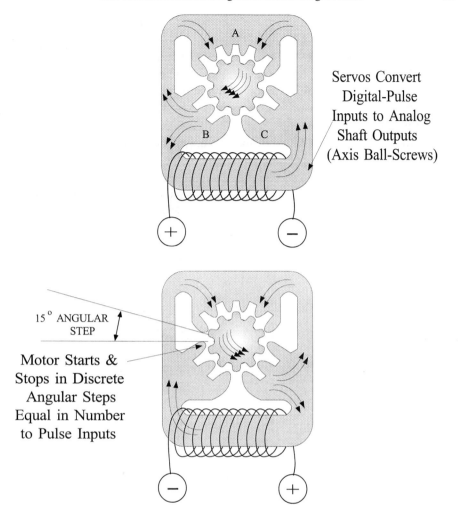

Servos Convert
Digital-Pulse
Inputs to Analog
Shaft Outputs
(Axis Ball-Screws)

15° ANGULAR
STEP

Motor Starts &
Stops in Discrete
Angular Steps
Equal in Number
to Pulse Inputs

Figure 2.5 *Stepping Motor—CNC Axis Servo Motors*

motor and provides a means for accurately positioning in a repeatable, uniform manner. Step angles range from as small as .72° to as large as 90°. Various means for electrically actuating stepping motors include DC pulses, square waves, and fixed logic sequence or multiphase square waves. Typical designs include selenoid-operated ratchets, permanent magnets, and variable reluctance.

The Electromagnetic Rotary Incremental Actuator (or stepping motor) operates by converting digital-pulse inputs to analog shaft-output motion. See Figure 2.5.

The motor shown starts and stops in discrete angular increments of equal magnitude (15°) to produce output steps always exactly proportional in number to the pulse inputs. There are two permanent magnets, connected in parallel for uniform flux distribution, bridging two portent poles (A and B) and one detent pole (C). The portent poles have three sets of teeth each spaced 36° apart and are positioned so that when one set of portent teeth aligns with three rotor teeth, the other set aligns with spaces between the rotor teeth. Three of six detent-pole teeth spaced 18° apart are also aligned with three rotor teeth. The rotor position establishes alternate flux paths. Every pulse of alternating polarity applied to the coil advances the rotor one single step by switching the magnetic flux from one path to the other. DC pulses of plus or minus polarity overcome the permanent magnetic detent and produce torque to advance the rotor from one detent to the next. On the CNC machine, this mechanism makes possible the conversion of calculated electronic units to precision machine movement.

Chapter 3

PROGRAMMING

CODED LANGUAGES

Although CNC has clearly moved ahead to Conversational Programming formats that have advanced the entire programming process to the instruction of the machine in everyday language, many part programs are stored in conventional Program System Formats such as EIA—RS 274D or G & M codes (program structure in accordance with DIN 66 025 resp. ISO 1056). Originally most NC machines were designed using this format and many tape-controlled machines are still controlled by this language today.

An example of this Program System Format for a CNC Turning Machine follows:

N   Block Number (00—999)

G   Preparatory Functions

         G00 = Rapid Traverse

         G01 = Linear Interpolation

         G02 = Circular Interpolation Clockwise

         G03 = Circular Interpolation Counterclockwise

         G04 = Dwell, programmable

         G25 = Subroutine Call-up

         G27 = Jump Instruction

         G64 = Feed Motors

         G65 = Disk/Tape Activation

         G73 = Chip-Breaking Cycle

         G78 = Threading Cycle

         G81 = Drilling Cycle

         G82 = Drilling Cycle with Dwell

         G83 = Deep-Hole Drilling Cycle

G84 = Roughing Cycle, Longitudinal
G85 = Reaming Cycle
G88 = Roughing Cycle, Facing
G89 = Reaming & Drilling with Dwell
G90 = Absolute Value Programming
G91 = Incremental Value Programming
G92 = Offset of Reference Point
G94 = Feed in IPM (inch per min)
G95 = Feed in IPR (inch per rev)

X and Z = Dimensional Data
F = Feedrate
T = Tool Address
M = Miscellaneous Function
L = Subroutine Call-up
I and K = Partial Arc Interpolation
M = Miscellaneous Functions
M00 = Program Stop
M03 = Spindle On (RH)
M05 = Spindle Off
M06 = Tool Change and Cutter Compensation
M08 = Switching Functions
M17 = Jump back to Main Program
M30 = End of Program
M98 = Automatic Ball-Screw Compensation
M99 = Circular Interpolation Parameters

All these NC commands or selectable subroutines are very powerful. Each executes a series of instructions to the Control, using the inputted variables to move the machine axis in desired directions at specific feedrates. The following is a sample of an NC Program that is machining an operation in a Turning Center. Identifiable are commonly used commands such as

G00 = RAPID TRAVERSE
G01 = LINEAR INTERPOLATION (Straight-line moves of Measurement)
G02 = CLOCKWISE CIRCULAR INTERPOLATION (Cutting a Radius)

Also easily identifiable are some of the axis coordinates that follow the commands:

Z 1.2368 X 4.5(000)
Z 3.1637 X 4.3(000)

The Program can be viewed on the NC Control CRT. See Figure 3.1.

```
 ┌─────────────────────────────────────────────────┐
 │ Lathe   NC 2                      ALT - H   HELP  │
 │                                                   │
 │   NO765G00Z5.0                                    │
 │   NO770G01X4.6                                    │
 │   NO775Z1.2368                                    │
 │   NO780G02Z1.1477X4.7KO.28510.3380                │
 │   NO785G00Z5.0                                    │
 │   NO790G01X4.5                                    │
 │   NO795Z2.9637                                    │
 │   NO800Z2.9637X4.5                                │
 │   NO805Z1.5153                                    │
 │   NO810G02Z1.2368X4.6K0.010.4380                  │
 │   NO815G00Z5.0                                    │
 │   NO820G01X4.4                                    │
 │   NO825Z3.0637                                    │
 │   NO830Z2.9637X4.5                                │
 │   NO835G00Z5.0                                    │
 │   NO840G01X4.3                                    │
 │   NO845Z3.1637                                    │
 │   NO850Z3.0637X4.4                                │
 │   NO855G00Z5.0                                    │
 │   NO860G01X4.2                                    │
 │   NO865Z3.2637                                    │
 │   NO870Z3.1637X4.3                                │
 │   NO875G00Z5.0                                    │
 └─────────────────────────────────────────────────┘
```

(CONTROL CRT Screen)

Figure 3.1 *An NC Turning Program (Sample)*

NC Programs require the knowledge of ASCII (American Standard Code for Information Interchange) and/or EIA (Electronic Industry Association) codes. The Programs look more complex and the NC machine must strictly adhere to the program. In CNC, the same program format may be recognized or the program contained in the memory is more flexible for editing purposes, allowing the execution of program segments and enabling single cycling for specific tools. Success in CNC programming, however, is founded on strong fundamentals of basic machining, NC understanding, and the powerful infusion of today's computers into the system.

CONVERSATIONAL FORMAT

Many new CNC machine Controls use a Conversational Format for programming. This format is an interface between the machine language, which directly controls the machine movement, and the programmer/operator.

In certain selected cycles/subroutines, the Control accepts the actual values on blueprints and allows the dimensions to be entered directly into the Control. Inputs made by the programmer/operator can also be displayed as graphics. Even the dimensions of complex workpieces can be calculated by the Control itself, a feature that speeds up programming considerably. Cutter Compensation automatically references the tool diameter from the Tool Library and compensates for the tool radius by calculating the necessary trigonometric formulas in the computer. The canned cycles, subroutines, and fixed programs into which only the required dimensions have to be entered have dramatically changed programming. Many modern Controls use a complete system of graphical displays and plotter graphics that help to check the program that has been created. A simulated machining sequence shows the run of a program without the actual machine axes ever moving. Toolpaths can be displayed just as easily as the finished contour with these cycles. Portions of a workpiece can be enlarged on many Control CRTs, with the workpieces being displayed in three dimensions.

Computer Numerical Controls (CNCs) can also simulate the complete machining process. Many shops are switching over to CNCs simply because of ease of use. There are less complicated code languages to learn, the programs do not require a specialist to read, and the fact that they allow job shops to improve profits, deliveries, production, and expand machining capabilities are definite advantages.

DIMENSIONS in CONVERSATIONAL CNC CONTROLS

Dimensions can be directly inputted into Conversational CNC Controls for the following:

- Milling, drilling, boring, tapping, and C'Boring
- Milling squares, rectangles, pockets, circles, and arcs
- Creation of ellipses and splines using linear or arc approximation
- Creation of lines using polar, end points, or tangents
- Creation of arcs using polar, end points, or tangents to one, two, or three objects
- Dynamic tool display, animated or static display, and toolpath increment display set by the user
- Spiral pocketing, island avoidance, look-ahead cutter compensation, and automatic roughing passes for contouring
- Projection onto planes, cylinders, cones, spheres, or combinations thereof
- Automatic speed and feed calculators (input materials, numbers of flutes, and cutter diameter)
- Cycle time available for milling or turning for constant **IPM** or **IPR**.

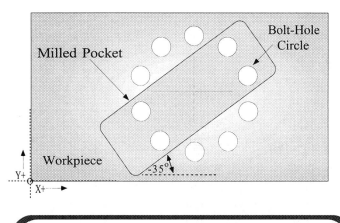

BLOCK #	OPER	X	Y	Z	FDRATE	TL #
1	PL/DR	5.125	3.375	-.6872	3.5	2
	BOLT CIRCLE START			12 DEG. CW		
	2.125 RADIUS		10 HOLES			
2	PL/DR	5.125	3.375	-.6872	3.5	3
	BOLT CIRCLE START			12 DEG. CW		
	2.125 RADIUS		10 HOLES			
3	PL/DR	3.1632	.8590	-.3750	5.0	4
4	MILL POCKET	ANGLED CCW	-35 DEG.			4
5	XL 5.5500	YW 1.9870			4.5	4

Only 5 Blocks of Program Space Required

(CRT Screen)

Figure 3.2 *A CNC Milling Program (Sample)*

- Tool Tables. New toolpath editing function. Program one part, use edited toolpath to rotate other 2D or 3D parts about any Plane. Mirror, translate or scale the NC part program
- Reverse postprocess existing NC programs. Create screen geometry from the NC program or postprocess to a different machine. Three-dimensional backplotting in any view

A sample CNC Milling program can be seen in Figure 3.2. The simple selection of Subroutines for milling a Pocket feature that is skewed at −35° to the part axis, and drilling the hole pattern requires only five Blocks of program space.

All dimensions are entered as Absolute Dimensions from X.000 Y.000 (Origin), eliminating a great amount of computation for the milling operation alone. All calculations for Cutter Compensation are performed in the CNC Control's microprocessor *while* the program is in operation. See Figure 3.2.

STRAIGHT-LINE, POINT-to-POINT MACHINING: LINEAR INTERPOLATION

Linear Interpolation is a straight-line motion in one or two axes. The only coordinate requirement is a motion Starting Point and End Point. If an Angular move is made, moving two axes at once, yet in a straight line, the Control plots a series of high-resolution steps (stairway form). The higher the resolution of the machine axes, the closer and smaller are the stepped increments. Today's CNC machines produce finishes as fine on angular moves as are produced in one-axis motions, due to very high-resolution interpolation systems.

During straight-line motion, the Control must receive a feedrate. Various machine designs require different programmed motion rates. Machining and Turning Centers usually specify an F____ word with the numerical value following, represented in inches per minute (IPM), or inches per revolution (IPR).

Milling Centers use straight-line motions for milling moves and for hole-pattern coordinates. However, some Controls do not require the tool to adhere to strict Linear Interpolation when rapid traversing between Hole Coordinates. Check Control Manuals for individual machine functions.

Two- and Three-Axis Simultaneous Machining

Two-Dimensional Arcs. Arcs for programming purposes require varying amounts of information. Typically, for a two-dimensional arc to be completed by the machine Control, the Arc Starting-Point, Arc-Center, and Arc End-Point coordinates need to be established. For Milling Centers, 2D Arcs can exist in any two-axis planes: XY, XZ, YZ, with XY being the most common. If the Radius remains constant from the Arc Center, the Arcs can be defined as Quarter Circles in many newer CNC Controls (when an Arc spans 90°), clockwise or counterclockwise. A common Two-Dimensional Arc is programmed in Figure 3.3, with the coordinates measured from the XY Zero Origin. Notice that all data are contained in only three Blocks of Program space.

Three-Dimensional Arcs and Helix. Three-Dimensional Arcs involve the simultaneous movement of three axes around a single or moving Arc Center equidistant or of varying radii. A Helix is created when three axes move simultaneously around an XY Arc Center at equidistant radii. Typically, the angle of ascent or descent is determined by the Starting-Point and End-Point Coordinates. Cutting these multiaxis movements calls for special cutting tool require-

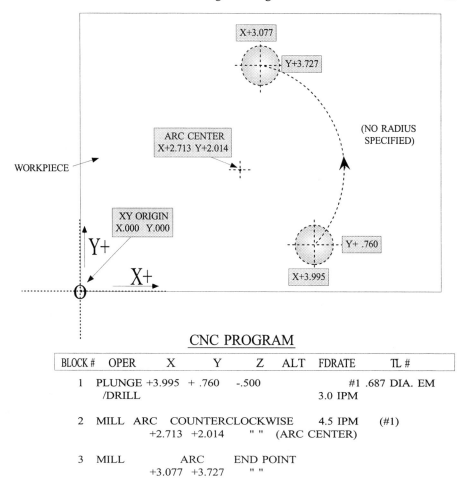

CNC PROGRAM

BLOCK #	OPER	X	Y	Z	ALT	FDRATE	TL #
1	PLUNGE /DRILL	+3.995	+ .760	-.500		#1 3.0 IPM	.687 DIA. EM
2	MILL ARC COUNTERCLOCKWISE	+2.713	+2.014	" "		4.5 IPM (ARC CENTER)	(#1)
3	MILL ARC	+3.077	+3.727	END POINT " "			

Figure 3.3 *Milling Two-Axis Arc*

ments to allow for axial relief on newly cut surface areas. Turning inserts with generous radii and spherical (or ball) Endmills allow for adequate clearance on Three-Dimensional machining operations. See Figure 3.4.

SPECIAL CNC CONTROL: GEOMETRY CAPABILITY

Today's CNC Controls offer very powerful features to aid in Programming simple to complex part geometries. The following are a few examples of popular features. Chapters 6 to 9 offer in-depth selections of many features and their direct applications to Programming. The examples offered in this chapter represent some directional advancements made in the CNC field.

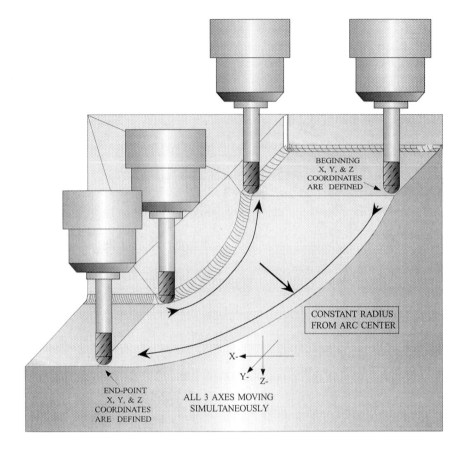

BEGINNING
X, Y, & Z
COORDINATES
ARE DEFINED

CONSTANT RADIUS
FROM ARC CENTER

X-

Y- Z-

END-POINT
X, Y, & Z
COORDINATES
ARE DEFINED

ALL 3 AXES MOVING
SIMULTANEOUSLY

Figure 3.4 *CNC Milling of a Helix—Simultaneous Three-Axis Milling*

Scaling

Most Controls have the capability to proportionally reduce or increase the size of selected sections of the CNC program. This is an exceptionally powerful tool when working with engineering drawings where some specifications are not finalized. It is also used frequently when Z depths change on specific mold components requiring a 15% or 20% increase in depth from job lot to lot. Scaling selections can be made in all axis directions and independently affect only those dimensions in the selected axis. Typical operations of this function are (1) to choose the Program Blocks that are to be scaled, (2) to specify the direction of scaling (i.e., X+ axis), and (3) to specify the scaling (i.e., 30%).

The CNC program sample in Figure 3.5 shows six Blocks of a Milling program that require scaling. The Blocks are selected in the Scaling Dialog Box and necessary information is inputted to accomplish the Scaling operation. The actual program is altered in the *X axis* to the *Positive direction*. This function

BLOCK #	OPER	X	Y	Z	FDRATE	TL #
12	MILL	6.123	3.937	-.98721	3.5	2
13	MILL	5.143	3.937	-.98721	3.5	2
14	MILL	5.143	4.250	-.98721	3.5	2
15	PL/DR	2.937	1.500	-.6250	4.0	2
16	MILL	3.125	1.500	-.62501	3.5	2
17	MILL	3.125	3.750	-.62501	3.5	2
18	MILL	6.123	3.750	-.62501	3.5	2
19	MILL	6.123	4.972	-.62501	3.5	2
20	MILL	7.263	4.972	-.62501	3.5	2
21	SCALE	BLOCKS #15-20		Z- .1613		3
22	PL/DR			-.7613	2.5	3
	MILL			-.7613	6.5	3

BLOCKS SELECTED BEFORE SCALING

BLOCK #	OPER	X	Y	Z	FDRATE	TL #
12	MILL	6.123	3.937	-.98721	3.5	2
13	MILL	5.143	3.937	-.98721	3.5	2
14	MILL	5.143	4.250	-.98721	3.5	2
15	PL/DR	2.937	1.500	-.7613	2.5	3
16	MILL	3.125	1.500	-.7613	6.5	3
17	MILL	3.125	3.750	-.7613	6.5	3
18	MILL	6.123	3.750	-.7613	6.5	3
19	MILL	6.123	4.972	-.7613	6.5	3
20	MILL	7.263	4.972	-.7613	6.5	3

BLOCKS SELECTED AFTER SCALING

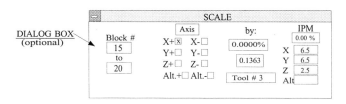

DIALOG BOX (optional)

Figure 3.5 *Scaling of a Program*

overwrites the previous values in machine memory. Always save backup on memory storage media before scaling.

Rotating

Rotating is a Transformation function that analyzes the orientation of the part geometry in any of the three, four, or five dimensions of machine-axis travel. The three standard axes of machine-axis travel can be individually ro-

SELECTED BLOCKS for ROTATION

BLOCK #	OPER	X	Y	Z	FDRATE	TL #
12	PL/DR	5.125	3.375	-.68722	3.5	2
13	PL/DR	5.125	-2.750	-.68722	3.5	2
14	PL/DR	4.000	-2.750	-.68722	3.5	2
15	PL/DR	4.000	-1.500	-.68722	3.5	2
16	PL/DR	3.125	-1.500	-.68722	3.5	2
17	PL/DR	3.250	-3.750	-.68722	3.5	2
18	PL/DR	6.125	-3.500	-.68722	3.5	2
19	PL/DR	7.187	-4.973	-.68722	3.5	2
20	PL/DR	7.2632	-9.4788	-.68722	3.5	2
21	ROTATE BLOCKS	#12-20		90 DEG. CCW		
22	XY AXIS	XY CENTER	.000	.000	3.5	

SELECTED BLOCKS after ROTATION

BLOCK #	OPER	X	Y	Z	FDRATE	TL #
12	PL/DR	3.375	5.125	-.68722	2.5	2
13	PL/DR	-2.750	5.125	-.68722	2.5	2
14	PL/DR	-2.750	4.000	-.68722	2.5	2
15	PL/DR	-1.500	4.000	-.68722	2.5	2
16	PL/DR	-1.500	3.125	-.68722	2.5	2
17	PL/DR	-3.750	3.250	-.68722	2.5	2
18	PL/DR	-3.500	6.125	-.68722	2.5	2
19	PL/DR	-4.973	7.187	-.68722	2.5	2
20	PL/DR	-9.4788	7.2632	-.68722	2.5	2

DIALOG BOX (OPTIONAL)

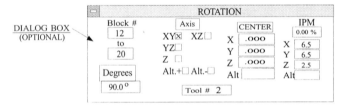

Figure 3.6 *Rotation of a Program*

tated or rotated in two and three axis directions. Rotation is an advanced function that individually recalculates every coordinate in a selected axis (or axes) and changes the X, Y, and/or Z values in the program.

X and Y, X and Z axes are typically rotated in unison; the XY combination for Milling Machines and the XZ combination for Turning Machines are the [Default] selections in most Control's Rotation function. Figure 3.6 shows a Ten-Block Program excerpt that requires rotation. The Blocks are selected to be Rotated and a Dialog Box (optional) is shown to contain the values that must be entered for rotation. A Degree value is entered; an Axis Combination

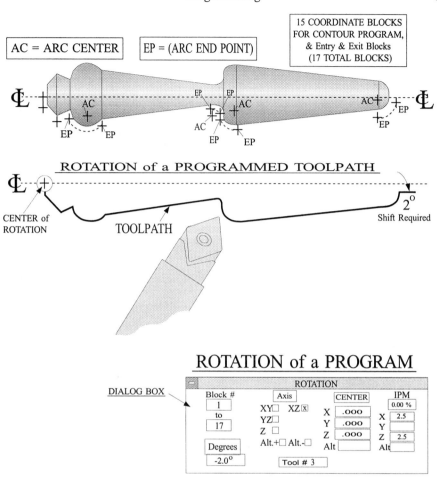

Figure 3.7 *Rotation Used in a Turning Program*

is entered; a Rotation Center, Origin, or other XY Dimension (around which the rotation is to take place) is specified; and the function is performed. Notice that the second program sample shows the changes in all of the X and Y co-ordinates of the selected blocks.

This transformation tool is particularly useful for hole patterns that require rotation from their previous design configuration; milled pockets or slots that require reorientation; turning operations that increase tapering orientation; setup reorientation where fixturing is indexed from its original location.

A Turning operation is shown in Figure 3.7, which also shows an intended change to be made in the contour. The change is a frequent engineering revision that requires that the tapered contour is to be increased in the Y– direction, with all the features to remain in the proper X+ location. Many prototype job

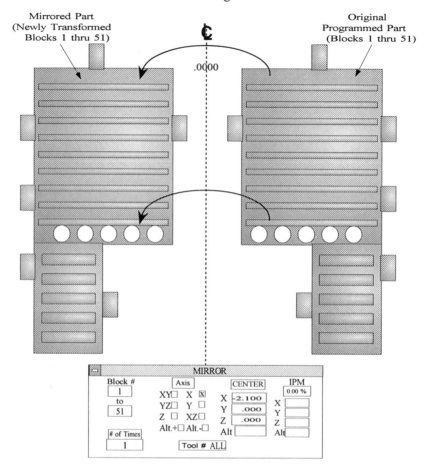

Figure 3.8 *Mirroring a Part Program*

lots require sets of 5 or 10 parts to have increased tapers in positive or negative degrees. This transformation tool saves hours of trigonometric calculations to adjust semicomplex or complex contours for prototype purposes. Often used in combination with the graphical toolpath features, the desired contour can be viewed on the CRT before any machining is performed.

Mirroring

The Mirroring Control function is designed to "flip" the selected Program Blocks around the axis or axes chosen. This is especially useful for mating parts that require a mirrored-part Program to be written. The computer orients the part geometry and its relationship to the XYZ origin, compensates for the requested axis direction of Mirroring, and completes the function. See Figure 3.8.

Shown is a workpiece with hole patterns, milling operations, bosses, etc. To recalculate all the XY coordinates of the mirrored axis would be a programming task equal to the original Program creation in actual work time. By selecting the Mirror function, inserting the required values for a successful "flip" to the desired mirror location around the XY origin (orientation), the Mirroring is completed. Shown is the finished geometric "mirror" within the computer's graphic display and the Program Blocks that were affected by the Mirror function.

Copy

Copy is a function used very often when programming CNC Controls. It is used to duplicate a selected section of a Program. Before duplication, a Dialog Box requires information about the duplication: Blocks selected for duplication; changes made in the Blocks copied (offsets in X, Y, or Z axis, offset amounts); desired renumbering of created Blocks; and Tool depths are required factors. The Copy function is powerful; it can rewrite a large and complex program without the programmer going over every Block to make changes and revisions. See Figure 3.9.

Shown is a Program sample and Dialog Box asking for the required values needed to complete the Copy function. The intended purpose is to rewrite Blocks 25 through 72, changing all the Z– dimensions by increasing their depths by –.2500. In Block 73, the Copy function is selected and the Dialog Box then requests the values be entered. Some Controls vary on the method and value input terminology, but ultimate functions are the same.

Particularly important is the selection of changing all Z– (Z negative) values by -.250. The end result of a Copy function on this particular program is the reproduction of Blocks 25 through 72, now renumbered as 100 through 146; Block 73, which created the copied blocks, is left blank after the operation. All Milling Blocks still begin their Plunge Points at +.0050; all Drilling and Boring operations still begin at +.010. Only the Z– dimensions are extended to a negative .2500 beyond their previous depths. The value of Z– was the critical input that searched and changed all the negative Z's to a value of greater depth with all tools. This is very useful for job lots that have variations on Z levels for different part assemblies, requiring only that one master program be written and copied to cover the variations.

Display of Working Environments

Modern CNC Controls have the graphical capability and the powerful microprocessors to maintain an awareness of the location and physical boundaries of all the components in and around the machine's work area. This is particularly important because of the power, speed, and cost of the machine tool under automated control. Spindles are being produced on Turning Centers with

BLOCK #	OPER	X	Y	Z	FDRATE	TL #
64	MILL	6.123	3.937	-.50021	3.5	2
65	MILL	5.143	3.937	-.50021	3.5	2
66	MILL	5.143	4.250	-.50021	3.5	2
67	PL/DR	2.937	1.500	-.6250	4.0	2
68	MILL	3.125	1.500	-.62501	3.5	2
69	MILL	3.125	3.750	-.62501	3.5	2
70	MILL	6.123	3.750	-.62501	3.5	2
71	MILL	6.123	4.972	-.62501	3.5	2
72	MILL	7.263	4.972	-.62501	3.5	2
73	COPY	BLOCKS		#25 - 72		
74	OFFSETS:	.000	.000	Z	-.250 ALL	TOOLS

BLOCK #	OPER	X	Y	Z	FDRATE	TL #
138	MILL	6.123	3.937	-.7502	13.5	2
139	MILL	5.143	3.937	-.7502	13.5	2
140	MILL	5.143	4.250	-.7502	13.5	2
141	PL/DR	2.937	1.500	-.7750	4.0	2
142	MILL	3.125	1.500	-.7750	13.5	2
143	MILL	3.125	3.750	-.7750	13.5	2
144	MILL	6.123	3.750	-.7750	13.5	2
145	MILL	6.123	4.972	-.7750	13.5	2
146	MILL	7.263	4.972	-.7750	13.5	2
147						

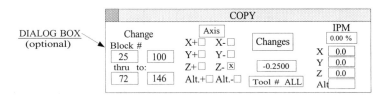

Figure 3.9 *Copying a Program*

.000020 concentricity guarantees; Z-axis heads and X and Y axes on machining centers are in production with .000040 resolution over the full length of table travel. All of these factors, together with the HP ratings of spindles and drive servos, require that extreme care be taken during programming so that no physical interference or unintended contact occurs between anything other than the cutting tool and the workpiece during intended machining conditions.

The ability to "dry run" using the CRT's Graphical Display of the outline periphery of all components in the work area has dramatically reduced CNC crashes that have in the past proved very costly. In a Machining Center, the work area includes all areas on and immediately near the table's complete travel zone; the machine spindle and included coolant feed lines; the Automatic Tool Changer (ATC) and its full range of motion, rotation, and current tool lengths; and any interchangeable pallets in the work area during the Program's operation. In a Turning Center, the work area includes all areas on and immediately near the cross-slide or carriage's complete travel zone; the machine spindle and included coolant feed lines; Tool Posts and Turrets; the Automatic Tool Changer (ATC) and its full range of motion, rotation, and current tool lengths; and any interchangeable Chucks, Jaws, Collets, or Workholding Fixtures that will be in the work area during the program's operation. See Figures 3.10(a) and 3.10(b).

Workpiece

Part Programs and the input of the finished dimensions for workpieces indicate to the Control's computer the overall dimensions of a workpiece. Programmers also input the dimensions for premachining materials, castings, forgings, and so on, which indicate to the Control the overall dimensions that the machine's cutting tool must avoid. By establishing graphical boundaries for the workpiece, Rapid Traverse motions by any axis crossing the theoretical boundary signals the Control of an upcoming interference. Especially helpful is the Control's ability to avoid interference when directions of travel stray from the original programmed move and cutter path. For example, when a revision is made to a program with a Stop Block added and a tool change occurring in a new area, the interference may not have been anticipated after the revision. See Figure 3.11.

Clamps

Outlines of Clamps, Threaded Posts, Packing Blocks, and their alternative positions are the most frequently unknown areas for the Programmer. Clamping-related features are the leading causes for interference crashes during CNC machining. Because the exact location of clamps can change from part to part due to operators replacing clamping items inconsistently, the full range of clamping positions need to be inputted into the Control's memory. Threaded Posts and Bolts can "back out" of their seats and move into cutter-traverse paths. Packing Blocks can be changed during part runs and extend into the traverse paths. See Figure 3.12.

Fixtures

Fixtures include all plates, blocks, custom positioning tools, and so on, that hold workpieces in correct location for machining. Fixtures are generally the

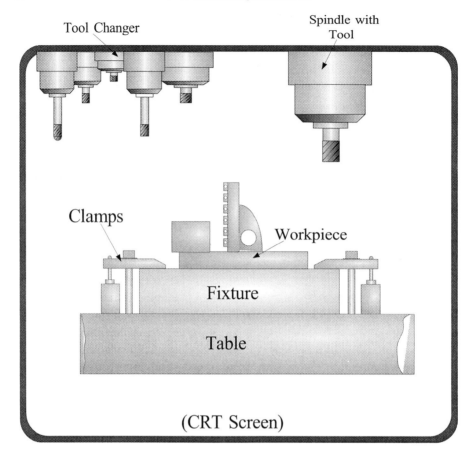

Figure 3.10(a) *Display of a Working Environment*

most time-consuming component of the setup process, requiring toolmaking skills to design the proper features into them for ultimate part location and machining stability. The Control must "know" all of the outside dimensions, overall heights, possible indexing movements of any moving fixture components, and where the workpiece locates on the fixture. See Figure 3.13.

Tools and Toolholders

Tools in Toolholders are the variables that can lead to "confusion" for a CNC Milling Machine Control. In the Tool Library, the Diameter, Length, RPM, and Tool Geometry are stored for each tool. The variation of Tool Length and Tool Diameter from tool to tool can be large. The Control, "thinking" a shorter tool or tool of smaller diameter is in the spindle, can rapidly position (traverse) into

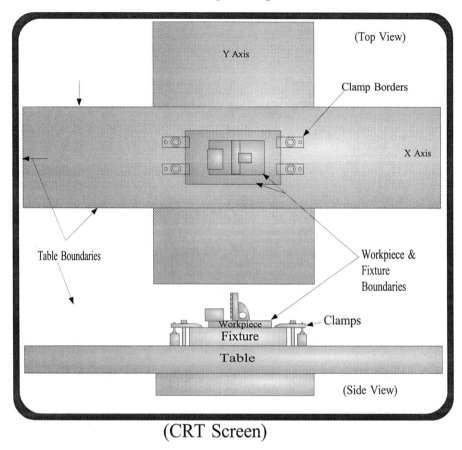

Figure 3.10(b) *Display of a Working Environment (Milling Center)*

the workpiece, fixture, or even the machine table. Not only will this ruin the part setup and workpiece, but the machine table and machine spindle after this crash can be very expensive to repair. Various Toolholder types can be entered into many Control memories, usually in the Tool Library. See Figure 3.14.

Turrets

Turrets are the indexable tool posts on many CNC Turning machines. Tools and Toolholders are mounted in Turrets. When a tool change is required, the Turret indexes to the required position, enabling the desired tool to be in the correct position to machine the next operation. Turrets are designed in "octagonal drums" (8 tool positions), "dodecagonal drums" (12 tool positions), and other combinations, allowing workpieces to be machined with as many tools

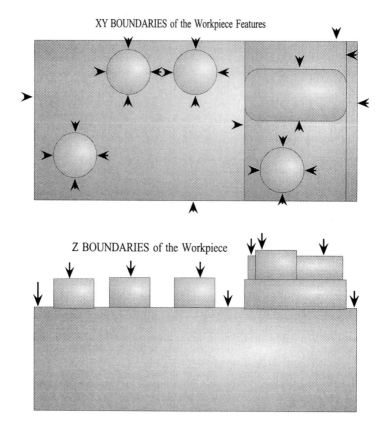

Figure 3.11 *Graphical Boundaries of the Workpiece*

as possible in one part clamping. Most important of all the dimensions entered for the working environment is the dimension for the longest and largest tool mounted on the Turret. When the Turret is indexing, assurance that every tool has clearance of all components in the work area *is* a priority. See Figure 3.15.

Jaws

Lathes and Turning Machines increasingly are using Jaws for Chucks that are machineable to suit specific jobs. The Jaws are of many different shapes and sizes, so the variables need to be entered into the working environment section of Control memory. Jaws extend away from the spindle center and

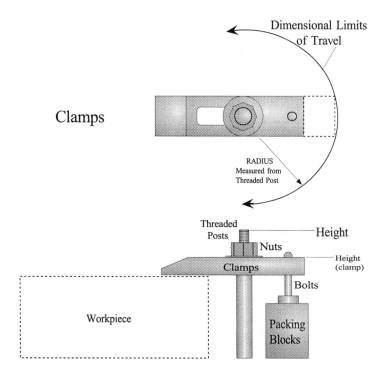

Figure 3.12 *Graphical Display of Clamps and Related Dimensions*

represent the radius of a full diameter that requires interference avoidance. See Figure 3.16.

TOOL LIBRARIES for CUTTERS

Tool Calibrations

Each tool in the CNC Program is Calibrated at Datum Zero (Z 00.0000) for Milling Centers, (XZ 00.0000) for Turning Centers, individually. Typically, a Z or XZ Zero is chosen on the fixture or workpiece surface and all cutting tools are calibrated on that surface. Drilling, Boring, Tapping, and other hole-related tools are usually calibrated at .0000 from the surface into which they are cutting the hole. Often hole-related tools are calibrated at Zero (.0000) by zeroing in on a nominal gage block such as a 1.000 block to use as a spacer/feeler gage (and calibrating at +1.000). Tool Calibrations are critical, especially on milling

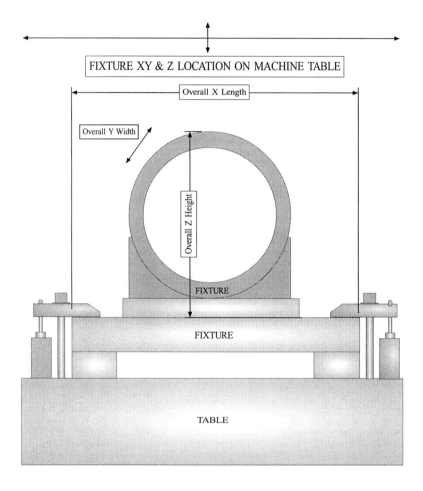

Figure 3.13 *Graphical Display of Fixture Boundaries*

and turning tools, where surface blends must be seamless. Modern electronic calibration, where memory adjustments are possible, makes the tool-blending tasks easier. Once a machining trial run has been completed and a mismatch blend between two or more tool calibrations is discovered, a determination of the difference between calibrations can be compensated for. The Zero (00.0000) for the tools can be adjusted for perfect blends at the Tool Calibration file in the Control memory. See Figure 3.17.

Storing Cutter Geometry

Advanced Controls have memory areas to store Cutter Geometry. This includes the number of Flutes on cutters; Bottom-cutting capabilities; Cutter Ma-

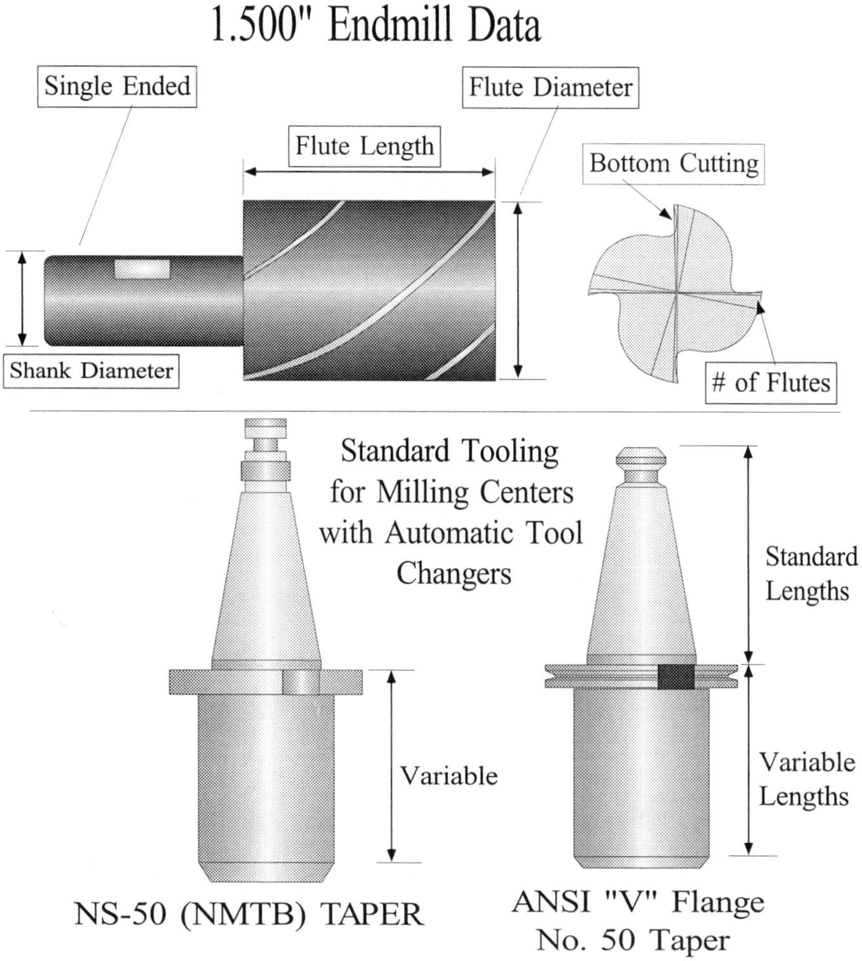

1.500" Endmill Data

Single Ended

Flute Diameter

Flute Length

Bottom Cutting

Shank Diameter

# of Flutes

Standard Tooling
for Milling Centers
with Automatic Tool
Changers

Standard
Lengths

Variable

Variable
Lengths

NS-50 (NMTB) TAPER

ANSI "V" Flange
No. 50 Taper

Figure 3.14 *Graphical Display of Tool Library in Memory*

terial (cobalt, coated); High-helix flutes; Lathe tool, RH, LH; Radii on tools;
special-form tools; Thread Pitches on taps, tools; C'Bore and C'Sink Sizes and
angles; Flute lengths; Shank Sizes; Single- or Double-ended tools. Other data
can also be noted, such as the best RPM previously tested. See Figure 3.18.

(The previous examples of Working Environment, Tool Libraries, and Tool
Calibrations and Geometry were generalized for insight into today's CNC Control capabilities. Chapters 9 and 10 provide in-depth coverage of these topics
with direct application to Programming.)

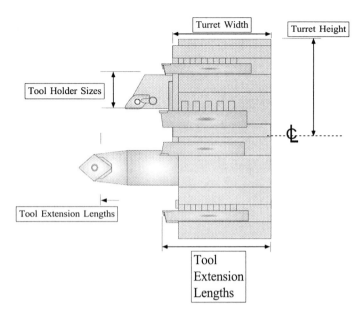

Figure 3.15   Graphical Display of Turret with Tools

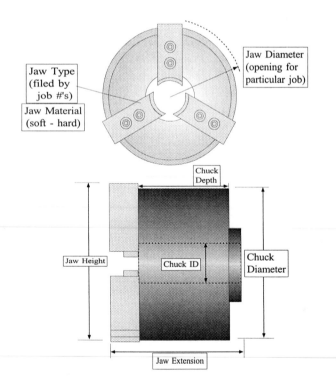

Figure 3.16   *Graphical Display of Chuck Jaws*

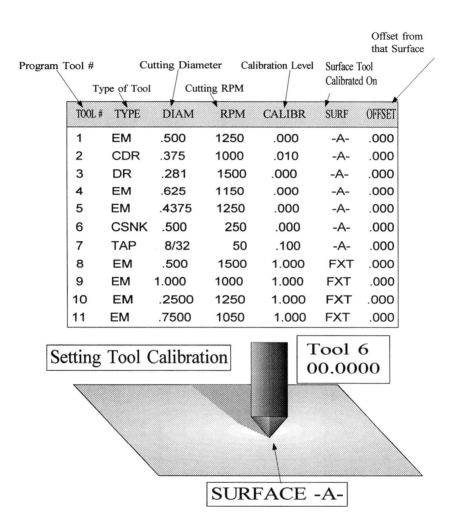

TOOL #	TYPE	DIAM	RPM	CALIBR	SURF	OFFSET
1	EM	.500	1250	.000	-A-	.000
2	CDR	.375	1000	.010	-A-	.000
3	DR	.281	1500	.000	-A-	.000
4	EM	.625	1150	.000	-A-	.000
5	EM	.4375	1250	.000	-A-	.000
6	CSNK	.500	250	.000	-A-	.000
7	TAP	8/32	50	.100	-A-	.000
8	EM	.500	1500	1.000	FXT	.000
9	EM	1.000	1000	1.000	FXT	.000
10	EM	.2500	1250	1.000	FXT	.000
11	EM	.7500	1050	1.000	FXT	.000

Figure 3.17   *Graphical Display of Tool Calibration (Programmable)*

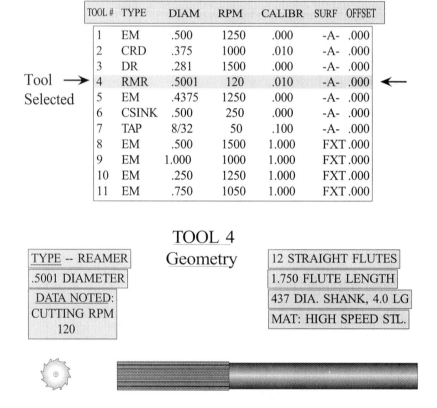

TOOL #	TYPE	DIAM	RPM	CALIBR	SURF	OFFSET
1	EM	.500	1250	.000	-A-	.000
2	CRD	.375	1000	.010	-A-	.000
3	DR	.281	1500	.000	-A-	.000
4	RMR	.5001	120	.010	-A-	.000
5	EM	.4375	1250	.000	-A-	.000
6	CSINK	.500	250	.000	-A-	.000
7	TAP	8/32	50	.100	-A-	.000
8	EM	.500	1500	1.000	FXT	.000
9	EM	1.000	1000	1.000	FXT	.000
10	EM	.250	1250	1.000	FXT	.000
11	EM	.750	1050	1.000	FXT	.000

Tool → 4
Selected ←

TOOL 4
Geometry

TYPE -- REAMER

.5001 DIAMETER

DATA NOTED:
CUTTING RPM
120

12 STRAIGHT FLUTES

1.750 FLUTE LENGTH

437 DIA. SHANK, 4.0 LG

MAT: HIGH SPEED STL.

Figure 3.18   *Graphical Display of Tool Geometry*

CHAPTER 4

PROGRAMMING TOOL MOVES

STRAIGHT-CUT LINEAR MILLING

Absolute Dimension Coordinates: Moves from Absolute Part Zero

This is the most popular and frequently used form of a dimensional programming format. It uses "absolute" measurements from Part Zero or Datum Zero in the part setup. The format is ideal to "program in" because of its universal application to many stages of the workpiece production process.

Initial part layout is normally performed using absolute measurements from Part Zero. All workpiece features can be located and established using the same dimensions furnished on part prints. Each and every feature (boss, surface, hole, slot, pocket, etc.) is dimensioned directly from the same Zero in all axes (X, Y, and Z).

Calculating absolute dimensions means establishing the direct measurement from the Datum Origin. The distance is measured exactly from Zero for every feature on the workpiece. Slots and pockets are calculated from Zero, and tool centers are chosen in both X and Y Axes. Allowances for finish cuts are made to the tool-center coordinates. The specified Radius (Rad.) is a governing factor usually presented with a tolerance. This allows a movement of the tool for finish passes. Adding and subtracting for the finish cut of .010 or less is done by calculating the finished coordinates and moving away on the initial rough passes. See Figure 4.1.

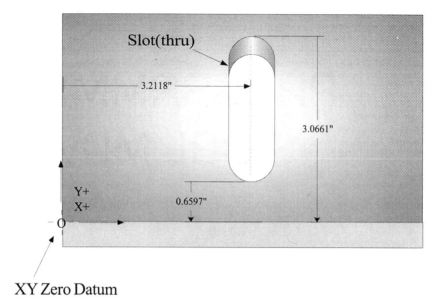

XY Zero Datum

Figure 4.1 *Absolute Dimensions from Zero Datum*

By using today's machine technology, the most accurate way to hold work-piece tolerances specified from Part Zero is to design your program in absolute dimension coordinates. The CNC machine's control cross-checks one dimension instead of combining several dimensions together (where increased instances of measurement error can develop between the incremental machine moves).

More complex moves can be programmed using (and transferring) absolute dimensions from blueprint to part program. Extremely accurate and intricate tool movements are assembled into sequential moves using the standard milling techniques. See Figure 4.2.

A program sheet is made up with the tool moves in the sequence selected for proper cutting procedure. An example follows for climb-milling with a .500-dia. cutter. The allowances are for the .250 Radius of the tool added or subtracted in either direction the cutter is to be placed with respect to a workpiece feature.

Block #	X Axis	Y Axis	Z Depth	Ref.
1	+3.9313	+.9872	−.437	Plunge
2	+5.7760	+.9872	−.437	Mill
3	+5.7760	+2.5440	−.437	Mill
4	+3.9313	+2.5440	−.437	Mill

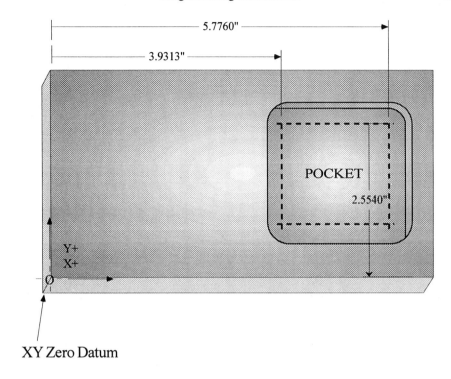

Figure 4.2 *Tool Centers from Absolute Zero*

INCREMENTAL MILLING: POINT to POINT

Milling can be programmed and executed in the Incremental Mode, which involves the virtual resetting of Zero after every move. Older machine controls used this type of programming. Today, it is still used in certain circumstances. It is helpful in operations where some features change from job lot to job lot. It does have disadvantages in its use: compounding of errors between moves (building upon each other); failure to return to the absolute mode in the proper location; programming and control problems when stopping in incremental blocks. See Figure 4.3.

Special circumstances warrant the use of incremental blocks being inserted into a program based otherwise on absolute blocks. When, as the following example illustrates, a slot feature varies from one part to another, a [Stop Block] can be added. The Control can be switched to the [Incremental Mode] and a single move can be added to accommodate a fluctuating dimensional feature. See Figure 4.4.

The program sheet that follows details an example of switching into the [In-

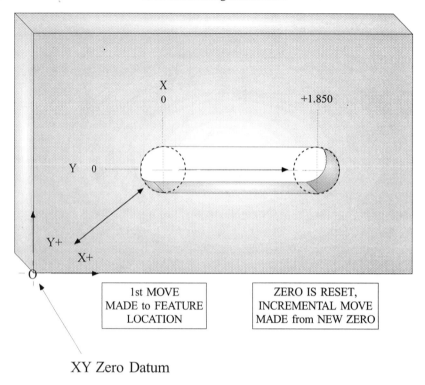

XY Zero Datum

Figure 4.3 *Incremental Milling: Point-to-Point*

cremental] mode, leaving the variable-dimension block open for the specific -X- move to be added when the part is in the machining sequence.

Block #	X Axis	Y Axis	Z Depth	Ref.
11	+3.250	+1.675	+.500	Retract
12	+ .850	+ .625	+.500	Abs. Pos.
13	0.000	0.000	+.500	Incr. Mode
14	0.000	0.000	−.500	Plunge
15	+1.850	0.000	−.500	Mill

PRECISION FINISH MILLING: ATTAINING ULTRA-CLOSE TOLERANCES

Machine Controls that are programmable in increments as small as 50 millionths (.00005) are available. Simply because the programmed machine coordinate is assigned to make a high-resolution move accurate to five decimal places does not mean the machine will move in that small an increment accu-

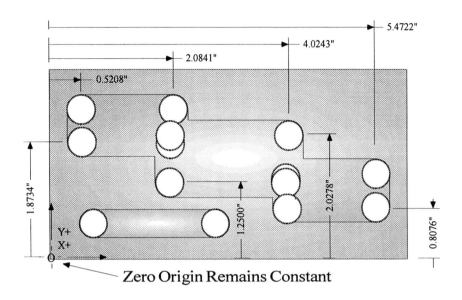

Zero Origin Remains Constant

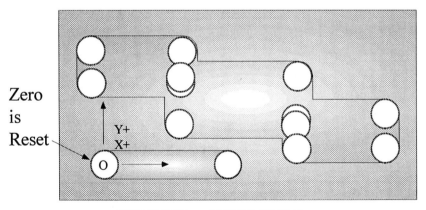

SWITCHED to INCREMENTAL
for SINGLE FEATURE

Figure 4.4 *Change in Program from Absolute*

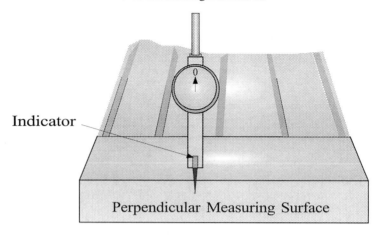

Indicator

Perpendicular Measuring Surface

X	Y	Yes/No
.00005	.00005	+?- +?-
.0001	.0001	+?- +?-
.0005	.0005	+?- +?-

Pos./Neg.
Move Direction

Figure 4.5 *Detecting Smallest Machine Movement*

rately. The smallest actual movement depends on many factors: Resolution of Stepping Motors, Cross-Check Readout accuracy, Machine Screw Repeatability, and others.

To measure the actual "smallest increment" the machine moves, mount a Dial Indicator into the machine spindle with the tip "loaded" against a straight surface mounted perpendicularly across the table of a Milling Machine or on the cross-slide of a Turning Machine. See Figure 4.5.

1. Set the Indicator at -0-.
2. Program in the smallest increment (.00005; .0001; or .0005).
3. Activate the Control's [Single Cycle/Spindle OFF] move capability (Manual Positioning will not represent a Control move).

Detect the smallest move to which the machine responds and repeat it in the opposite direction. This will indicate whether the machine will be consistent it both -X- and -Y- directions of movement.

Once the smallest straight-line indication is determined in the form of an

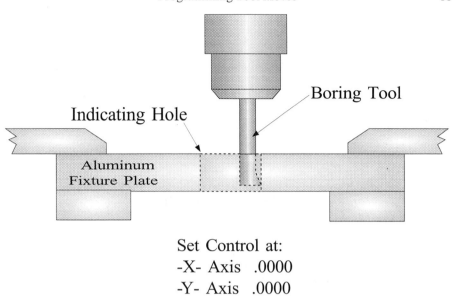

Figure 4.6 *Boring Hole for Indication*

actual increment that the machine Control is capable of moving (via the Program Data Block), another test is necessary to establish accuracy in movement under Rapid Traverse Control power. An aluminum plate has to be mounted directly on the machine table so that a Boring operation is possible. It is advised, through common toolmaking practice, to elevate the plate with blocks (or use a blank aluminum disk held in a Turning Machine). See Figure 4.6.

The figure shows a precision hole being bored into an aluminum plate. The bore requires a high/fine finish on its walls to benefit indicator measurement. The Control is boring on the -X- .0000 -Y- .0000 location [Table Zero] for the future positioning test in Rapid Traverse operation.

After the hole is bored on [.0000.0000] location using machine Control, check for concentricity using a high-resolution Dial Indicator.

1. Move the table off location using manual table jogging. Move off in both X and Y directions to a diagonal location on the table.
2. Using the machine control, "program in" a Rapid Traverse positioning move to X.0000, Y.0000 [Single cycle/Spindle OFF].
3. Measure the concentricity of the bored hole.
4. Repeat in four diagonal directions and note all readings at .0000.0000 achieving this location under the machine's Control Power.

This test gives a very accurate indication of the machine's ability to attain

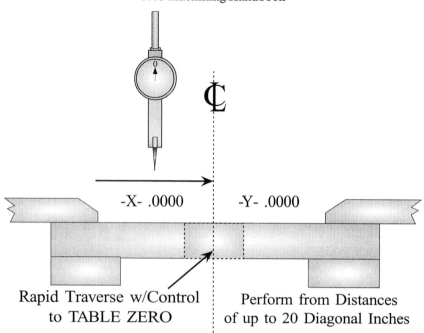

-X- .0000   -Y- .0000

Rapid Traverse w/Control   Perform from Distances
     to TABLE ZERO   of up to 20 Diagonal Inches

Figure 4.7 *Precision Cross-Checking of Machine Accuracy (Under Power)*

the precision positioning for which it is certified. An additional variable can be
added by programming in the smallest increment that the machine is supposed
to move, in addition to the .0000.0000 location, such as +.0002.0000, which
should register an -X- reading of .0002 to the positive. This shows that not only
does the machine repeat to its original home Zero, but that it achieves the
smallest incremental move beyond Zero. See Figure 4.7.

   This procedure gives the knowledge needed to mill and bore as accurately as
the machine will allow, using every known directional advantage to specific
machines. Extremely accurate milling cuts can be made by approaching surfaces with tools, repeating passes of .002 or less for finish passes in aluminum,
and recutting some surfaces on the same coordinate many times. The following
program example utilizes the smallest increment movable in a milling routine.
It is "nested" after the standard milling routine, and protected by a [Stop] Block
so that the operator can use it after gaging or choose not to. It continues to
move in only .0002" (two ten-thousandths) per pass, with one pass chosen after
every plunge.

When the [Stop] Block stops the machine, and if an additional cut is needed to bring in the dimension, the Control is then restarted.

Block #	-X-	-Y-	Z Depth	Ref.
11	+3.250	+1.750	-.562	Mill
12	+3.937	+1.750	-.562	Mill
13	+3.937	+1.750	[Retract]	[STOP]
14	+3.250	+1.7498	-.560	PLUNGE
15	+3.937	+1.7498	-.560	MILL
16	+3.937	+1.7498	[Retract]	[STOP]

At this point in the program, Block 11 is a standard [Mill] block, bringing the cutter into position where the -Y- axis is at +1.750. This Y position is a critical dimension on the part print and must be within .001 of that position from the -Y- Datum Zero (Generic Control Commands).

Due to cutter deflection, wear, flute inconsistencies, and so on, the dimension may not fall into tolerance even though the coordinates are on target and the cutter is machining to the proper size. The [Stop] Block is then executed and the Control stops the machine for a measurement of the workpiece.

If it is necessary to take a finish cut, most Controls allow the Block number to be punched up (Block 14 in this case), and the Control is restarted. The tool plunges, mills one pass .0002" farther in the -Y- direction, and the Control again runs into a [Stop] Block. There, the Control waits for a Block number to continue. If after gaging, the workpiece has to be recut, another .0002 can be machined or the Control can be instructed to continue. Do not remove the cutter from the spindle. By using a proven part-locating procedure, the achievement of ultra-close tolerances can be expected from any Machining Center. After establishing what the machine will move and repeat consistently as the smallest increment (.0005;.0002;.00005), check the workpiece on an angle-plate/granite-surface plate with an electronic indicator to verify the surface dimensions against the intended sizes or part print. If additional cutting is needed, replace the part on the fixture (that has been checked for repeat/replaceability). See Figure 4.8.

It is recommended in the CNC Fixtures section (Chapter 10) to use Horberg[R] tapered locating pins that repeat to within .0001 or less when replacing the workpiece on the fixture continuously. These are necessary to provide precision replacement. After an additional cut is determined to be needed, record the amount necessary to bring the surface into print tolerance. Replace the workpiece onto the fixturing, pushing the locating pins into the same depth as the previous cut.

Return to the [Plunge] Block before the last mill cut and begin cutting and gaging from that point in the program.

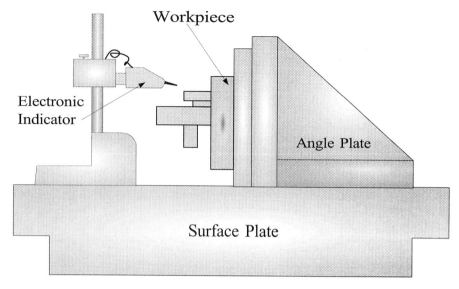

Figure 4.8 *Confirming Precision Mill Cut*

IDEAL CUTTER PATHS

Optimal Cutter Selections: Diameters and Lengths

A blueprint assessment will reveal Toolpath Widths and Radius specs that allow or restrict cutter selections. Most aerospace and **MIL SPEC** workpieces allow very little tolerance when it comes to Radius sizes in corners, pockets, and so on.

- Determine the *largest allowable* Radius specified in the corners of milling features. Double this for cutter diameter and scan the print views for clearance problems with features in close proximity of each other.
- Use the *largest cutter possible* that will fit between features, accommodate Radius requirements, and be held with stability in the machine spindle.

This determination enables the job to be milled efficiently with the cutter diameter large enough to provide maximum surface coverage; to provide cutter stability; to decrease vibration tendencies and allow cutting capacity; and to fit into a wide variety of Radii needs on the workpiece. Concentricity can suffer over the 1.000" Diameter size, especially a cutter with more than two flutes. A cutter diameter that is too small can be programmed to generate larger Radii, but will compromise other areas: vibration, cutting width (requiring more passes), tool wear, and so on. Figure 4.9 shows the cutter diameter selected out of multiple radii and cutter clearances required on the workpiece.

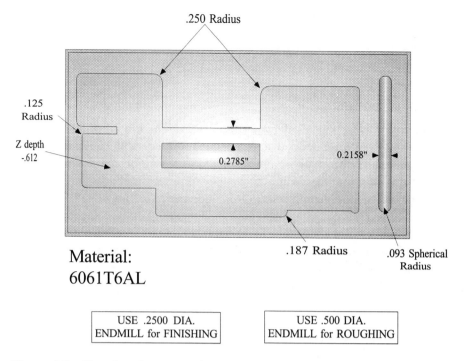

Figure 4.9 *Choosing Correct Tool Diameter*

There are a few choices to make. Because the material is 6061 Aluminum, which is easy to machine, the comparison between the smallest tool clearance and the Z Depth of –.612 must be considered. Here, the depth is more than double the size of cutter width allowed in the slot. Therefore, the most rigid tools should be selected with a minimum of tool changes. The ideal selection would be starting out with a .500-dia., two-flute Endmill. One with .750 of two-flute length would accommodate chip removal yet retain rigidity. The good cutter span covers in a minimum of passes and cuts half of the corner radii on the workpiece. One tool change to a .250-dia., two-flute Endmill will cut the remaining Radii, and the .187 radii have to be generated into and out of the corners, which is easy with CNC. Another alternative is to cut the entire part with a .250 Endmill, although it would be a time-consuming and tool-wasting procedure. Another tool choice is an intermediate tool change to a .375 or .312 dia., which would cut the slot with stability and cut the .187 corners. A .250-dia. Endmill cuts well in aluminum and the time consumed making a tool change does not warrant the extra cutter added.

During tool section it is important to consider the following:

- The number of Radii that are required on a workpiece view
- The amount of surface area on a particular surface

- The range of Radii, from the smallest to the largest size
- A balance of preceding factors, with primary interest being given to covering the most cutting-surface area.

Depth of Cutting

Choice of tools for cutting depth can make or break job productivity. A tool held improperly or extended too far out of the Toolholder can cause a multitude of problems: excessive wear, chipping, breakage, vibration marks on the walls and bottom, minimum material removal per minute.

Factors in CNC tool-length selection include the following:

- Maintain solid shanks down *to the surfaces* being cut, by custom grinding when necessary. Fluted areas of Endmills are the weakest points.
- Select only flute lengths that are required; no cutting edges need extend beyond 1/32 above cut surfaces.
- Use only solid NC Toolholders *whenever* possible.

Notice that the tool choice in what follows illustrates the preceding principles in some detail. See Figure 4.10.

One pass with this .500-dia. Endmill could cause the tool to shatter because

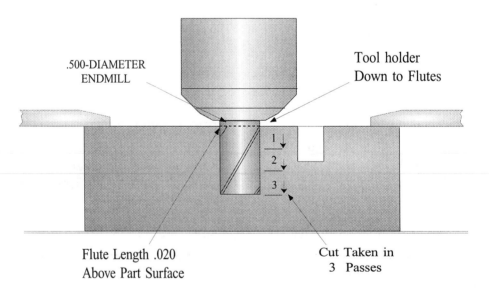

.500-DIAMETER
ENDMILL

Tool holder
Down to Flutes

1
2
3

Flute Length .020
Above Part Surface

Cut Taken in
3 Passes

Figure 4.10 *Optimum Tool-Length Selection*

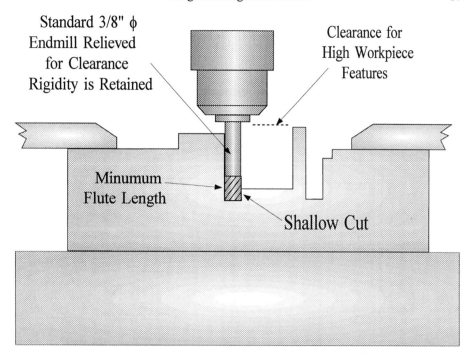

Standard 3/8" φ
Endmill Relieved
for Clearance
Rigidity is Retained

Clearance for
High Workpiece
Features

Minumum
Flute Length

Shallow Cut

Figure 4.11 *Extended Tool Lengths*

chip removal would be diminished because the flute channels are blocked during the full-depth pass. Three passes are chosen at a higher XY feedrate, with rigidity maintained by keeping the toolholder "choked down" near the cutting flutes. If the tool were extended, the amount of tool deflection/flex would decrease the effectiveness of the tool completely. Here, in aluminum, the feedrate could be as high as 20 IPM with an adequate spray mist.

If a tool is required to cut down along a higher wall, long-fluted Endmills are not the best choice. The principle used here is that of *minimum* flute exposure. Even though a tool is required to be extended for clearance to the cutting site, next to a workpiece feature, for example, *no more* flute exposure than necessary is the general rule. See Figure 4.11.

If an extended length is required on a special feature, such as the groove being cut in the preceding component, a relieved Endmill will reach down into very difficult spots and transfer the maximum rigidity from the machine spindle to the cutting edge without the extra vibration that comes into play using a tool that has lengthy flutes.

- Always limit the flute length to the surface being cut; any extra cutting edges only add to vibration and remove critical stiffening material from the shank.

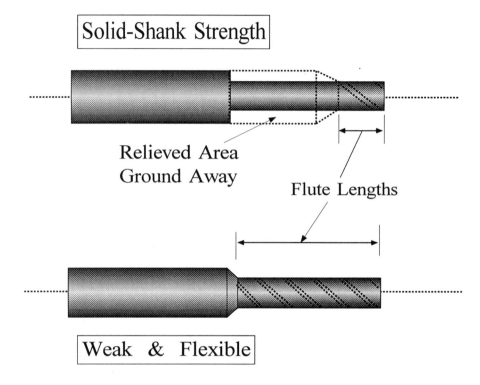

Figure 4.12 *Relieved Endmill Advantages*

- Relieve cutters using a grinding fixture under a coolant to prevent weakening of the tool shank and loss of heat treatment to the cutting edges.
- Relieve only the material needed to clear features on the workpiece from cutting tools.
- In Machining Centers, hold the tools whenever possible in a solid Toolholder. Collets cause additional vibration and allow tools to move during heavy cuts. See Figure 4.12.

Cutter-Path Decisions

Experience dictates several cutter-path decisions be made prior to milling complex and simple shapes and contours. The material being machined is a determining factor. Most steels require conventional milling to keep the machine from causing the workpiece to pull into the cutter. Aluminum, magnesium, and plastic should be climb-milled whenever possible to allow faster material removal and cleaner surfaces. Figure 4.13 details both types of machining directions that are very important for CNC machining. Most milling

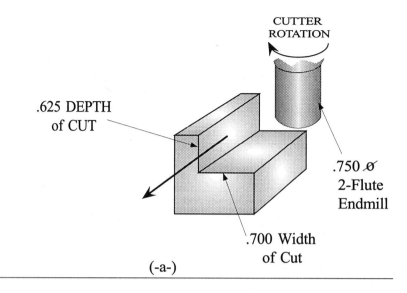

.625 DEPTH
of CUT

.750 ∅
2-Flute
Endmill

CUTTER
ROTATION

.700 Width
of Cut

(-a-)

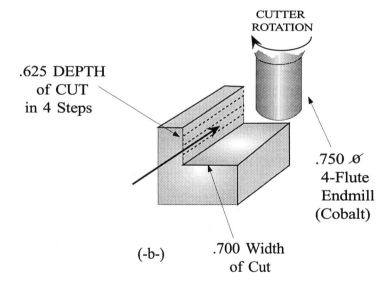

.625 DEPTH
of CUT
in 4 Steps

.750 ∅
4-Flute
Endmill
(Cobalt)

CUTTER
ROTATION

(-b-)

.700 Width
of Cut

Figure 4.13 *(a) Climb-Milling: Aluminum; (b) Conventional Milling: Steel*

programs are written strictly in conventional or climb-milling directions; however, certain operations require "toggling" to the opposite direction.

Paths need to be carefully planned. They can very well determine whether
the finished workpiece, though within dimensional tolerance, will fall within
flatness requirements, perpendicularity notations, and squareness dictations.
Excessive tool force in the wrong direction on a workpiece can build stress
lines within a part. Upon clamping release, stress built up during machining
will cause flexing. This is an undesirable condition that will result in "scrapping
out" otherwise good parts.

- Open areas ideally should be cut from the center out, spiraling outwardly
  from the plunge point.
- Open channels need to be milled in the center first, removing a majority
  of the material for tool and chip clearance.
- Side walls should be saved for final machining, and bottom surfaces
  roughed and finished first. This keeps the tool flex, when milling walls,
  from "tilting" the cutter bottom and rippling the finished bottom with
  vibration marks.
- Small Radii should be the very last operations completed because of the
  fragile tools used.

When moving from one area to another that needs to be milled, and constant
plunging to the center of pockets is unpractical, the approach should be to
move the tool to the center, where the most material has to be removed. There,
tool passes should be made in the center sections first. Moves can then be made

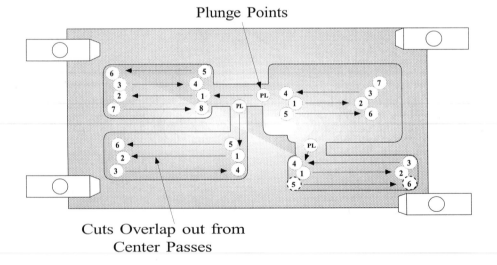

Figure 4.14 Milling Center Pocket Sections First

outwardly toward the walls to be machined. This practice decreases part stress and flex that result from center lifting and stress lines incurred by the tool leverage on center slugs. See Figure 4.14.

Small radii require special attention be given to the direction of milling. Consider the example of milling a small corner in 304 stainless steel, using a .125 Endmill reaching down –.500 deep. Most milling operations performed in stainless steel are done by conventional milling. This pulls the tool into the work, which is desirable using a small tool on stainless steel. If a small tool were used to climb-mill into stainless, the tool would climb up and over the material before it would cut into it. Eventually, the tool would snap. Aluminum and magnesium milling react differently than steel, and a reasonable amount of these materials can be cut in the climb-milling direction with a small tool climbing over them.

CHAPTER 5

CNC OPERATION
SELECTION

CHOOSING the BEST PROGRAM FEATURES
From Blueprint to Machine Control

Blueprint assessment is perhaps the best investment of time on which anyone can focus during the component production process. One patient hour can equate to 60 or more machining hours saved on a 100-piece job lot. A conscious evaluation of *all* the features on *every* view of *each* surface is the first task at hand.

- Color coding of print features helps to distinguish surface depths from each other on complex print views.
- Close-tolerance dimensions need special attention; allowances must be made for extra material left on these surfaces for final finishing.
- Print Notations and Legends must be reviewed and specs applied to the dimensions where necessary.
- Additional noninclusive but pertinent standards that apply to the components being manufactured must be researched (such as Zone Tolerances; Target Dimensions; Hardware and feature specs that require special site machining).
- Material history and documentation if applicable; material grain directions; and inspection documentation if required.

Be well advised to first scan all prints associated with the job for every operation that has to be performed. Next, the creation of "Absolute Dimension

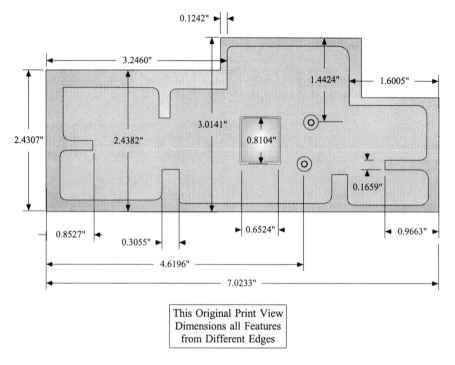

Figure 5.1 *Machine Print View*

Sheets" for each view is a requirement of all successful CNC programs. The Print View, shown in Figure 5.1, and the Absolute Dimension Sheet show in detail how features translate to absolute dimensions, which are used for many sections of the machining.

Absolute Dimension Sheets

A good overview of all the machined features on one face or view is best accomplished by making up these sheets. Their importance will resurface time after time throughout the machining process. Absolute Dimensions Sheets should be made up for every view of a workpiece requiring machining.

Ideally, programs should be designed, when possible, with the X and Y (or X and Z for Turning) Zero Datum (origin) in the lower left-hand corner of the dimension sheet. (If an axes configuration is different for a specific machine, locate the Zero Datum where the two main axes travel *away* from *Zero* in *two positive* directions.) At times, this means that the dimensions have to be recalculated from the given Print Datums or part edges. The end result is well worth the effort because most of the machine moves are X+ (positive) and Y+ (positive), eliminating many crossovers into the negatives on axis moves. Also, because X .0000 and Y .0000 are usually on both exterior edges (flat surfaces), inspection is therefore less involved.

On this Absolute Dimension Sheet, every machined edge of every feature in the view is assigned an "absolute" dimension from the Zero of that axis.

- Begin by making an outline of the features on the face to be programmed; include all machined walls, features, and workpiece edges.
- Calculate, by using print dimensions, all of the absolute sizes of every edge of every feature from the Zero (.0000) of that axis.
- Assign their absolute distances to the feature lines on the new "dimension sheet."
- When angle intersections and arc centers are given, include them on the sheet.

After calculating and assigning every edge and surface a dimension in both the X and Y axes, *cross-check each number*. Initially, this might seem like a drawn-out unnecessary task, but as in all tried-and-proven methods, it is a very important operation in the programming sequence.

The sheet is used first to lay out the workpiece, with each dimension in perfect position for laying out with a height gage from Datum .0000 in the X and Y directions. Once the layout is done, visual inspections quickly reveal errors in calculations, material allowances, and blueprint engineering errors. Windows and pockets, diameters and faces can be checked with calipers for length and width of openings, steps, shoulders, and so on. If everything checks out visually, in the correct place and to scale, a good amount of work has already been cross-checked. Consider that the dimensions have been: transferred from the blueprint to the sheet; inspected during layout of the part; and visually evaluated for scale, feature symmetry, and locations. A triple-checking process has been used. These same "absolute numbers" (dimensions) are used for inspection after the part is machined. See Figure 5.2.

Optimizing the Use of Subroutines in Control

Subroutines offered by today's software programs should, whenever possible, be selected for milling, drilling, facing, turning, and boring operations. "Pocket" and "Frame" subroutines eliminate countless calculations when milling square and rectangular features, compensating for machine backlash while requiring only the finished dimensions be entered in most cases.

Scanning prints for symmetry in hole patterns helps in the application of the drilling and boring routines included in today's software. Bolt-hole patterns can be programmed in two simple blocks that run hundreds of holes. Symmetrical rows of hundreds to thousands of equally spaced holes are programmed in two

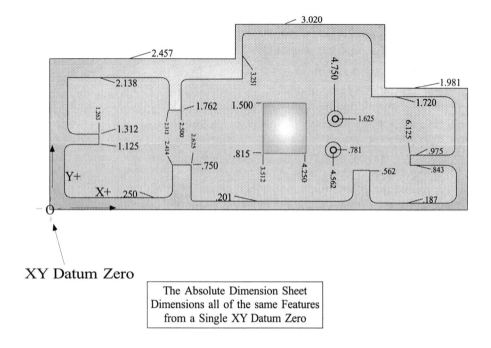

XY Datum Zero

> The Absolute Dimension Sheet
> Dimensions all of the same Features
> from a Single XY Datum Zero

Figure 5.2 *Absolute Dimension Sheet*

simple blocks. Identifying these patterns on the blueprints and using the appropriate subroutines save hundreds of blocks of program space. Selecting subroutines enables the execution of miniprograms, or "macros," to be applied to your particular features on the workpiece. See Figure 5.3.

Specific tools and operations require point-to-point moves by the machine table. Allocate time to select plunge-point coordinates and choose the best direction in which the tool is desired to move. Use the Absolute Dimension Sheet to add or subtract the tool radius (1/2 of the tool diameter).

- Remember to plan moves so that they clear clamps and locating pins.
- Any path can be easily programmed by sketching (or printing out a hard copy), adding or subtracting the tool radius, and writing in the tool coordinates on the E/M Toolpath Sheets.

Also noted on these sheets are the tool calibrations for each tool diameter. See Figure 5.4.

Many straight-line coordinate moves need to be planned and executed in single block moves. A general rule applies to both subroutines and straight-line moves:

- Accomplish as many operations with one tool (without changing) as possible.

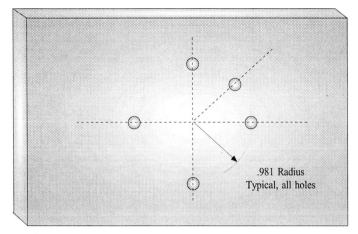

.981 Radius
Typical, all holes

Hole Center Defined, Radius, and # of Holes

SUBROUTINE Used for
Symmetrical Hole Patterns

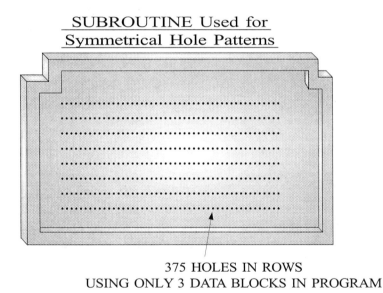

375 HOLES IN ROWS
USING ONLY 3 DATA BLOCKS IN PROGRAM

Figure 5.3   Bolt-Hole Subroutine Used

In the following example, a workpiece to be machined has one pocket with .062 Radius in the corners. Also, there are also two bores, 1.281 Diameter typical. A general rule applies here:

- Use an Endmill radius *equal to* or *smaller than* the *smallest* radius specified on the machined features of a workpiece.

The pocket with the .062 Radius requires a .125 Endmill or smaller for finishing. *Every* feature can be effectively milled first with a .500-Dia. Endmill,

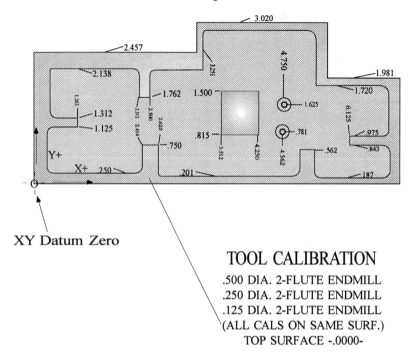

XY Datum Zero

TOOL CALIBRATION

.500 DIA. 2-FLUTE ENDMILL
.250 DIA. 2-FLUTE ENDMILL
.125 DIA. 2-FLUTE ENDMILL
(ALL CALS ON SAME SURF.)
TOP SURFACE -.0000-

Figure 5.4 *Absolute Dimension Sheet Tool Calibration*

roughing and finishing the pocket floor and bore diameters. This ties together all the dimensions on each feature; it also eliminates multiple tool changes and calibration differences that are always a possible source of error. Of course, this principle is governed by the tools that remove material effectively. Slow finishing feedrates with a .125 Endmill can then complete the pocket corners, requiring only one tool change to finish machining the features. See Figure 5.5.

- A Radius in one pocket that requires a .125 Endmill will not dictate roughing larger bores with this fragile tool.

If single-block calculations must be made to mill point to point around radii or complex arcs that blend together, it is a wise idea to choose an Endmill smaller than the smallest radii required.

- Try to choose an Endmill *ON* an even fraction size such as .500-Dia. E/M or a .250-Dia. E/M.

This not only allows for each replacement or the tool after wear or breakage, but reduces "odd digit error" for future numerical calculations that can potentially cause error.

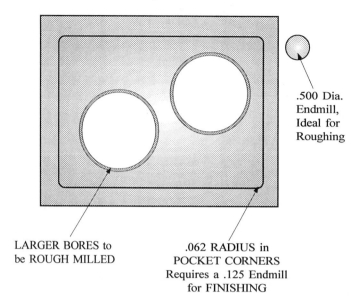

.500 Dia.
Endmill,
Ideal for
Roughing

LARGER BORES to
be ROUGH MILLED

.062 RADIUS in
POCKET CORNERS
Requires a .125 Endmill
for FINISHING

Figure 5.5 *Feature Requirements vs. Tool Diameters*

- An even number on a tool diameter or a multiple of 10 creates many less digits during manual computation (inspection, dimension sheets).
- Choose tools that have the shortest shanks possible and ones that *complete* as many operations as possible.

The sequence of operations is as important as any other factor in program design. All milling operations (except for the very close-tolerance surfaces) need to be completed on one side of a workpiece before any other operations are done. On parts where thickness and flatness tolerances are critically close, all milling operations should be completed prior to holes and bores being finished. This allows for stress relief and part flexing after most of the material is removed. Mill as many surfaces as possible to remove most of the material to allow for proper drilling- and boring-tool access. It also establishes depths from which other operations are measured in all three axes. See Figure 5.6.

- Be well aware of the subroutines offered in the software user manuals.

Cutter compensation, Pockets, Frames, Circles, Ellipses, Arcs, Helixes, and other subroutines save program space and untold hours of math computation time. They execute trigonometric and geometric formulas requiring programmers to only fill in the blueprint dimensions. Most even return the cutter to

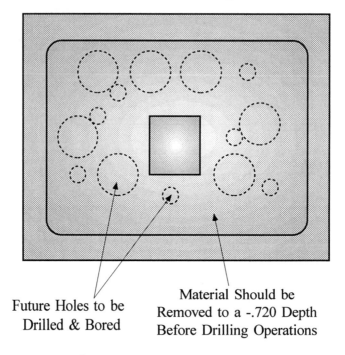

Large Amounts of
Material Removed
Cause
Part Stress and Flexing

Future Holes to be
Drilled & Bored

Material Should be
Removed to a -.720 Depth
Before Drilling Operations

Figure 5.6 *Sequence of Operations*

the starting point and perform finishing passes automatically—using only one
or two blocks of program space. (See Chapter 8 for complete subroutine listing
and description.)

Subroutines used in combination to create more complex workpiece features
make the most efficient use of the machine Control. The miniprograms can create
shapes with finish passes included (that execute both tool directions and variable
material amounts on roughing and finishing passes) with menu-driven input parameters all contained in one or two blocks of the subroutine's program space.

Hole Patterns for Drilling

After milling operations have been performed on part programs, dril-
ling/rough-boring is the next operation to be executed. Surfaces that have been
finish-milled can provide dimensional pickup points for hole patterns (while
the workpiece is still clamped, if possible).

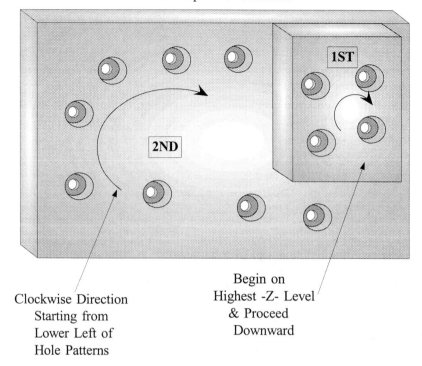

Figure 5.7 *Sequence of Hold Drilling*

- Choose a Centerdrill that allows the pilot/centerdrilling of all the holes to be machined on one surface or side of the workpiece—this saves Tool Changes and extra Stop Blocks.

If complex hole patterns are scattered all over the workpiece face without any symmetry, select all the holes on the same Z (axis) level and start in a clockwise direction with the selection. Clockwise selection of drill features enables all the coordinates to progress in an increasing Y+ then X+ direction first (if the Zero Origin was ideally in the lower left-hand corner). Proceed to lower and lower -Z- levels, completing the centerdrilling, "pecking" 5 to 10 times on each centerdrilling spot (for most materials). See Figure 5.7.

- Pecking, included in most machining software, not only removes/relieves the chips from the tool's cutting edge, it also tends to rebore locationwise with each downward motion of the tool through the previously drilled pilot, correcting some deflection in the centerdrilling process.

Generally, centerdrill to a depth that creates a diameter .010 larger than the finished drilled hole that will be following. This allows for proper centering without too large of a chamfer left on the hole diameter.

Most programming softwares allow for [Copy Blocks] to be made after the original centerdrilling operations are completed. Once the centerdrilling operations have passed inspection for XY locations and are proven accurate to blueprint specs, the sequential tools such as drills, countersinks, and counterbores can make use of the [Copy Blocks]. These blocks copy all of the previous X and Y coordinates that have been checked through inspections, and enable the new blocks to be created instantly without inputting all the X and Y dimensions again. One or two keystrokes with the new tool diameter and Z depths specified, the Control creates new blocks instantly. This enables all of the previous drill blocks to be copied without the chance of a typographical error inputting the XY coordinates. See the following program sample.

Block #	Operation	-X-	-Y-	-Z-	REF.
21	[COPY]	-ALL-	-ALL-	NEW-Z-Depth	Copy 1–20
22	Drill Tool #4	+1.2500	+3.7500	−.396	12 pecks
23	Drill Tool #4	+3.6880	+3.7500	−.396	12 pecks

If material and coolant conditions permit, insert 10 or more pecks into the drill blocks to allow for chip removal, coolant influx, and tool cooling. [Pecks] happen so fast that their virtual time consumption is quickly made up by less downtime for tool wear and breakage.

Subroutines for Drilling/Boring/Tapping in most controls can also be very powerful and data-intensive with as little as one to three Blocks of program space. Consider the hole configuration in Figure 5.8.

The Program Sheet that follows uses Subroutines to cover the entire irregular and largely unsymmetrical hole pattern shown in Figure 5.8 using only [15] Blocks of program space.

Block #	Operation	-X-	-Y-	-Z-	Comments
1	Plunge/Dr.	1.25	3.38	−0.25	Tool #1
2	Repeat	0.6	−0.75	−0.25	C'Drill
3	# of Times	7 times	1 time	−0.25	Subrout.
4	Drill	0.8	0.95	−0.25	
5	Drill	0.98	1.33	−0.25	(Individual
6	Drill	1.33	1.33	−0.25	Blocks)
7	Drill	2.02	1.8	−0.25	

Countersinking and Counterboring

Counterboring depths can be easily set and inspected to meet blueprint specs. All dimensions (depths, diameters) repeat consistently when the program is ready for production. Use single-fluted Countersinks where possible and Endmills or boring tools to counterbore where material conditions permit.

Symmetrical Rows of Holes

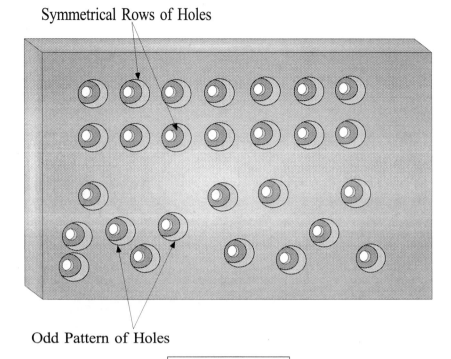

Odd Pattern of Holes

This 27-Hole Pattern
is Programmed in only
15 Blocks of
Program Space

Figure 5.8 *Drilling/Boring/Tapping Using Subroutines*

- Pilots on Countersinks and Counterbores should be avoided wherever possible. They tend to inhibit chip removal, score pilot holes, and slow feedrates.
- Low tool RPMs and fast feedrates IPMs function ideally.
- Flood Coolant leaves the best finish for both operations (on most materials).
- Use solid Toolholders and medium extension lengths from toolholders to allow Countersinks and Counterbores to flex and follow pilot holes on downfeed.

Notice the countersinks and the corresponding material in which they perform best, as shown in Figure 5.9.

Finish-Boring Operations

Finish-boring (and finish-milling) operations on close-tolerance dimensions should be the last operations to be completed on any surface or side of a work-

For Large Holes &
Chamfers in:
ALL MATERIALS
SEMIHARDENED STEEL
CERAMICS

Insert Tool (Carbide)

For Small Holes
& Chamfers in:
ALUMINUM
BRASS
MAGNESIUM
SOFT STEEL

Single-Flute High-Speed Steel

For Small to
Large Holes &
Chamfers in:
STEELS
STRINGY ALLOYS
INTERRUPTED HOLE
WALLS

Multi-flute Countersink
(High-Speed Steel)

Figure 5.9 *Countersinks and Their Best Suited Materials*

piece. These operations are last, even after chamfering holes and milling 45's
on surface edges. Milling out large quantities of material on any surface causes
flexing after the stress lines in a part change. Even drilling and rough boring
large holes have the same twisting effect on a part surface. Close-tolerance sizes
and boring passes are therefore placed as the last Program Blocks before a
workpiece side is finally finished. Highlight these surface lines on the Absolute
Dimension Sheet so that an extra .005 to .007 is left on these surfaces and
diameters.

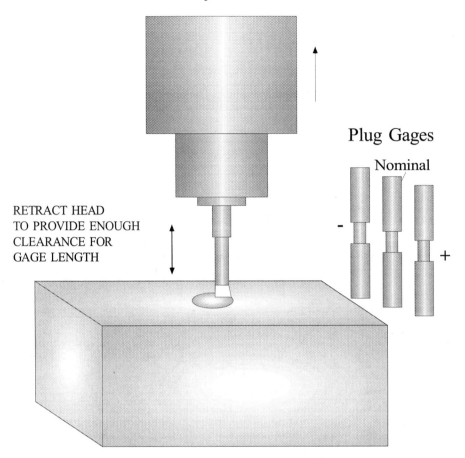

Figure 5.10 *Stop Block: Retracting Boring Head for Gaging*

- Place [Stop] Blocks in the program preceding boring and finishing operations to clean tool tapers and prepare gages to measure each close-tolerance dimension after it is completed.
- If additional boring cuts/finishing passes are needed, restart the machine at the last [Stop] Block, remachine/reinspect the workpiece at the [Stop] Block.

See Figure 5.10.

ARCS

Quarter-Circle Arcs

An Arc that begins and ends covering 1/4 of a circle, 90°, with a constant radius revolving around one common Arc Center is a Quarter-Circle Arc. It can

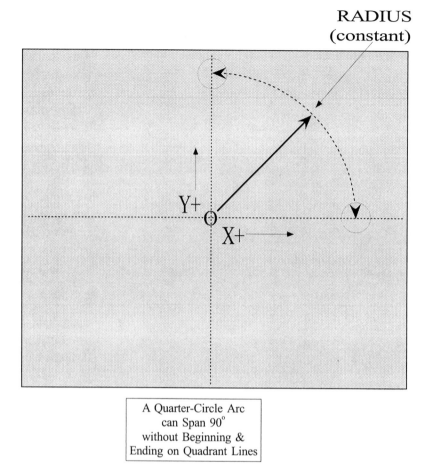

A Quarter-Circle Arc
can Span 90°
without Beginning &
Ending on Quadrant Lines

Figure 5.11 *Quarter-Circle Arc*

progress from its origin to its End Point in the Clockwise or Counterclockwise direction. This common Arc, which is used in toolpath programming, forms a right triangle and is shown in Figure 5.11.

Many times when there is room to use this type of Arc, it is a good choice to incorporate it because of the ease of computation, the guarantee of angular representation (45° to –45°, 90°), the ability to adjust the coordinates equally after inspection, and the simple program data input.

Sector Arcs

Sector Arcs range from 0° to 360°. They begin and end covering the range of degrees with a constant radius revolving around one common Arc Center.

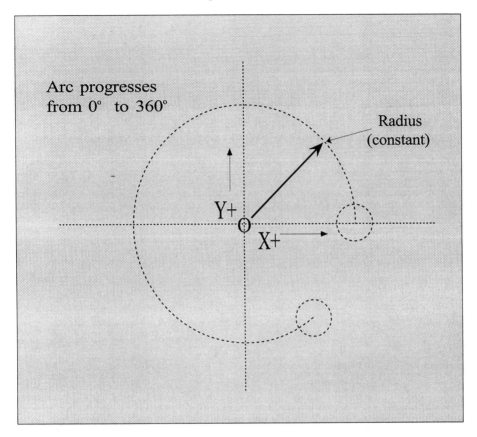

Figure 5.12   *Sector Arcs*

Sector Arcs can progress from their origin to their End Point in the Clockwise or Counterclockwise direction. These are commonly used in Toolpath programming, especially when full-circle mill paths have obstructions that prohibit an entire circular milling pass. See Figure 5.12.

Elliptical Arcs

An Elliptical Arc follows a path where the Arc Center changes between the locus of points for which the sum of the distances from each point to two fixed points is equal. This Arc is much more complex and requires accurate blend points where the toolpaths intersect. Elliptical Arcs are frequently used for cam and eccentric fabrication. As Figure 5.13 shows, four Arc Centers are controlling two Radii, transferring the toolpath in a smooth transition between them. Many Arcs require an elliptical path to be configured to blend two Arcs together.

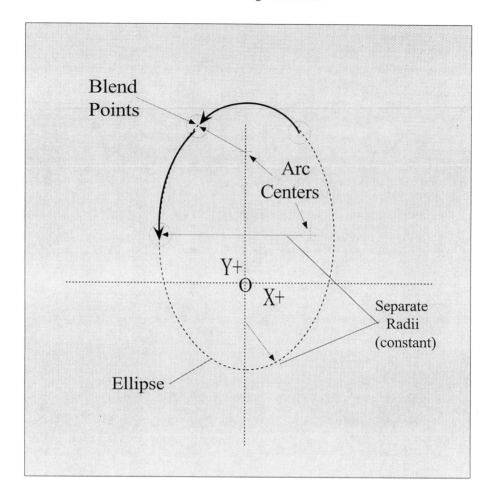

Figure 5.13 *Elliptical Arcs*

Circular Curves

A Circular Curve from a mathematical standpoint is an Arc having a constant radius, but it is used as a general heading in CNC Programming to cover simple, compound, and reversed curves. The headings accurately describe coordinate locations that are required to enable Controls to achieve desired contours with minimal data calculation and input.

A Curve made up of two or more simple Curves, each having a common tangent point at their junction and lying on the same side of the tangent, is called a Common Curve. Compound Curves have an advantage over simple Arcs because they may be easily adapted to the natural topography of a particular location. See Figure 5.14(a).

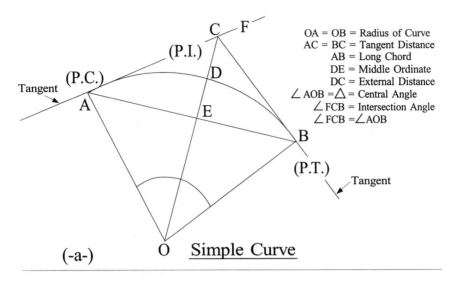

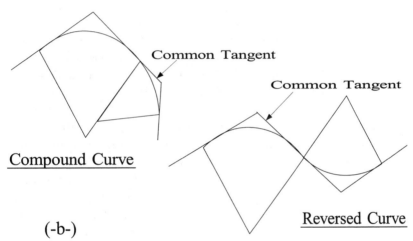

Figure 5.14 *(a) Circular Curves and Circular Arcs; (b) Compound and Reversed Curves*

In Figure 5.14(a), point A is called the Point of Curvature (P.C.) and point B the Point of Tangency (P.T.). Point C is known as the Point of Intersection (P.I.) of the Tangents. In Programming, the P.I. is an essential dimension because it represents the absolute machine-axis coordinate intersection. It would make up the intersection point of machined surfaces if radii were not specified or if sharp corners were theoretically achieved.

A Curve or Arc made up of two simple Curves having a common tangency at their junction and lying on opposite sides of the common tangent is called a Reversed Curve. This type of Curve is advantageous for blending two or more Arcs into one another without steps or mathematical mismatches. Many CNC Controls have capabilities to calculate and blend multiple Arcs together with minimal data input or calculation. However, all critically dimensioned contours *require* programmers to *know* how to make fine coordinate adjustments to Arcs, Curves, and Contours. Revising a preprogrammed coordinate for the blend point of the Common Tangent in a Compound Curve or Reversed Curve is a common practice in CNC machining. See Figure 5.14(b).

Parabolic Toolpaths

To understand where the toolpath is to be traveling in more than two axes, for example, in 3-, 4-, and 5-Axis Milling and Turning Programs, a thorough understanding of a Parabolic Curve is necessary. The Parabolic Curve is symmetrical around an axis. The Parabola is a simple portion of space occupied or chosen by the path traced out in a plane by a point moving in accordance with a simple law. The Curve is used as an accepted and recognized format for many advanced CNC Control systems. See Figure 5.15(a).

Briefly stated, point P is equidistant from a fixed point S (the Focus) and a fixed line ZM (the Directrix). This allows a further relevant comparison between the Parabola (PS/PM = 1) and other Conic sections, the Ellipse (PS/PM < 1), and the Hyperbola (PS/PM > 1). See Figure 5.15(b).

Since the marriage by Descartes (1596–1650) of geometry to algebra, it has been possible to represent the Parabola in shorthand: $y^2 = 4ax$; this provides a powerful tool for revealing the properties of the Curve. The viewpoint from which the Parabola is seen in its most relevant aspect to CNC Programming is the special section of a right circular cone (Figure 5.15(b)). The most general conic section is an ellipse (AA'), which has two extreme forms—the Circle and the Parabola. In Figure 5.15(b), P'OP, Q'OQ represent generators of a right circular cone, AA' being a section of the cone by a plane that makes an angle with the axis of the cone greater than half the vertical angle AOA'. When this angle is equal to one-half of AOA', the major axis AA' of the ellipse is parallel to the generator of the cone and therefore of infinite length. This extreme form of the Ellipse is the Parabola. All successful Advanced CNC Programmers need to become familiar with the Parabolic Arc. See Figure 5.16(a).

The spheres inscribed touch the cone in circles, and the cross-section of the ellipse slices this plane at the Foci S, S'. This is directly translated to three- and four-axis CNC Toolpaths for machining centers where tools move in Parabolic Planes in relation to Arc Centers (or Foci). In Figure 5.16(a), the planes containing the circles of contact between spheres and the cone intersect the plane of the Ellipse in two lines, which are the Directrices. This geometric plane Curve can seem complex in comparison to 2-Dimensional Arcs, but its simplicity in design allow it to be applied to *any* of the geometric multiaxis Toolpaths in

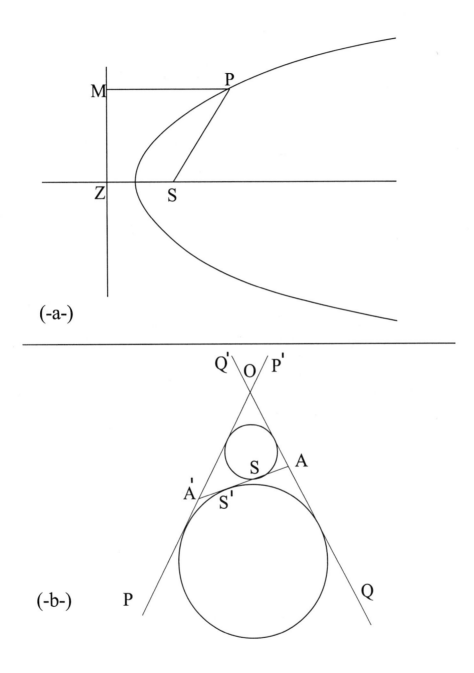

(-a-)

(-b-)

Figure 5.15 *(a) Parabolic Arc; (b) Conic-Section Ellipse*

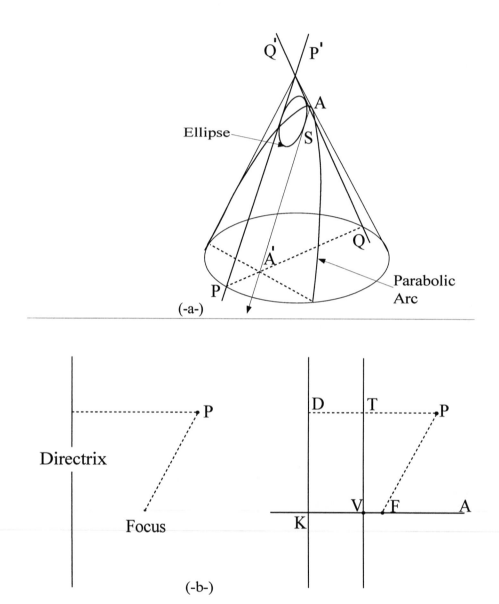

Figure 5.16 *(a) Parabolic Arc: Conic Section; (b) Parabola Construction*

CNC Programming. It is selected for its adaptability to many multiaxis shapes and contours.

Direct Application to CNC Programming

A Parabola is the locus of a point whose undirected distance from a fixed point is equal to its undirected distance from a fixed line. The fixed point is the Focus and the fixed line is the Directrix of the Parabola. See Figure 5.16(b).

Line A through the Focus, perpendicular to the Directrix, meets the Directrix at K. Point V, midway between K and the Focus, is a point on the Parabola. T is the line through V, parallel to the Directrix. All points on the side of T away from the Focus are nearer the Directrix than the Focus and cannot lie on the Parabola. Therefore, the Parabola is entirely on the same side of T as is the focus. Given Directrix D and Focus F of a Parabola, it is possible to pinpoint as many coordinates in direct relation to machine axes as desired. Any straight-line machine move can be visualized by line L to the right of T and parallel to it. See Figure 5.17.

This line is a certain distance from the Directrix. With this distance as a Radius and the Focus as an Arc Center, Arcs intersecting L in P and P′ can be visualized. These two points are by definition on the Parabolic Arc. By continuing this process, this entire Arc can be determined and the required data gleaned for a CNC Control to accomplish up to the most complex 3-, 4-, and 5-axis contouring.

In Figure 5.18, line A is called the Axis, V the Vertex, and T the Vertex-Tangent of the Parabola. The chord cut by the Parabolic Arc from the line through the focus perpendicular to the axis is called the Latus Rectum. Its length is twice the distance between the Directrix and the Focus.

Parabolic Arcs and CNC Control

A Parabolic Arc follows a path where the Arc Center changes between the locus of points formed equidistant from a fixed line and a fixed point not on the line. This Arc is also much more complex and requires a series of accurate blend points where the toolpath consistently adjusts to a moving Arc Center. Parabolic Arcs are one of the most complicated that will ever be encountered during programming. They require a constant reinforming (updating) method to instruct the Control where the Arc Center progresses to and at what small increment the Toolpath and Arc Center update themselves. Most advanced Controls employ macros that simply require the variables be inputted: Arc Center Path; Base and Height Dimensions; and Toolpath and Arc Center update increments. Figures 5.19 and 5.20, respectively, show the formulas for the Parabolic Arc and an example.

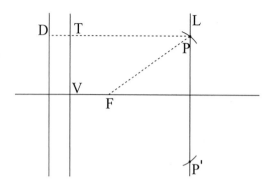

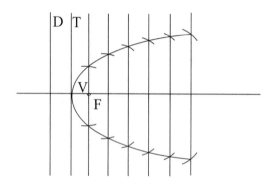

Figure 5.17 *Parabola: (a) Directrix and Focus; (b) Arc Intersection*

Contours

CNC functions well to provide machine contours without interruption. Many companies purchase CNC machines and Machining Centers for the sole purpose of machining complex shapes and contours.

Ideally, the programmer should design the toolpath to take finish passes from feature to feature, leaving a stepless, seamless contouring surface. This is accomplished through numerical commands sent from the control to the axes motors. If the toolpath is geometrically possible—that is, allows a tool small enough to fit into corners and small areas; and the print dimensions are correct—any seamless transition from feature to feature is possible through the

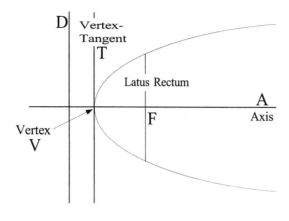

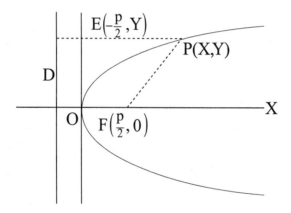

Figure 5.18 *Parabolic Arcs: (a) Axis and Vertex; (b) Axis and Vertex (formulas)*

use of a precision program structure and the efficient use of the Control's software features.

Today's Controls employ Cutter-Compensation features that minimize the computations needed to machine complex contours and shapes. Cutter Compensation allows the programmer to input the absolute dimensions of a workpiece, the actual finished dimensions that each feature is assigned from absolute Datum Zero.

The Control's computer makes mathematical compensations to move the cut-

It is worthwhile to note the Equation of a Parabolic Arc with its Vertex at the Origin of a system of coordinates with the Focus on the (Positive) = X Axis. Denote the distance between the Directrix and Focus by P.

The coordinates of F are: $\left(\dfrac{P}{2}, 0\right)$

And, the Equation of D is: $X = -\dfrac{P}{2}$

By industry-accepted definition, the Curve of the Locus of a point P that satisfies the condition: $FP = EP$

But $FP = \sqrt{\left(X - \dfrac{P}{2}\right)^2 + Y^2}$

And the undirected distance EP is: $\left| X + \dfrac{P}{2} \right|$

The Algebraic counterpart of the Parabolic Arc is therefore: $\sqrt{\left(X - \dfrac{P}{2}\right)^2 + Y^2} + \left| X + \dfrac{P}{2} \right|$

Upon squaring & simplifying, this becomes: $Y^2 = 2 P X$

Because no XY coordinates can satisfy the complement of the Parabolic Arc, the simplification gives an equivalent Equation. This is the standard Equation for the Parabolic Arc.

CNC Controls use Linear, Circular, and Parabolic Interpolation to calculate and maintain precision Toolpaths that allow the tool to follow complex geometries such as the Parabolic Arcs through constant real-time calculation in the machine's processor. Zero-based interpolation is the maximum deviation of the actual characteristic (average of upscale and downscale readings) from theoretically perfect lines or curves so positioned to coincide with the actual characteristic at the lower tangent value and to minimize the maximum deviation from the ideal Toolpath.

Figure 5.19 *Standard Equations for Parabolic Arcs*

ter right or left of the feature, predicts blend points and tool tangents, and even allows for programmable finish passes and finish feedrates. While the tool is in motion, the control is constantly updating the cutting-edge position and tool-center distance from absolute Datum Zero.

Cutter Compensation is definitely a time-saving subroutine that should be used wherever possible. However, in the workplace, where a variety of complex programs are encountered on a regular basis, knowledge of Conventional Point-to-Point Contour Programming methods is still a prerequisite to mastering CNC programming and program design.

The significant difference between Conventional Point-to-Point Programming and Cutter Compensation is the measuring distance from Datum Zero, which

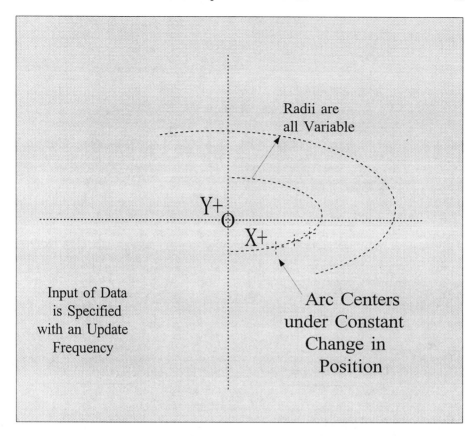

Figure 5.20 *Parabolic Toolpath Arcs*

is dimensioned to the tool center in the point-to-point mode and dimensioned to the finished workpiece surface in cutter-compensation mode. Primarily, there is an additional triangle whose trigonometry is computed to find the point where the cutting edge is tangent to the finished contouring surface that is being milled or turned. Many of the more complex and close-tolerance contours require that conventional programming be used to input the axis coordinates into the CNC control.

Figures 5.21 and 5.22 show the use of Conventional Tool-Center programming and Cutter Compensation being used on the same contour. It details where triangles and formulas are required for computation to locate the tangent cutting edge. Notice the areas where angled surfaces blend into arcs and the tool-tangent triangles that correspond to their geometry. The important comparison made between the contours in Figures 5.21 and 5.22 reveals that the amount

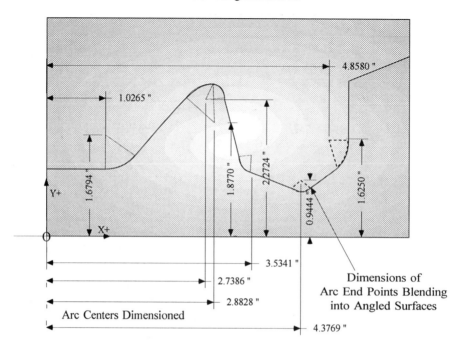

Figure 5.21 *Conventional Tool-Center Programming Dimensions*

of mathematical computation is greatly reduced using Cutter Compensation. Only the finished dimensions are required for entry. The triangles are computed within the Control while machining. (See Chapter 8.)

Continuous Feature-to-Feature Milling: Ideal Toolpaths

After material has been roughed from a workpiece, a toolpath needs to be designed and plotted to move the tool from feature to feature on the same -Z-level without retracting the tool. This allows the precision finishing of the feature wall surfaces and sizing/gaging operations to be performed.

[Stop] Blocks can be nested between finishing operations to allow for gaging access during close-tolerance milling. The workpiece in Figure 5.23 has precision features both in its XY location and dimensionally. Notice how the tool moves from a single Plunge Point, which maintains an accurate -Z- dimension, and approaches the center bosses first. The plotted path moves the shortest distance from the center features toward the outside of the workpiece face, finally finishing the outer walls. All passes are performed in the Climb-Milling direction because the workpiece machined is Magnesium.

Ideal toolpaths involve the best choices to optimize cutter travel from feature

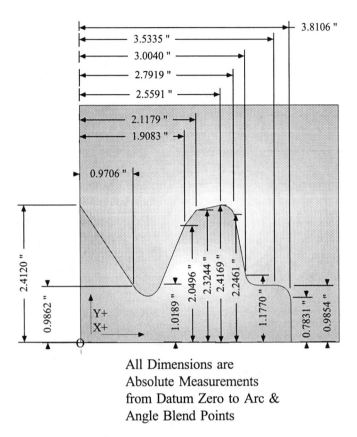

All Dimensions are
Absolute Measurements
from Datum Zero to Arc &
Angle Blend Points

Figure 5.22 *Dimensions for Cutter Compensation*

to feature. This normally requires several factors to be considered: the material being cut; the tolerance requirements in the X, Y, and Z directions; and the finishes required.

The material being machined is a major variable that controls toolpaths considerably. Aluminum and Magnesium parts can capitalize on free machining, deep cuts, and fast feedrates/spindle RPMs. Mild Steels, stringy Stainless, and space-age Alloys such as Inconel and Monel require careful strategy, custom tooling, and force/leverage predictions for toolpath designs.

Figure 5.24 shows the two basic principles used to create ideal paths for roughing—one in Steel, taking stepping passes; the other in Aluminum, using a circular motion after allowing for a center boss.

When XYZ dimensions are close enough to require special attention (.002 or closer in any direction), it should be paid to every roughing cut, especially the

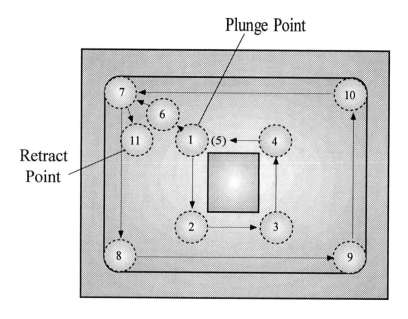

Block #12 -- [STOP] BLOCK
allowing for Gaging Operation

Figure 5.23 *Stop Block in Finishing Tool Moves*

last rough cut. Z-depth dimensions need to be "stepped" in most cases, leaving a finish cut large enough to avoid "work hardening" in Steel, where the tool rides over small amounts of material instead of cutting it.

Figure 5.25 shows step cuts in Steel leaving an amount of finish-cut material larger than the Aluminum example, which shows one large roughing cut and a small skim cut for finishing.

Figure 5.26 shows the Roughing/Finishing depth-of-cut relationship between mild Steel and softer Aluminum and Magnesium, with corresponding XY Feedrates/Spindle RPMs. These can be used as general guidelines for starting parameters when writing programs. When the XY feedrates are tested during actual cutting conditions, overrides can be used on the Control to fine-tune the cutting of the material with XY feedrates, spindle speeds, and end-result surface finishes.

Plunge Points should never be directly adjacent to finished features. Tool deflection and out-of-concentricity movements during plunging can gouge into material that would end up as finished feature walls. Generally, plunge .125 to .250 away from the finished surfaces. During the plunge, divide the depth to be cut by the number of passes, still allowing for the finish-cut material. Figure

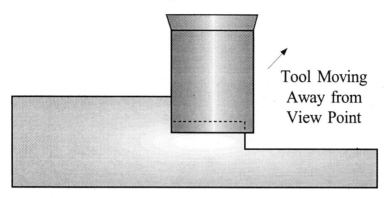

Tool Moving
Away from
View Point

CIRCULAR TOOLPATHS
in ALUMINUM

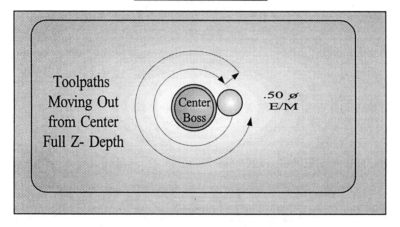

Toolpaths
Moving Out
from Center
Full Z- Depth

Center
Boss

.50 ø
E/M

Figure 5.24 *(a) Step Passes in Steel: Conventional Milling; (b) Circular Toolpaths in Aluminum*

5.27 shows a Plunge Point .125 away from a critically dimensioned pad, stepping the cutter down one of three passes and still allowing for a .006 finish cut in the AL 6061. Slowly feed into the feature surface at an angle from the axis feed that will be used for the finished machining. Use a 25% reduced feedrate from the finish feedrate for the feature.

Surface Approaches are a critical part of toolpaths. They allow the tool to ease into a surface to avoid cutter digging, overtravel, and material pull-ins to occur. These imperfections can be discovered after the part is finished-machined. A surface, especially one controlled by close tolerances and finish notations, has to be approached at an angle skewed from the direct perpendicular intersection. Design the path, where space permits, to approach in a parallel

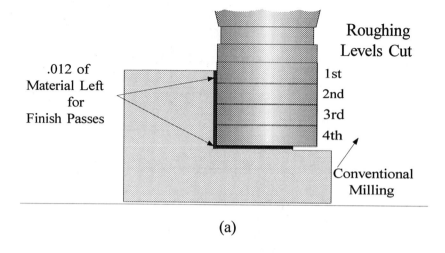

(a)

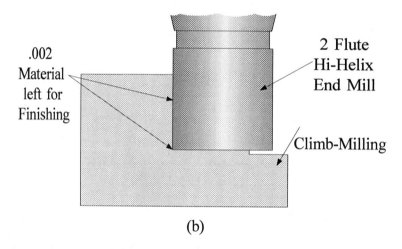

(b)

Figure 5.25 *(a) Step Cuts in Steel; (b) Roughing Full Pass in Aluminum*

direction, angling into the surface (15°) at a 25% decreased feedrate from the designated feedrate to be used when the surface is reached. See Figure 5.28.

Corner feedrates are critical especially in materials that tend to grab and pull up workpieces and pull in cutters. Ideally, "design-in" a "ramp-down" condition before and after the actual corner to prevent this and other problems that will leave surface imperfections. Choose a point .030 before and after the radius washout in the existing roughed corner. Figure 5.29 demonstrates the ideal ramp-down condition that should be used in every critical corner. Some newer Controls feature this process automatically.

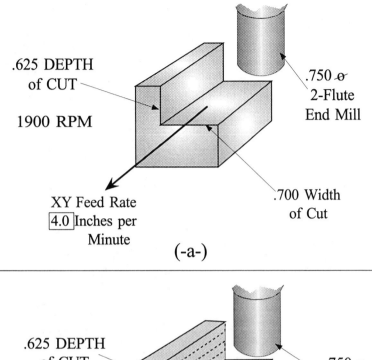

.625 DEPTH
of CUT

1900 RPM

.750 ⌀
2-Flute
End Mill

XY Feed Rate
4.0 Inches per
Minute

.700 Width
of Cut

(-a-)

.625 DEPTH
of CUT
in 4 Steps

680 RPM

XY Feed Rate
1.2 Inches per
Minute

.750 ⌀
4-Flute
End Mill
(Cobalt)

.700 Width
of Cut

(-b-)

Figure 5.26 *Feedrates: (a) Aluminum; (b) Steel*

Exit Points should mirror the principles used for Plunge Points. Move the tool out at an angle from the last movement. Feedrates can be constant from the last mill block because no new material is being cut. After the desired distance is achieved, the spindle can be retracted. See Figure 5.30.

Cutter Compensation is usually presented as an individual subroutine, separate from other milling subroutines that use Cutter Compensation as well as Circle, Frame, Pocket, and so on. The individual Cutter Compensation subrou-

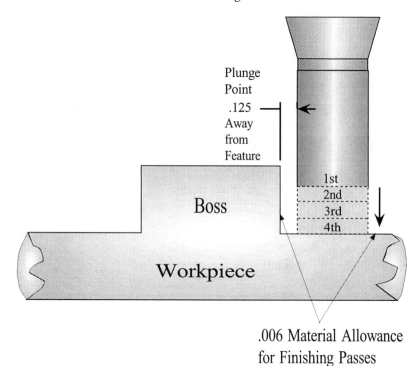

Figure 5.27   *Plunge Parameters*

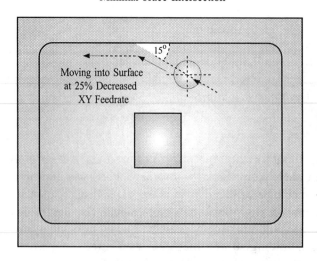

Figure 5.28   *Finish-Pass Tool and Surface Intersection*

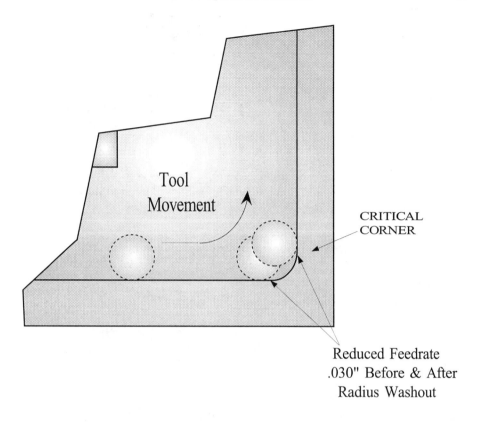

Tool Movement

CRITICAL CORNER

Reduced Feedrate
.030" Before & After
Radius Washout

Figure 5.29 *Ideal Ramp-Down Condition for Corners*

tines used for contouring are Cutter Comp (Left) and Cutter Comp (Right). By viewing at the cutter level looking past the tool to the workpiece, Cutter Comp (Left) places the tool to the left of the surface to be cut; Cutter Comp (Right) places the tool to the right of the surface to be cut. Therefore, Cutter Comp (Left) Climb-Mills into the surface and is the most commonly used of the two. Cutter Comp (Right) places the control in the Conventional Milling mode and is used more for Steel and heavy milling operations and those particular operations that require the tool to be on that side of a surface. Various control manufacturers use different names for subroutines that are the same as the preceding versions. (See Chapter 8.)

Figure 5.31 shows examples of Cutter Compensation: Cutter Left, and Cutter Right. Notice that the point of view is toward the tool and workpiece, as described.

Many subroutines are two-pass routines that have fully programmable parameters:

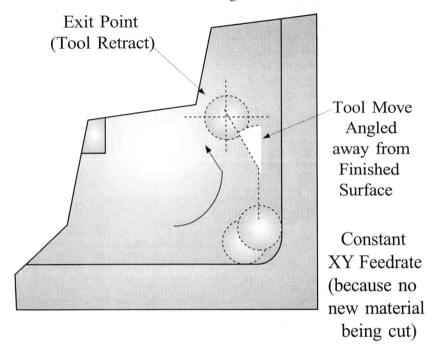

Figure 5.30   *Tool Exit Point*

- Rough Pass Material Allowance/Finish Pass
- Rough Pass Feedrates/Finish Pass Feedrates
- Rough Pass Spindle RPM/Finish Pass Spindle RPM

These combinations of variables make the subroutine of Cutter Compensation a very versatile and time-saving feature. Combined with the ability to input basic dimensions, there are true advantages to this software power.

Normal material allowances in Cutter Compensation modes are typical of other milling operations. For Climb-Milling in Aluminum and Magnesium, allowances are .002 to .010 for the finishing passes. Material allowances for Steel and similar Alloys are generally .008 to .015 for the finishing passes, depending on the machinability.

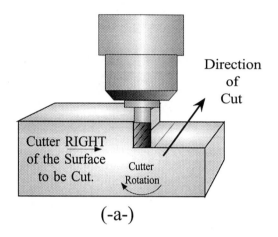

Direction
of
Cut

Cutter RIGHT
of the Surface
to be Cut.

Cutter
Rotation

(-a-)

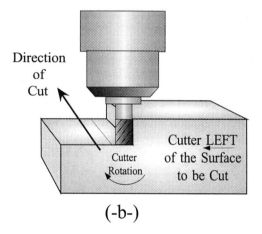

Direction
of
Cut

Cutter
Rotation

Cutter LEFT
of the Surface
to be Cut

(-b-)

Figure 5.31 *Cutter Comp: (a) Cutter Right; (b) Cutter Left*

Part II

Programming CNC Machine Motions

To this point in the *CNC Handbook*, many elements essential to CNC Programming and the operation of a number of CNC machine-types have been covered.

In Part II, specific Commands are listed. Each Command is referenced with the machine movement/toolpath it produces when executed in a program. Also provided with each Command are two programming Formats, the Command's Conventional programming Format and its Conversational Format.

When writing, editing, entering or debugging programs, Part II can be a very helpful ready reference to guide the user through Commands by the actual machine movement/toolpath each individual Command will cause upon execution. Often, in the process of writing a complex program or searching for a command name, the programmer will find a need for the logical organization of all graphically illustrated CNC Commands to index-through. In the following chapters, all commonly used Commands can be found quickly and easily in an organized, consistent manner.

Some Controls may label their individual Commands differently. Typically, the programming requirements for specific Commands may vary slightly from

Control to Control. But the type of information entered, the number of data Blocks per Command, and other pertinent parameters are very much the same.

Therefore, industry-standard generic Command names or headings have been selected. A consideration of all the major Controls has been assessed for this text. A single Command and accompanying illustration have been provided for every commonly used machine movement/toolpath. Two formats are provided for each Command: Conventional and Conversational. The Conventional Format represents an industry-standard for Controls that use conventional programming language. Conversational Format represents an example of conversational programming words that are used by today's state-of-the-art user-friendly Controls.

CHAPTER 6

MILLING- AND BORING-CENTER MACHINE MOTIONS

PROGRAMMING STANDARD MILLING and BORING-CENTER MOVES (for VERTICAL MACHINING CENTER)

Spindle On

Conventional CNC Format

M03: TURN ON SPINDLE in a CLOCKWISE Direction

The M word <u>M03</u> is universal on almost every CNC using conventional language to <u>TURN ON</u> the spindle in a Clockwise direction.

M04: TURN ON SPINDLE in a COUNTERCLOCKWISE Direction

Universally used to TURN ON the spindle in a Counterclockwise direction.

Conversational CNC Format

DRILL, PLUNGE, POSITION, and other Spindle Rotating Commands automatically **TURN ON** the machine spindle when selected in an initial Program Block (line). A Tool # is specified that has the +RPM (Clockwise) or –RPM (Counterclockwise) for spindle rotation recorded for that Tool in memory in the Tool Library. See Figure 6.1.

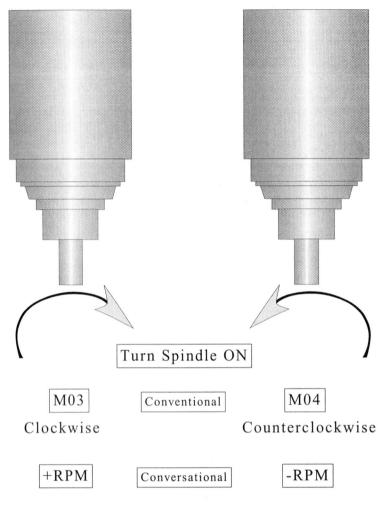

Figure 6.1 *Spindle-Rotation Commands*

Rapid Position/Rapid Traverse

Conventional CNC Format
G00: Instructs the machine to **POSITION** at the **MAXIMUM FEEDRATE**.

Conversational CNC Format
POSITION: Followed by XYZ Coordinates **POSITIONS** to that location at **MAXIMUM FEEDRATE**.

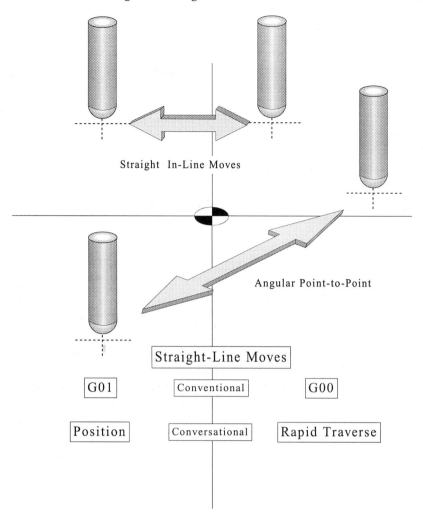

Straight In-Line Moves

Angular Point-to-Point

Straight-Line Moves

| G01 | Conventional | G00 |

| Position | Conversational | Rapid Traverse |

Figure 6.2 *Linear Interpolation/Straight-Line Moves*

Straight-Line Move/Linear Interpolation

Conventional CNC Format

G01: POSITIONS the specified axis to a location in a **STRAIGHT-LINE MOVE.**

G01 F___: POSITIONS the specified axis to a location in a **STRAIGHT-LINE MOVE** at a specified **FEEDRATE**.

Conversational CNC Format

MILL, DRILL, or **POSITION** moves the specified axis in a **STRAIGHT-LINE MOVE** at the **FEEDRATE** specified in that program line or block. See Figure 6.2.

Dwell

Conventional CNC Format

G04: Instructs all axis motion to **Pause**, spindle rotation unchanged, for a **specified length of time** (i.e., **G04 1.5** would cause the motion to be held for **1.5 seconds**).

Conversational CNC Format

DWELL _____: Instructs all axis motion to **Pause**, spindle rotation unchanged, for a **specified length of time** (i.e., **DWELL 1.5** would cause the motion to be held for **1.5 seconds**).

Some CNC Conversational Formats simply have Dwell times programmable for individual operations, and so on, such as all drill dwells set at .9 second.

Arcs or Circular Interpolation

Conventional CNC Format

G02: Instructs machine axes to move in a **CLOCKWISE** direction around a specified **ARC CENTER** maintaining a set **RADIUS** (cutting a standard two-axis **ARC** in a Clockwise direction a set distance, or **Radius**, away from a fixed **Arc Center**).

G03: Instructs machine axes to move in a **COUNTERCLOCKWISE** direction around a specified **ARC CENTER** maintaining a set **RADIUS** (cutting a standard two-axis **ARC** in a Counterclockwise direction a set distance, or **Radius**, away from a fixed **Arc Center**).

(Certain Turning Center Controls reverse these two commands. Check the Manuals.)

Conversational CNC Format

MILL ARC CW: Instructs machine axes to move in a **CLOCKWISE** direction around a specified **ARC CENTER** maintaining a set **RADIUS** (cutting a standard two-axis **ARC** in a Clockwise direction a set distance, or **Radius**, away from a fixed **Arc Center).**

MILL ARC CCW: Instructs machine axes to move in a **COUNTERCLOCKWISE** direction around a specified **ARC CENTER** maintaining a set **RADIUS** (cutting a standard two-axis **ARC** in a Counterclockwise direction a set distance, or **Radius**, away from a fixed **Arc Center**). See Figure 6.3.

Quarter-Circle Arcs

Conventional CNC Format

G02 X__ Y__ R__: Instructs machine axes to move from its present **XY Location** (specified in the previous program line), continuing in a **Clockwise Direction**

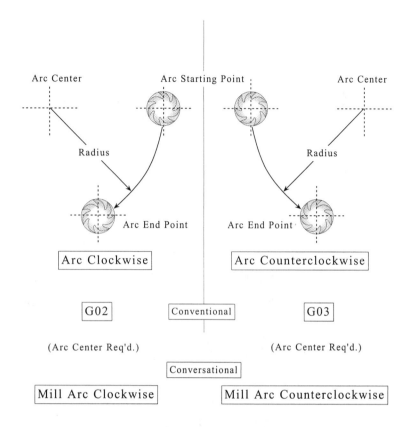

Figure 6.3 *Arc Clockwise and Counterclockwise Commands*

to the **End Point** on the **XY Location** stated in **this G02 line**, staying an equal distance from an unspecified **Arc Center** by the **R__** specified. The **Starting-Point** and **Arc End-Point** coordinates are the only locations that need to be entered (on Quadrant Lines).

G03 X__ Y__ R__: Instructs machine axes to move from its present **XY Location** (specified in the previous program line), continuing in a **Counterclockwise Direction** to the **End Point** on the **XY Location** stated in **this G02 line**, staying an equal distance from an unspecified **Arc Center** by the **R__** specified. The **Starting-Point** and **Arc End-Point** coordinates are the only locations that need to be entered (on Quadrant Lines).

Conversational CNC Format

MILL QUARTER-CIRCLE ARC CW: Instructs machine axes to move one full **Quadrant**, beginning on an **Axis Quadrant Line** and continuing in a **Clockwise Direction** to an **End Point** on the next Axis Quadrant Line, staying an

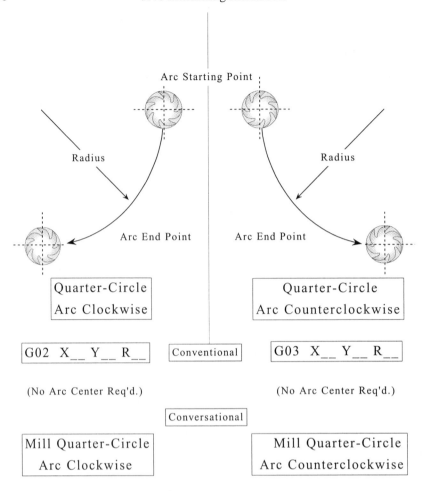

Figure 6.4 *Quarter-Circle Arcs (No Arc Center Required)*

equal distance from an unspecified **Arc Center**. The **Starting-Point** and **Arc End-Point** coordinates are the only locations that need to be specified (on Quadrant Lines).

MILL QUARTER-CIRCLE ARC CCW: Instructs machine axes to move one full **Quadrant**, beginning on an **Axis Quadrant Line** and continuing in a **Counterclockwise Direction** to an **End Point** on the next Axis Quadrant Line, staying an equal distance from an unspecified **Arc Center**. The **Starting-Point** and **Arc End-Point** coordinates are the only locations that need to be specified (on Quadrant Lines). See Figure 6.4.

Full-Circle Arcs

Conventional CNC Format

G02 J-1: After the previous Program Line defines the **Arc Starting Point**, the **G02 J-1** command is given that causes the machine axes to move in a **Clockwise direction**, establishing its own unspecified **Arc Center** cutting a **Full Clockwise Circle**, to an **End Point** that is the same coordinate as specified in the previous program line.

G03 J-1: After the previous Program Line defines the **Arc Starting Point**, the **G03 J-1** command is given that causes the machine axes to move in a **Counterclockwise direction**, establishing its own unspecified **Arc Center** cutting a **Full Clockwise Circle**, to an **End Point** that is the same coordinate as specified in the previous program line.

(Some older Controls will not allow crossing multiple quadrant lines using this command.)

Conversational CNC Format

MILL CIRCLE CW (In/Out) R__: Instructs the machine axes to move around the specified **Arc Center** in a **Clockwise direction**, maintaining an equidistant **Radius (R__)**, on the selected **Inside or Outside** of the circle. Most features have Ramp-in/Ramp-out toolpath angles that leave minimal tool-mark blends.

MILL CIRCLE CCW (In/Out) R__: Instructs the machine axes to move around the specified **Arc Center** in a **Counterclockwise direction**, maintaining an equidistant **Radius (R__)**, on the selected **Inside or Outside** of the circle. Most features have Ramp-in/Ramp-out toolpath angles that leave minimal tool-mark blends. See Figure 6.5.

Arc—Center Defined

Conventional CNC Format

G01 X__ Y__ F__

G02 X__ Y__ I__ J__: Instructs axes to position to the **XY Coordinate** specified in the **G01** line, then move at the **F__** (feedrate) in a **Clockwise direction G02**, to the **XY coordinates** in the **G02** line, staying away an equidistant **Radius** from the **I__ J__ Arc Center**.

G01 X__ Y__ F__

G03 X__ Y__ I__ J__: Instructs axes to position to the **XY Coordinate** specified in the **G01** line, then move at the **F__** (feedrate) in a **Counterclockwise direction G03**, to the **XY coordinates** in the **G03** line, staying away an equidistant **Radius** from the **I__ J__ Arc Center**.

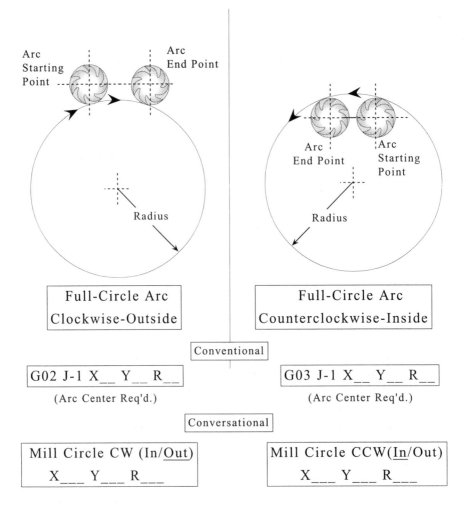

Figure 6.5 *Full-Circle Arcs*

I__ :   X axis Center Point of an Arc
J__ :   Y axis Center Point of an Arc
K__ :   Z axis Center Point of an Arc
R__ :   Defines Arc Radius if used instead of Center Point

Conversational CNC Format

MILL ARC CW: Instructs machine axes to move around the specified **Arc Center** in a **Clockwise direction** from the XY coordinate in the previous block, maintaining the equidistant **Radius** entered, to the next XY End-Point block.

MILL ARC CCW: Instructs machine axes to move around the specified **Arc Center** in a **Counterclockwise direction** from the XY coordinate in the previous block, maintaining the equidistant **Radius** entered, to the next XY End-Point block. See Figure 6.6.

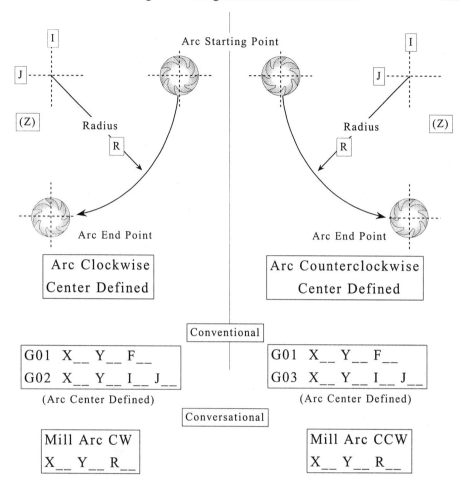

Figure 6.6 *Arcs—Center Defined*

Rapid Motion/Position/Traverse

Conventional CNC Format

G00: Instructs the machine to move at its **Fastest** possible traveling **Feedrate**, to a specified **XY (Z) location**.

Conversational CNC Format

POSITION or

RAPID TRAVERSE: Instructs the machine to move at its **Fastest** possible traveling **Feedrate**, to a specified **XY (Z) location**.

(Normally, a machine will access its highest IPM rating for all axes and use this for a Rapid Traverse feedrate.)

Program Startup

Conventional CNC Format

Actual input values such as speeds, feedrates, tool numbers, axis coordinates, and so on are variable from workpiece to workpiece. However, the fundamental Format for beginning a new program is consistent every time a new Program is written in Conventional CNC language.

(for Vertical machining center)

O000 (program number; line #; Block #)

N005 G91 G28 X0 Y0 Z0 (verifies axes are at their Reference Zeros)

N010 G54 (set the current Program Zero)

N015 G90 S300 M03 T02 (activates Absolute mode, Spindle ON Clockwise, 300 RPM, initializes Tool #2)

N020 G00 X7. Y4.3 (position to first XY location for tool)

N025 G43 H01 Z.1 (activate Tool-Length Compensation, position to first Z location)

N030 M08 (switch Coolant ON)

N035 G01 F1.8 (Feedrate 1.8 IPM)

(brief explanation of commands; full, expanded <u>definition of each command in</u> <u>Chapter 9</u>)

O = Program #; Block #; Line #

G00 = Rapid Positioning; Rapid Traverse

G01 = Straight-Line move; Linear Interpolation

G28 = Send Machine Axes to Reference Point

G43 = Tool-Length Compensation

G54 = Assign Program Zero

G90 = Activates Absolute Mode of Positioning

G91 = Activates Incremental Mode of Positioning

F__ = Feedrate (in Inches per Minute)

M03 = Turn Spindle on in Clockwise Direction

M08 = Turn ON Coolant

T02 = Tool Number 2

X0 = X Axis 000.000 (Zero)

Y0 = Y Axis 000.000 (Zero)

Z0 = Z Axis 000.000 (Zero)

Conversational CNC Format

Block #

1 Drill / Plunge X 2.821 Y 2.125 Zup .1 Zdn −.5 F 2.0 TL 1

(starts spindle at rpm in Tool 1's specs; rapid positions to the XY location; plunges to −Z)

2 Mill X 2.821 Y 2.500 Zdn –.5 F 3.2 TL1

> (mills from past position, to new XY location specified at the new feedrate, at same –Z)

3 Mill X 3.456 Y 2.500 Zdn –.5 F 3.2 TL1

> (mills to new XY location)

4 Stop X 3.456 Y 2.500 TL1

> (retracts Z axis rapidly; stops all axis movement; turns off spindle; brake on for tool change)

(Every command word given in conversational format executes a combination of instructions to the machine.)

Tool Change

Conventional CNC Format

G91 G28 G49 Z0 M19

M01: Instructs the machine to send the **Z-Axis** to the **Tool-Change position**, **cancels** the **Tool Length** in memory, **orients the Tool** in the spindle for a **Tool Change. M01** instructs the **Optional Stop** to occur.

Conversational CNC Format

STOP / (New Tool #)

or **CHANGE TOOL**: Instructs the machine to **Retract the Z-Axis** to its **Tool-Change Position**, **Orients the Spindle**, and causes a **Stop Axis Movement** to take place.

(Full Tool-Changer Commands are documented in Chapter 10.)

Drill

Conventional CNC Format

G81 F__: Instructs the **Tool** (Z-Axis spindle) to **feed into** the hole location at a **specified Feedrate**, then a **Rapid-out Retraction** from the hole feature takes place.

G73 F__: Instructs the **Tool** (Z-Axis spindle) to **feed into** the hole location at a **specified Feedrate**, with intermittent chip-breaking retractions (pecking), then a **Rapid-out Retraction** from the hole feature takes place, to the "R," or "Reference Level."

Conversational CNC Format

DRILL

(Peck #): Instructs the **Tool** (Z-Axis spindle) to **feed into** the hole location at a **specified Feedrate**, after achieving the Depth required, then a **Rapid-out Retraction** from the hole feature takes place. If a number is entered into the

Peck # Box, the Control will divide up the Z drilling distance by the # of Pecks specified.

Bore/Ream

Conventional CNC Format

G86 F__: Instructs Axis (Z) to feed into the hole at a specified feedrate, then spindle will **Stop, Rapid feed out** of the hole.

G85 F__: Instructs Axis (Z) to feed into the hole at a specified feedrate, then spindle will **Stop, and Reverse** its feed at the **same Feedrate out** of the hole.

Conversational CNC Format

BORE: Instructs Axis (Z) to feed into the hole at a specified feedrate, then spindle will **Stop, Rapid feed out** of the hole.

REAM: Instructs Axis (Z) to feed into the hole at a specified feedrate, then spindle will **Stop, and Reverse** its feed at the **same Feedrate out** of the hole. See Figure 6.7.

Tap

Conventional CNC Format

G84 F__: Instructs the machine axis (Z) to feed into the hole, at a **specified Feedrate**, with the spindle **rotating** in a **Clockwise direction (M03)**. Upon reaching the required depth, the Tap (in a special Tap-holder) will **Reverse Rotation** and the Z Axis **retracts** from the hole. Once the hole feature is cleared, the spindle Stops and Reverses rotation to a Clockwise direction again.

G74 F__: Instructs the machine axis (Z) to feed into the hole, at a **specified Feedrate**, with the spindle **rotating** in a **Counterclockwise direction (M04)**. Upon reaching the required depth, the Tap (in a special Tap-holder) will **Reverse Rotation** and the Z Axis **retracts** from the hole. Once the hole feature is cleared, the spindle Stops and Reverses rotation to a Counterclockwise direction again.

(See Chapter 9 for CNC Tapping Speeds and Feeds Table.)

Conversational CNC Format

TAP (STD/RH): Instructs the machine axis (Z) to feed into the hole, at a **specified Feedrate**, with the spindle **rotating** in a **Clockwise direction**. Upon reaching the required depth, the Tap (in a special Tap-holder) will **Reverse Rotation** and the Z Axis **retracts** from the hole. Once the hole feature is cleared, the spindle Stops and Reverses rotation to a Clockwise direction again.

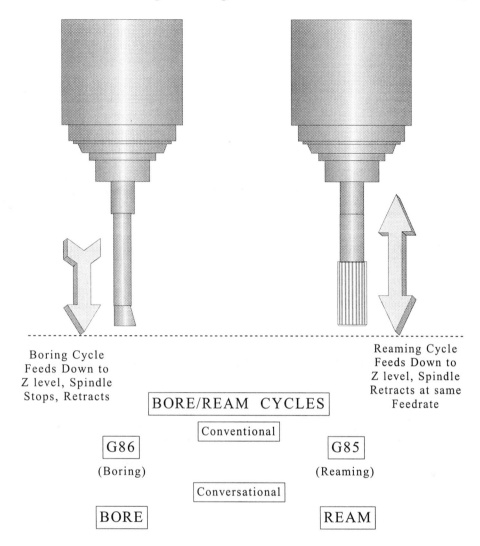

Figure 6.7 *Bore/Ream Commands*

TAP (L/H): Instructs the machine axis (Z) to feed into the hole, at a **specified Feedrate**, with the spindle **rotating** in a **Counterclockwise direction**. Upon reaching the required depth, the Tap (in a special Tap-holder) will **Reverse Rotation** and the Z-Axis **retracts** from the hole. Once the hole feature is cleared, the spindle Stops and Reverses rotation to a Counterclockwise direction again.

(G84, Clockwise or the Right-handed Tapping cycle is the commonly used cycle; very few left-handed threads are tapped by CNC.)

Tool Restart/Restartup

Conventional CNC Format

G90 S450 M03 T03

G00 X_ Y_: Instructs the machine to **Restart after a Tool Change** by selecting **Absolute Mode**, **Turning on** the **Spindle** (to 450 RPM), ready the **next
Tool (Tool 3** in this example). Next, the machine **Rapid Traverses** to a
specified **X_ Y_ Location.**

Conversational CNC Format

DRILL, PLUNGE, POSITION, and other Spindle Rotating Commands automatically **TURN ON** the machine spindle when selected in an initial Program
Block (line). A Tool # is specified that has the +RPM (Clockwise) or –RPM
(Counterclockwise) for spindle rotation recorded for that Tool in memory in
the Tool Library.

(Conversational Format in many instances includes multiple Commands within
its simple one- and two-word command selections.)

Stop/Optional Stop/End of Program

Conventional CNC Format

M00: Program Stop

M01: Optional Stop. Instructs the machine to **Stop executing the program**;
the **Spindle, Coolant**, and anything in motion will be switched **OFF.**

M30: Instructs the machine to switch **OFF** anything in motion, rewind or send
Control memory to beginning of the program. **Some Controls substitute
M02** for this command.

Conversational CNC Format

STOP or

END PROGRAM: Instructs Control to **STOP All Motion**. Program can be restarted by entering any Block # of a Spindle Rotation Command.

Absolute/Incremental

Conventional CNC Format

G90: Specifies the ABSOLUTE mode of Programming be used for positioning
of the machine axis.

G91: Specifies the INCREMENTAL mode of Programming be used for positioning of the machine axis.

Conversational CNC Format

ABSOLUTE/INCREMENTAL

(ABS/INC): Console button selection that instructs the Control to use either mode selected for machine-axis positioning.

Inch/Metric (MM)

Conventional CNC Format

G20: Inch Mode, Thousandths of an Inch.
G21: Metric Mode, Millimeters.

Conversational CNC Format

INCH / METRIC

(IN/MM): Switch on console toggles between inches or millimeters, for input while Programming.

Zero Reference Return/Table Zero

Conventional CNC Format

G92: Includes the **measured** distance **from Axis Zero** to the **XY Location** where **Program Zero is established** (i.e., **G92 X12.1611 Y9.3221 Z8.0919**).

Conversational CNC Format

TABLE ZERO or

MACHINE ZERO: Includes the **measured** distance **from Axis Zero** to the **XY Location** where **Program Zero is established** (i.e., **X12.1611 Y9.3221 Z8.0919**). See Figure 6.8.

Program Zero/Fixture Offsets (Zero)

Conventional CNC Format

G50: Program Zero Designator.
G54 through **G59**: Fixture Offsets (from Machine Zero).

Conversational CNC Format

PROGRAM ZERO or

ZERO: Program Zero Designator, XY Location where current Program in Control originates its coordinate measurements. See Figure 6.9.

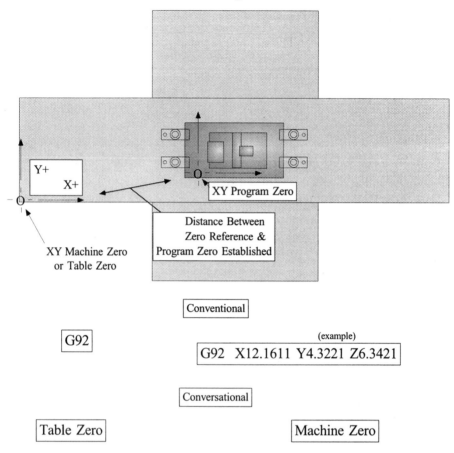

Figure 6.8 *Zero Reference Return/Table Zero*

Feedrates

Conventional CNC Format

F___: **Feedrates** for **Axis Motions** (if Control is in **Inch Mode**, it uses Inches per Minute, **IPM**; if in **Metric Mode**, it uses Millimeters per Minute, **MM** or MMM.

Conversational CNC Format
FEEDRATE

(FD): **Feedrates** for **Axis Motions** (if Control is in **Inch Mode**, it uses Inches per Minute, **IPM**; if in **Metric Mode**, it uses Millimeters per Minute, **MM** or MMM.

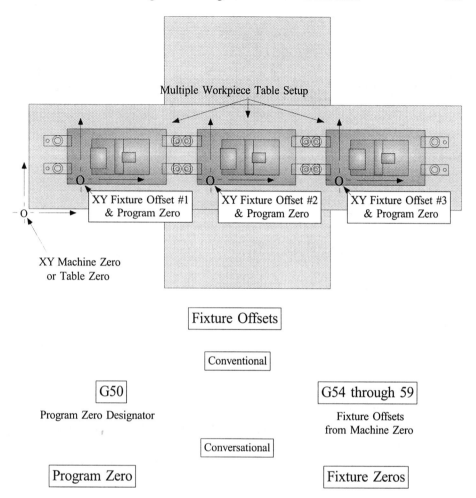

Figure 6.9 Zero Reference Return/Table Zero

RPM

Conventional CNC Format

S___: Instructs the spindle (after a revolution command); the **Spindle Speed in RPMs** (Revolutions per Minute).

Conversational CNC Format

RPM: Instructions for this value are stored in the **Tool Library**; the selection of a Tool # in a Program Block accesses the **RPM set for that Tool #**.

Coolants

Conventional CNC Format

M07: **Mist** Coolant **ON**.
M08: **Flood** Coolant **ON**.
M09: Coolant **OFF** (cancels **BOTH** Mist and Flood Coolant Flow).

Conversational CNC Format

MIST CLNT ON/OFF: Instructs **Mist** Coolant to Toggle **ON or OFF**.
FLOOD CLNT ON/OFF: Instructs **Flood** Coolant to Toggle **ON or OFF**.

PROGRAMMING COMPLEX MILLING and BORING MOVES

Single-Direction Approach

Conventional CNC Format

G60: Instructs positioning motions of the machine axis to "**Approach**" an **XY Location** from a **Single Direction.**
G64: Turns **OFF** Single-Direction Positioning.

Conversational CNC Format

_____ **AXIS APPROACH**: **Toggling ON** and entering an **Axis Direction** (**–X+Y**), preceding positioning Blocks, the Control will "**Approach**" XY Co-ordinates from that direction. By reentering and **toggling OFF** the Program Word, positioning returns to normal. See Figure 6.10.

Polar-Coordinate Rotation

Conventional CNC Format

G68 X __ Y__ R __ A __: Instructs machine axis to establish an **XY Center Location (X _ Y_)**, define a **Radius (R___)**, and **Orients** the first **Polar Coordinate**. (This feature is ideal to precede Subroutines such as milling Radial Slot configurations or unsymmetrical Bolt-hole circles.)

Conversational CNC Format

POLAR ROTATE X ____ Y____ R____ A____: Instructs machine axis to estab-lish an **XY Center Location (X _ Y_)**, define a **Radius (R___)**, and **Ori-ents** the first **Polar Coordinate**. (This feature is ideal to precede Subroutines such as milling Radial Slot configurations or Bolt-hole circles.) See Figure 6.11.

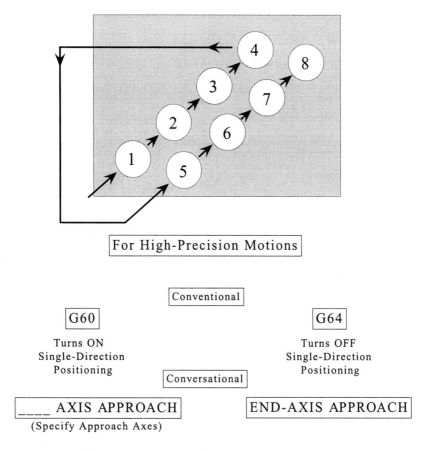

For High-Precision Motions

Conventional

G60   G64

Turns ON   Turns OFF
Single-Direction   Single-Direction
Positioning   Positioning

Conversational

_____ AXIS APPROACH   END-AXIS APPROACH

(Specify Approach Axes)

Figure 6.10 *Single-Direction Approach*

Curves

Conventional CNC Format
Not applicable in most Conventional formats.

Conversational CNC Format
CURVE CW/CCW X____ Y____ Z____ Blend Rad.____
CURVE ENDPOINT X____ Y____ Z____ F____: Instructs the two axes selected
to recognize an Arc Center and move in the directional rotation selected. The
Blend Radius value allows a minimum blend between consecutive Curve operations. This feature is ideal for cam operations that require an undefined
changing Arc Center. An example would be entering ten (10) Curve com-

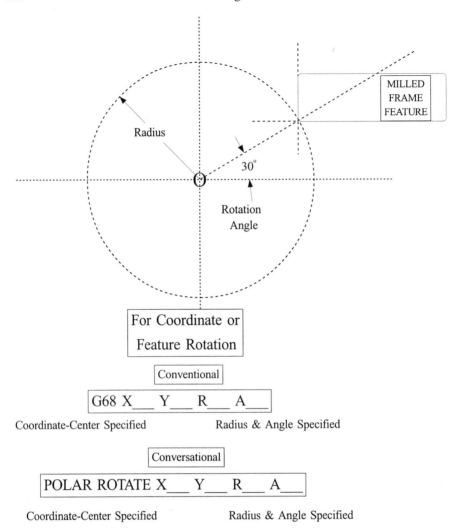

Figure 6.11 *Polar-Coordinate Rotation*

mands and Curve End Points consecutively, each dividing up a distance of
.500 that an Arc Center may move during a Cam-Cutting operation. The Blend
Radius allows minimum steps between Arcs. See Figure 6.12.

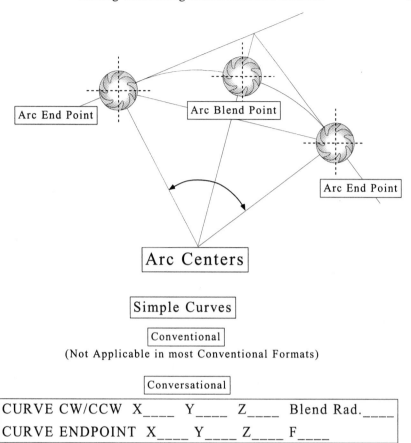

Arc Centers

Simple Curves

Conventional

(Not Applicable in most Conventional Formats)

Conversational

CURVE CW/CCW X____   Y____   Z____   Blend Rad.____
CURVE ENDPOINT X____   Y____   Z____   F____

Figure 6.12 *Curve Commands*

Reverse Curves

REV. CURVE BLEND RAD.___.___ CW/CCW CCW/CW
    ARC CENTER 1 X___ Y___ Z___ Fd___
    ARC END PT. 1 X___ Y___ Z___
    ARC CENTER 2 X___ Y___ Z___ Fd___
    ARC END PT. 2 X___ Y___ Z___: Instructs the two axes selected to
recognize an Arc Center and move in the directional rotation selected. The
second Arc (Arc 2) cuts in the opposite direction of rotation from the first
Arc. The Blend Radius value allows a minimum blend between consecutive
Curve operations. Additional Arcs can be inserted before and after the Reverse
Arc. See Figure 6.13.

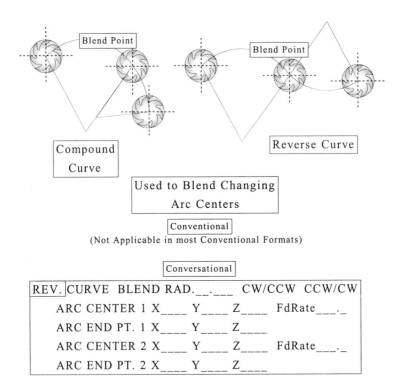

Figure 6.13 *Compound- and Reverse-Curve Commands*

Parabolic Arcs—Milling

Conventional CNC Format
Not applicable in most Conventional formats.

Conversational CNC Format
PARABOLIC ARC CW/CCW RAD.____
    ARC CENTER 1 X____ Y____ Z____ Alt____ Fd____
    ARC END PT. 1 X____ Y____ Z____
    ARC CENTER 2 X____ Y____ Z____ Alt____ Fd____
    ARC END PT. 2 X____ Y____ Z____: The use of the Parabolic Arc feature is normally dictated by the unique data specified in the workpiece dimensional measurements. The following workpiece feature criteria may require the Parabolic Arc to be used: 2- and 3-Axis Arcs with Radii unknown; 2- and 3-Axis Arcs with Remote Arc Centers; 3-, 4-, and 5-Axis Contours with a combination of these Arcs. See Figure 6.14.

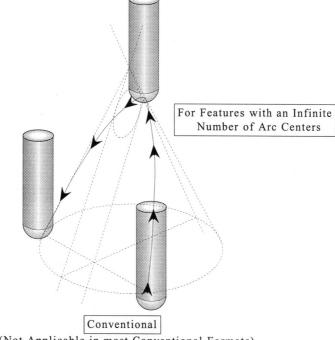

For Features with an Infinite
Number of Arc Centers

Conventional
(Not Applicable in most Conventional Formats)

Conversational

PARABOLIC ARC	CW/CCW	RAD 1____		RAD 2____	
ARC START1 X____	Y____	Z____	Alt____	FdRt____	
ARC ENDPT. X____	Y____	Z____	Alt____	FdRt____	
ARC START2 X____	Y____	Z____	Alt____	FdRt____	
ARC ENDPT. X____	Y____	Z____	Alt____	FdRt____	

Figure 6.14 *Parabolic-Arc Toolpath Commands*

Scaling

Conventional CNC Format

This Command is optional in some Conventional CNC formats. Consult the manuals.

Conversational CNC Format

SCALE X___ Y___ Z___ Factor___: Instructs the designated Axis Motion in current Control Program to be multiplied by the current Scale Factor and to be centralized on the XY (or Z) Center specified. See Figure 6.15.

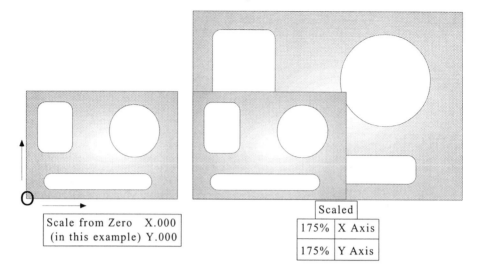

Scale from Zero   X.000
(in this example) Y.000

Scaled

175% | X Axis

175% | Y Axis

Conventional

(This Command is optional in some conventional CNC Formats,
Consult the Manuals)

Conversational

| SCALE CENTER | X____ Y____ Z____ Alt____ |
| FACTOR | X____ Y____ Z____ Alt____ |

Figure 6.15 *Scaling Compounds*

XY Axis—Exchange

Conventional CNC Format

G08: Instructs the (CNC) Control to **Transform all** the **X** and **Y values** in the program. Depending on the selection, all X values can be changed to Y values, and so on.

G09: **Cancels** the **XY Axis-Exchange** transformation.

Conversational CNC Format

TRANSLATION X___ Y___ Z___ Alt___: Instructs the (CNC) Control to **Transform all** the **X** and **Y values** in the program. Depending on the selection, all X values can be changed to Y values, and so on, of the X, Y, Z axes and any other alternate axis named. See Figure 6.16.

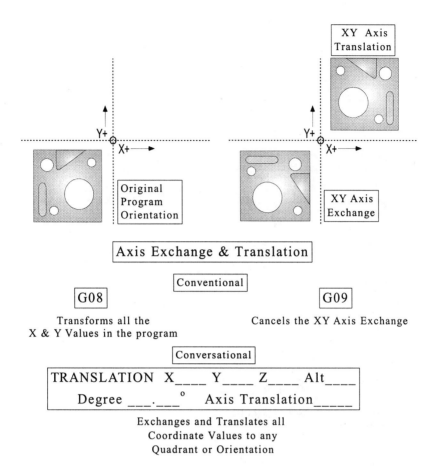

Figure 6.16 *XY Axis-Exchange Commands*

Mirror Image

Conventional CNC Format
G05: X AXIS MIRROR IMAGE
G06: Y AXIS MIRROR IMAGE
G07: Z AXIS MIRROR IMAGE
Each Command instructs the Control to generate a series of movements to occur in the Axis selected that represents the Mirror Image of a programmed Path or Coordinates.
G09: Cancels Mirror-Image Commands.

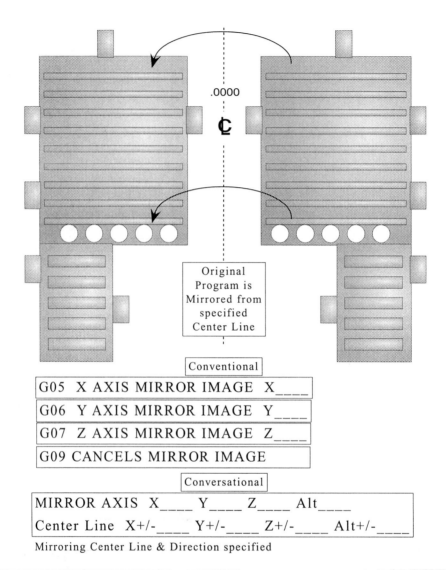

.0000

℄

Original
Program is
Mirrored from
specified
Center Line

Conventional	
G05 X AXIS MIRROR IMAGE X____	
G06 Y AXIS MIRROR IMAGE Y____	
G07 Z AXIS MIRROR IMAGE Z____	
G09 CANCELS MIRROR IMAGE	

Conversational			
MIRROR AXIS X____ Y____ Z____ Alt____			
Center Line X+/-____ Y+/-____ Z+/-____ Alt+/-____			

Mirroring Center Line & Direction specified

Figure 6.17 *Mirror-Image Commands*

Conversational CNC Format

MIRROR AXIS _____ **CL X___ Y___ Z___:** Each Command instructs the
Control to generate a series of movements that represents the Mirror Image
of a programmed Path or Coordinates; with a Mirroring Center Line specified
by Axis Coordinates. See Figure 6.17.

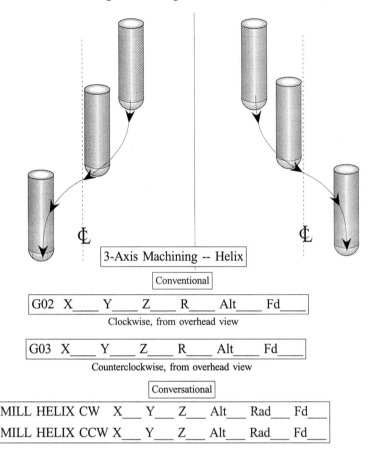

3-Axis Machining -- Helix

Conventional

G02 X___ Y___ Z___ R___ Alt___ Fd___

Clockwise, from overhead view

G03 X___ Y___ Z___ R___ Alt___ Fd___

Counterclockwise, from overhead view

Conversational

MILL HELIX CW X___ Y___ Z___ Alt___ Rad___ Fd___
MILL HELIX CCW X___ Y___ Z___ Alt___ Rad___ Fd___

Figure 6.18 Helical-Arc Command

Helical Arcs

Conventional CNC Format

G02 X____ Y____ Z____ R____ F____ (to)

G03 X____ Y____ Z____ R____ F____: Instructs the machine axis to move in a circular motion (G02 CW; G03 CCW), around a specified Axis Arc Center, at a specified Radius. The variation between the two Z____ values causes the Arc machined to move simultaneously in 3-Axis Motion.

Conversational CNC Format

MILL HELIX CW X____ Y____ Z____ RAD____

END HELIX CCW X____ Y____ Z____ RAD____: Instructs the machine axis to move in a circular motion (CW/CCW), around a specified Axis Arc Center, at a specified Radius, starting at the Mill-Helix coordinates and ending at the End-Helix coordinates. The variation between the two Z____ values causes the Arc machined to move simultaneously in 3-Axis Motion. See Figure 6.18.

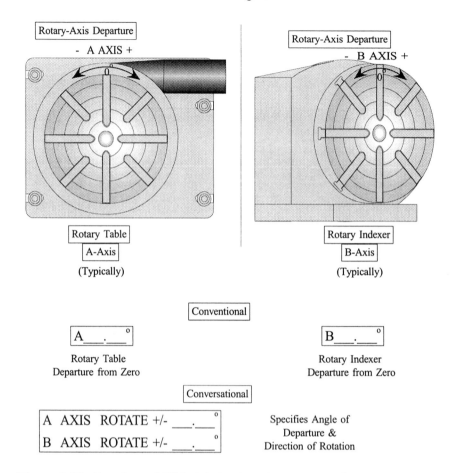

Figure 6.19 *Fourth- and Fifth-Axis Designation Commands*

Four- and Five-Axis Designation

Conventional CNC Format

A __.__°

B __.__°: Instructs the **Angular departure** of the **A Axis** or **B Axis** by the specified angular **+ or – degrees** (__.__°), from the standard XYZ.

Conversational CNC Format

A AXIS ROTATE__.__°

B AXIS ROTATE__.__°: Instructs the **Angular departure** of the **A Axis** or **B Axis** by the specified angular **+ or – degrees** (__.__°), from the standard XYZ. See Figure 6.19.

Rotary Tables

Conventional CNC Format

(Machine builders vary on Axis-name designation. For reference purposes in this text, the <u>A-Axis</u> designates <u>Rotary Tables</u> and the <u>B-Axis</u> designates <u>Rotary Indexers</u>.)

A ___.___°: This Rotary-Axis command instructs the Rotary Table to Index at the specified Angular departure from its 000.000° orientation.

Conversational CNC Format

(ROTARY) AXIS-A ___.___°: This Rotary-Axis command instructs the Rotary Table to Index at the specified Angular departure from its 000.000° orientation. See Figure 6.20.

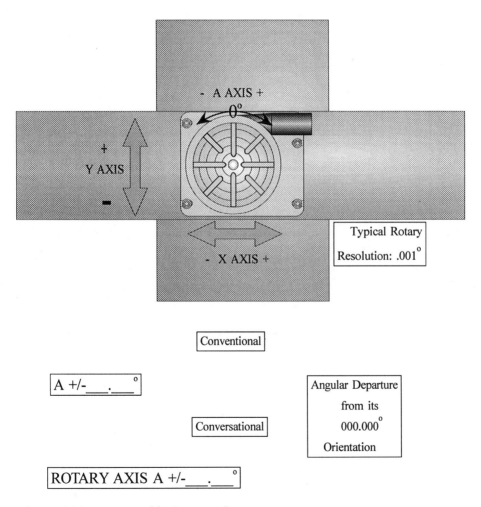

Figure 6.20 *Rotary-Table Commands*

Rotary Indexers

Conventional CNC Format

(Machine builders vary on Axis-name designation. For reference purposes in this text, the A-Axis designates Rotary Tables and the B-Axis designates Rotary Indexers.)

B ___.___°: This Rotary-Axis command instructs the Rotary Indexer to Index at the specified Angular departure from its 000.000° orientation.

Conversational CNC Format

(ROTARY) AXIS-B ___.___°: This Rotary-Axis command instructs the Rotary Indexer to Index at the specified Angular departure from its 000.000° orientation. See Figure 6.21.

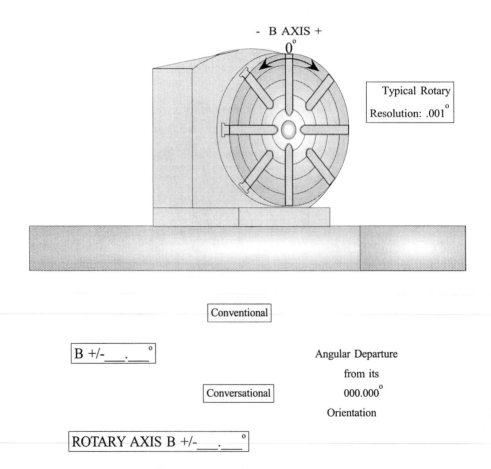

Figure 6.21 *Rotary-Indexer Commands*

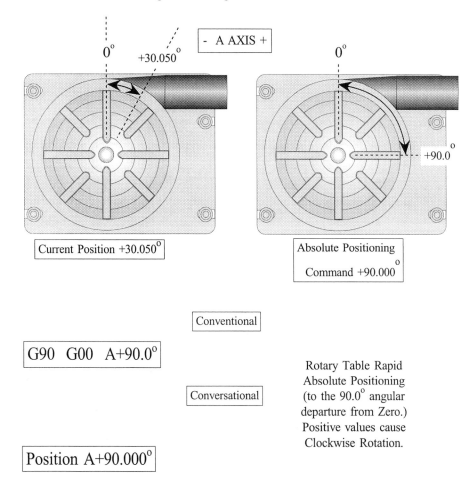

Figure 6.22 *Rotary Absolute-Positioning Commands*

Rotary—Absolute Mode

Conventional CNC Format

G90 G00 A(90.0)°: Causes the Rapid Positioning of the A-Axis in **Absolute Mode**, **Rotary motion** in a Clockwise direction (+90° in this example, therefore, clockwise).

Conversational CNC Format

POS(ition) A (+90.000)°: Causes the Rapid Positioning of the A-Axis in **Absolute Mode**, **Rotary motion** in a Clockwise direction (+90° in this example, therefore, clockwise). See Figure 6.22.

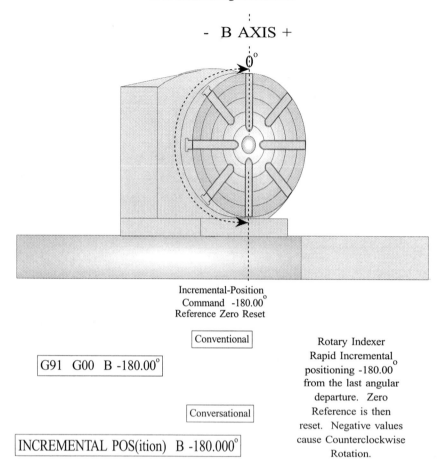

Figure 6.23 *Rotary incremental-Positioning Commands*

Rotary—Incremental Mode

Conventional CNC Format

G91 G00 B –180.00°: Causes the Rapid Positioning of the **B-Axis** in **Incremental Mode**, **Rotary motion** in a Counterclockwise direction (–180° in this example, therefore, clockwise from the last position), where Axis Zero is "Reset." The next Rotary Departure is from this Zero Reference Point.

Conversational CNC Format

INCREM(ental) POS B(–180.00°): Causes the Rapid Positioning of the **B-Axis** in **Incremental Mode**, **Rotary motion** in a Counterclockwise direction (–180° in this example, therefore, clockwise from the last position), where Axis Zero is "Reset." The next Rotary Departure is from this Zero Reference Point. See Figure 6.23.

Rotary—Feedrates

Conventional CNC Format

F___ (DPM): Degrees per Minute.

F___ (IPM): Inches per Minute.

Conversational CNC Format

Fd___ DPM / IPM: Entered value instructs Rotary Axis selected to be moved at the (Toggled) **Feedrate, IPM or DPM.**

Mill Pocket

Conventional CNC Format

Not applicable in most Conventional formats.

Conversational CNC Format

MILL POCKET XL___ YW___ ALT___ ZDp___ Fd___: Cleans out inner pocket-floor, rectangular or Alternate (toggled) arbitrary shape. Pocket clean-out selected from cutting methods: Spiral inside-out; Spiral outside-in; or ZigZagging at any angle with boss avoidance of up to 50 (specified) islands in some Controls. See Figure 6.24.

Mill Ruled Surface

Conventional CNC Format

Not applicable in most Conventional formats.

Conversational CNC Format

MILL RULED SURF(ace): Instructs machine axis to establish a Ruled Surface (a Linear cross-section blended surface) that is defined by following blocks containing defined 3-D contours (up to 100 blocks in some Controls).

Mill Lofted Surface

Conventional CNC Format

Not applicable in most Conventional formats.

Conversational CNC Format

MILL LOFTED SURF(ace): Instructs machine axis to establish a linear or parabolic 3-D surface defined by the following multiple Program Blocks containing the cross-section coordinates. Cross-sections consist of any combination of Points, Lines, Arcs, and Splines.

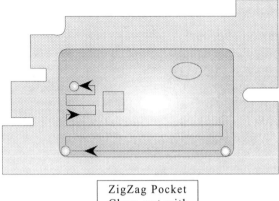

ZigZag Pocket
Clean-out with
Island Avoidance

Conventional

(Available as a Subroutine in some Controls -- see Manuals)

Conversational

MILL POCKET XL____	YW____	Alt____	ZDp____	XYFd____	
1 / 2 PASS ZigZag CLEANOUT		2	ISLANDS		
Island 1	X____	Y____	Rad.____		
Island 2	X____	Y____	Rad.____		

Figure 6.24 *Mill-Pocket Command*

Mill Filleted Surface

Conventional CNC Format
Not applicable in most Conventional formats.

Conversational CNC Format
MILL FILLETED SURF(ace): Instructs machine axis to establish a constant
or variable Filleted Toolpath between two Swept, Ruled, or Lofted surfaces.
The two selected surfaces (defined in following Program Blocks) are "assembled" in the Control's processor for a "best-fit" Fillet at each surface-intersec-
tion point. The proper application of this command produces a smooth
tangential transition between the two surfaces, using a minimum of program
space.

CHAPTER 7

TURNING- AND GRINDING-MACHINE MOTIONS

PROGRAMMING STANDARD TURNING MOTIONS (MOVES)

Many of the same G & M Codes and Conversational Commands apply to Turning Centers as well as Machining Centers. Turning-Center commands are listed here, whether they appeared before for ease of reference during programming.

Spindle Rotation—Spindle On (CW, CCW)

Conventional CNC Format

M03: TURN ON SPINDLE in a CLOCKWISE Direction

The M word <u>M03</u> is universal on almost every CNC using conventional language to <u>TURN ON</u> the spindle in a Clockwise direction.

M04: TURN ON SPINDLE in a COUNTERCLOCKWISE Direction

Universally used to TURN ON the spindle in a Counterclockwise direction.

Conversational CNC Format

SPINDLE ON and other Spindle Rotating Commands automatically **TURN ON** the machine spindle when selected in an initial Program Block (line). A Tool # is specified that has the +RPM (Clockwise) or –RPM (Counterclockwise) value for spindle rotation recorded for that Tool in memory in the Tool Library.

Rapid Position/Rapid Traverse

Conventional CNC Format

G00: Instructs the machine to **POSITION** at the **MAXIMUM FEEDRATE.**

Conversational CNC Format

POSITION: Followed by XZ Coordinates **POSITIONS** to that location at **MAXIMUM FEEDRATE.**

Straight-Line Move/Linear Interpolation

Conventional CNC Format

G01: **POSITIONS** the specified axis to a location in a **STRAIGHT-LINE MOVE.**

G01 F___: POSITIONS the specified axis to a location in a **STRAIGHT-LINE MOVE** at a specified **FEEDRATE.**

Conversational CNC Format

POSITION, TURN, or FACE moves the specified axis in a **STRAIGHT-LINE MOVE** at the **FEEDRATE** specified in that program line or block. See Figure 7.1.

Zero Reference Return/Machine Zero

Conventional CNC Format

G92: Includes the **measured** distance **from Axis Zero** to the **XZ Location** where **Program Zero is established** (i.e., **G92 X12.1611 Z8.0919**).

Conversational CNC Format

MACHINE ZERO or
REFERENCE ZERO: Includes the **measured** distance **from Axis Zero** to the **XY Location** where **Program Zero is established** (i.e., **X12.1611 Y9.3221 Z8.09**). See Figure 7.2.

Program Zero/Fixture Offsets (Zero)

Conventional CNC Format

G50: Program Zero Designator.
G54 through **G59**: Fixture Offsets (from Machine Zero).

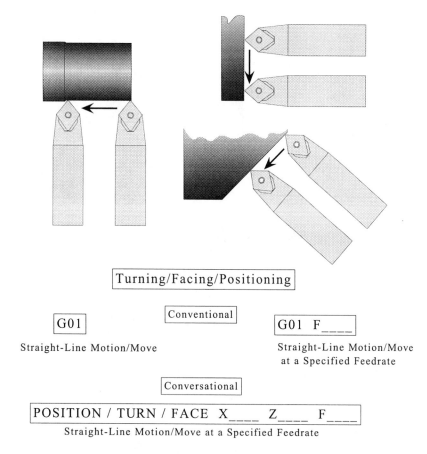

Turning/Facing/Positioning

Conventional

G01

Straight-Line Motion/Move

G01 F____

Straight-Line Motion/Move
at a Specified Feedrate

Conversational

POSITION / TURN / FACE X____ Z____ F____
Straight-Line Motion/Move at a Specified Feedrate

Figure 7.1 *Straight-Line Move/Linear Interpolation Command*

Conversational CNC Format
PROGRAM ZERO or

ZERO: Program Zero Designator, XZ Location where current Program in Control originates its coordinate measurements. See Figure 7.3.

Dwell

Conventional CNC Format
G04: Instructs all axis motion to **Pause**, spindle rotation unchanged, for a **specified length of time** (i.e., **G04 1.5** would cause the motion to be held for **1.5 seconds**).

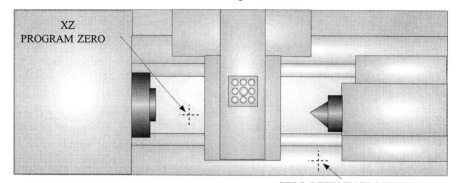

ZERO REFERENCE RETURN
(Zero Reference Return
may be located at another
Axis Limit Location)

Straight-Line Moves

Conventional

G92 X____ Z____

Conversational

This Command includes the
Measured Distance from
Axis Reference Zero to the
XZ Location -- Program Zero

MACHINE / REFERENCE ZERO
X____ Z____

Figure 7.2 *Zero Reference Return/Machine Zero Commands*

Conversational CNC Format

DWELL _____: Instructs all axis motion to **Pause**, spindle rotation unchanged, for a **specified length of time** (i.e., **DWELL 2.8** would cause the motion to be held for **2.8 seconds**).

Some CNC Conversational Formats simply have Dwell times programmable for individual operations, and so on, such as all Face dwells set at .9 second.

Absolute/Incremental

Conventional CNC Format

G90: Specifies the ABSOLUTE mode of Programming be used for positioning of the machine axis.

G91: Specifies the INCREMENTAL mode of Programming be used for positioning of the machine axis.

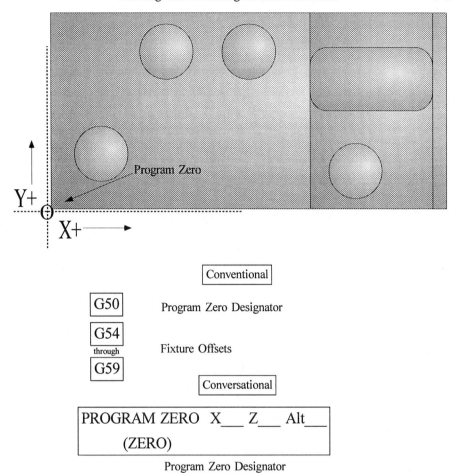

Figure 7.3 *Program Zero/Fixture Offsets (Zero) Commands*

Conversational CNC Format
ABSOLUTE/INCREMENTAL

(ABS/INC): Console button selection that instructs the Control to Toggle to either mode selected for machine-axis positioning.

Program Startup Format

Conventional CNC Format

Actual input values such as speeds, feedrates, tool numbers, axis coordinates, and so on, are variable from workpiece to workpiece. However, the fundamental Format for beginning a new program is consistent every time a new Program is written in Conventional CNC language.

(for Turning Centers)

    O000 (program number; line #; Block #)

    N005 G28 U0 W0 (cross-checking command to send axis to Reference Zero)

    N010 G50 X9.3764 Z5.3365 S2250 (Program Zero is assigned XZ; 2250 RPM)

    N015 G00 T101 M41 (Turret Index to first tool #1; spindle range specified)

    N020 G96 S750 M03 (select mode for spindle; RPM; switch ON spindle)

    N025 G00 X4.2410 Z3.7726 (first axis move to workpiece; switch ON coolant)

    N030 G01 X___ Z___ F____ (1st machining operation; insert feedrate)

Conversational CNC Format

Block #

    1 Position X 2.821 Z 2.125 F 2.0 TL 1

(starts spindle at RPM in Tool 1's specs; rapid positions to the XZ location; cuts to Z)

    2 Face X 2.821 Z 2.500 F 3.2 TL1

(faces from past position, to new XZ location specified at the new feedrate, at same Z)

    3 Turn X 3.456 Y 2.500 F 2.5 TL1

(Turn to new XZ location)

    4 Stop X 3.456 Y 2.500 TL1

(retracts Z axis rapidly; stops all axis movement; turns off spindle; Turret Rotation for tool change)

Every command word given in conversational format executes a combination of instructions to the machine saving Program space and programming time.

Feedrates

Conventional CNC Format

F___: Feedrates for **Axis Motions** (if Control is in **Inch Mode**, it uses Inches per Minute, **IPM**, and Surface Feet per Minute, **SFM**; if in **Metric Mode**, it uses Millimeters per Minute, **MM** or **MMM**.

G98: IPM, Inches per Minute.

G99: IPR, Inches per Revolution (Revolutions of the Spindle).

Conversational CNC Format

FEEDRATE

(FD): Feedrates for **Axis Motions** (if Control is in **Inch Mode**, it uses Inches per Minute, **IPM**, and Surface Feet per Minute, **SFM**; if in **Metric Mode**, it uses Millimeters per Minute, **MM** or MMM.

IPM: Inches per Minute.

IPR: Inches per Revolution (Revolutions of the Spindle).

Constant Surface Speed Control

Conventional CNC Format

G96: Designates spindle control to use Constant Surface Speed control (CSS).

G97: Designates spindle control to use RPMs (i.e., **G97 S500 M03**: causes the spindle to rotate at 500 RPM Clockwise).

Conversational CNC Format

RPM/CSS: Instructs the spindle to toggle between RPM or CSS. Constant Spindle Speed causes the tool to travel over the cutting surface at a constant speed; whether diameters increase or decrease during the operation, the RPMs will compensate accordingly.

RPM

Conventional CNC Format

S___: Instructs the spindle (after a revolution command); the **Spindle Speed in RPMs** (Revolutions per Minute), or SFM (Surface Feet per Minute).

Conversational CNC Format

RPM: Parameters for this value are stored in the **Tool Library**; the selection of a Tool # in a Program Block accesses the **RPM set for that Tool #**.

Spindle Power Ranges

Conventional CNC Format

M41: LOW Spindle Power Range.

M42: HIGH Spindle Power Range.

Conversational CNC Format

LOW RANGE: LOW Spindle Power Range.

HI RANGE: HIGH Spindle Power Range.

Coolants

Conventional CNC Format

M07: **Mist** Coolant **ON**.

M08: **Flood** Coolant **ON**.

M09: Coolant **OFF** (cancels **BOTH** Mist and Flood Coolant Flow).

Conversational CNC Format

MIST CLT ON/OFF: Instructs **Mist** Coolant to Toggle **ON or OFF**.

FLOOD CLT ON/OFF: Instructs **Flood** Coolant to Toggle **ON or OFF**.

Most Controls allow for the individual tools in the Tool Library to be Coolant-associated; or Coolant to be switched On and Off between Program Blocks.

Inch/Metric (MM)

Conventional CNC Format

G70: Inch Mode, Thousandths of an Inch (or divisions thereof).

G71: Metric Mode, Millimeters (or divisions thereof).

Conversational CNC Format

INCH/METRIC

(IN/MM): Switch on console toggles between Inches or Millimeters, for input while Programming.

Tool Change, Tools, and Turret Indexing

Conventional CNC Format

G91 G28 G49 Z0 M19

M01: Instructs the machine to send the **Z-Axis** to the **Tool-Change position**, **cancels** the **Tool Length** in memory, **orients the Tool** in the Turret or Cross-slide for a **Tool Change. M01** instructs the **Optional Stop** to occur.

T____: Turret Station and Offset # to instate.

Conversational CNC Format

STOP/(New Tool #)

or **CHANGE TOOL**: Instructs the machine to **Retract the Z-Axis** to its **Tool-Change Position**, **Orient the Turret**, and causes a **Stop Axis Movement** to take place. See Figure 7.4.

Full Tool Turret/Changer Commands are documented in Chapter 10.

Tool Restart/Restartup

Conventional CNC Format

G90 S450 M03 T03

G00 X____ Z____: Instructs the machine to **Restart after a Tool Change** by selecting **Absolute Mode**, **Turning on** the **Spindle** (to 450 RPM), ready the **next Tool (Tool 3** in this example). Next, the machine **Rapid Traverses** to a **specified X__ Z__ Location.**

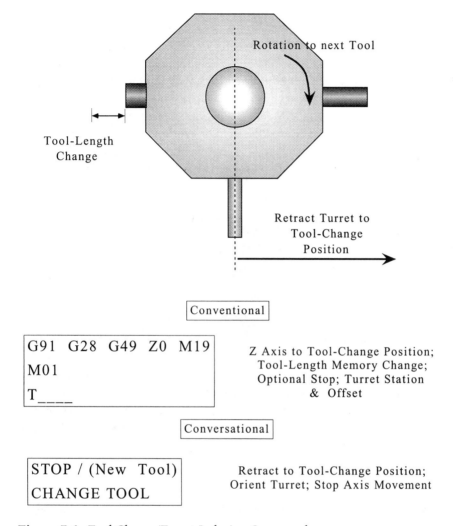

Figure 7.4 *Tool-Change/Turret Indexing Commands*

Conversational CNC Format

TURN, FACE, POSITION, and other Spindle Rotating Commands automatically **TURN ON** the machine spindle when selected in an initial Program Block (line). A Tool # is specified that has the +RPM (Clockwise) or –RPM (Counterclockwise) for spindle rotation recorded for that Tool in memory in the Tool Library.

Conversational Format in many instances includes multiple Commands within its simple one- and two-word command selections.

Tool Startup Format

Conventional CNC Format

N055 G50 X6.4489 Z3.8723 S2250 (Program Zero is set; Spindle Limit is 2250 RPM).

N060 G00 T0202 M42 (Turret is indexed to Station 2; Spindle Range is specified).

N065 G97 S750 M03 (Spindle Mode, Speed, and ON are selected).

N070 G00 X0.000 Z.1 M08 (Rapid Position to Workpiece, Coolant is switched ON).

N075 G01 Z4.5325 F3.5 (Machining move is made; Feedrate is specified).

Conversational CNC Format

POSITION X 6.1292 Z 3.6122 TOOL 2 RPM 1200
TURN X 6.1292 Z 1.5000 TOOL 2 Fd 3.1 IPM
POSITION X 6.0000 Z 3.8000 RAPID RATE
STOP　CHANGE TOOL　TOOL 3

Stop/Optional Stop/End of Program

Conventional CNC Format

M00: Program Stop

M01: Optional Stop: Instructs the machine to **Stop executing the program**; the **Spindle, Coolant**, and anything in motion will be switched **OFF**.

M30: Instructs the machine to switch **OFF** anything in motion, rewind or send control memory to the beginning of the program. **Some Controls substitute M02** for this command.

Conversational CNC Format

STOP or

END PROGRAM: Instructs Control to **STOP All Motion**. Program can be restarted by entering any Block # of a Spindle Rotation Command.

Program-Ending Format

Conventional CNC Format

N160 G00 X 5.3276 Z 5.6534 T0200

(Rapid Position back to Starting Point; Cancel current Tool Offset.)

N165 M30

(End of Program.)

Conversational CNC Format

STOP　RAPID POS X_____ Z_____ TOOL CHANGE　TOOL #_____: Instructs the machine axis to Rapid Traverse to the specified XZ location, Stop all motions, and ready the Turret Indexer with a new Station # for any upcoming Tool Change.

PROGRAMMING COMPLEX TURNING MOTIONS (MOVES)

Tool-Nose-Radius Compensation

Conventional CNC Format
G41: **LEFT**.

G42: **RIGHT**. Both instruct the machine axis to compensate for the **Tool Radius** (entered in the Tool Library) and cause the cutting edge to remain in constant tangent contact with workpiece surfaces. The Program lines (Blocks) entered after these commands contain the coordinate locations the Tool nose is required to achieve.

G40: Cancels both **Left** and **Right** commands.

Conversational CNC Format
TOOL LEFT:

TOOL RIGHT: Both instruct the machine axis to compensate for the **Tool Radius** (entered in the Tool Library) and cause the cutting edge to remain in constant tangent contact with workpiece surfaces. The Program lines (Blocks) entered after these commands contain the coordinate locations the Tool nose is required to achieve. **Both** are **Canceled** by entering a new **Turn, Face, Bore,** or a cutting operation, or **Stop** command, where Compensation is not instated. See Figure 7.5.

Arc Clockwise–Counterclockwise

Conventional CNC Format
G02 X___ Z___ Fd___: Instructs machine axes to move in a **CLOCKWISE** direction around a specified **ARC CENTER** maintaining a set **RADIUS** (cutting a standard 2-axis **ARC** in a Clockwise direction a set distance, or **Radius**, away from a fixed **Arc Center**).

G03 X___ Z___ Fd___: Instructs machine axes to move in a **COUNTERCLOCKWISE** direction around a specified **ARC CENTER** maintaining a set **RADIUS** (cutting a standard 2-axis **ARC** in a Counterclockwise direction a set distance, or **Radius**, away from a fixed **Arc Center**).

Certain Turning-Center Controls reverse these two commands [M032, M03]. Check manuals.

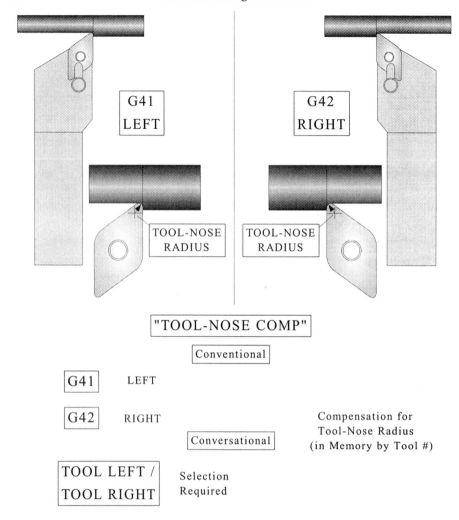

Figure 7.5 *Tool-Nose-Radius Compensation Commands*

Conversational CNC Format

TURN/FACE ARC CW: Instructs machine axes to move in a **CLOCKWISE** direction around a specified **ARC CENTER** maintaining a set **RADIUS** (cutting a standard 2-axis **ARC** in a Clockwise direction a set distance, or **Radius**, away from a fixed **Arc Center**).

TURN/FACE ARC CCW: Instructs machine axes to move in a **COUNTER-CLOCKWISE** direction around a specified **ARC CENTER** maintaining a set **RADIUS** (cutting a standard 2-axis **ARC** in a Counterclockwise direction a set distance, or **Radius**, away from a fixed **Arc Center**). See Figure 7.6.

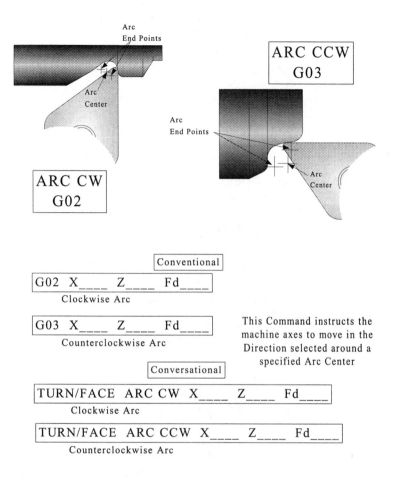

Figure 7.6 *Arc Clockwise–Counterclockwise Command*

Arc—Center Defined

Conventional CNC Format

G01 X__ Z__ F__

G02 X__ Z__ I__ K__: Instructs axes to position to the **XZ Coordinate** specified in the **G01** line, then move at the **F__** (feedrate) in a **Clockwise Direction G02**, to the **XZ coordinates** in the **G02** line, staying away an equidistant **Radius** from the **I__ K__ Arc Center**.

G01 X__ Z__ F__

G03 X__ Z__ I__ K__: Instructs axes to position to the **XZ Coordinate** specified in the **G01** line, then move at the **F__** (feedrate) in a **Counterclockwise Direction G03**, to the **XZ Coordinates** in the **G03** line, staying away an equidistant **Radius** from the **I__ K__ Arc Center**.

> **I__**: X axis Center Point of an Arc
> **K__**: Z axis Center Point of an Arc
> **R__**: Defines Arc Radius if used instead of Center Point

Some Controls on Turning Centers use "J" for the Z-Axis designation instead of "K." Check manuals.

Conversational CNC Format

TURN ARC CW: Instructs machine axes to move around the specified **Arc Center** in a **Clockwise Direction** from the XZ coordinate in the previous block, maintaining the equidistant **Radius** entered, to the next XZ End-Point block.

TURN ARC CCW: Instructs machine axes to move around the specified **Arc Center** in a **Counterclockwise Direction** from the XZ coordinate in the previous block, maintaining the equidistant **Radius** entered, to the next XZ End-Point block. See Figure 7.7.

Curves

Conventional CNC Format

Not applicable in most Conventional formats.

Conversational CNC Format

CURVE CW/CCW X____ Z____ Blend Rad.____

CURVE ENDPOINT X____ Z____ F____: Instructs the two axes selected to recognize an Arc Center and move in the directional rotation selected. The Blend Radius value allows a minimum blend between consecutive Curve operations. This feature is ideal for cam operations that require an undefined changing Arc Center. An example would be entering ten (10) Curve commands and Curve End Points consecutively, each dividing up a distance of .500 that an Arc Center may move during a Cam Contour Turning operation. The Blend Radius allows minimum steps between Arcs. See Figure 7.8.

Reverse Curves

REV. CURVE BLEND RAD.__ __ CW/CCW CCW/CW

> **ARC CENTER 1 X____ Z____ Fd____**
> **ARC END PT. 1 X____ Z____**
> **ARC CENTER 2 X____ Z____ Fd____**
> **ARC END PT. 2 X____ Z____**: Instructs the two axes selected to recognize

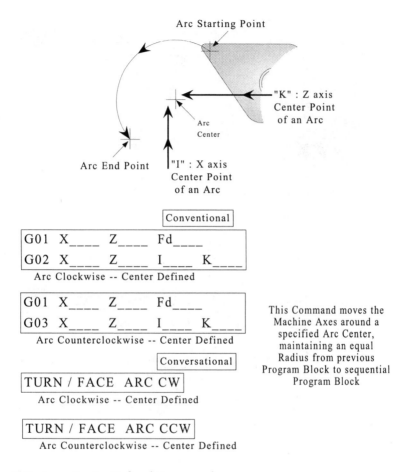

Arc Starting Point

"K" : Z axis
Center Point
of an Arc

Arc
Center

Arc End Point

"I" : X axis
Center Point
of an Arc

Conventional

G01 X____ Z____ Fd____
G02 X____ Z____ I____ K____

Arc Clockwise -- Center Defined

G01 X____ Z____ Fd____
G03 X____ Z____ I____ K____

Arc Counterclockwise -- Center Defined

This Command moves the
Machine Axes around a
specified Arc Center,
maintaining an equal
Radius from previous
Program Block to sequential
Program Block

Conversational

TURN / FACE ARC CW

Arc Clockwise -- Center Defined

TURN / FACE ARC CCW

Arc Counterclockwise -- Center Defined

Figure 7.7 *Arc—Center Defined Command*

an Arc Center and move in the directional rotation selected. The second
Arc (Reverse Arc 2) cuts in the opposite direction of rotation from the
first Arc. The Blend Radius value allows a minimum blend between consecutive Curve operations. Additional Arcs can be inserted before and
after the Reverse Arc. See Figure 7.9.

Parabolic Arcs—Turning

Conventional CNC Format

Not applicable in most Conventional formats.

CURVE COMMAND

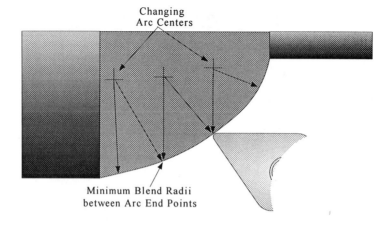

Figure 7.8 *Curve Command*

Conversational CNC Format

PARABOLIC ARC CW/CCW RAD.____

ARC CENTER 1 X____ Z____ Alt____ Fd____

ARC END PT. 1 X____ Z____

ARC CENTER 2 X____ Z____ Alt____ Fd____

ARC END PT. 2 X____ Z____: The use of the Parabolic Arc feature is normally dictated by the unique data specified in the workpiece dimensional measurements. The following workpiece feature criteria may require the Parabolic Arc to be used: 2- and 3-Axis Arcs with Radii unknown; 2- and 3-Axis Arcs with Remote Arc Centers; 3-, 4-, and 5-Axis Contours with a combination of these Arcs. See Figure 7.10.

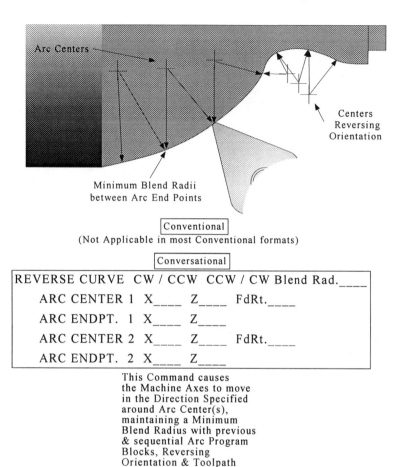

Figure 7.9 *Reverse-Curve Commands*

Alternate Axis Selection

Many Turning Centers feature 4- and 5-axis capabilities. The axis can be chosen and moved by entering the following commands.

Conventional & Conversational CNC Format

C ___.___°: Instructs the spindle to be indexed at the specified degree from 000°.

Y ____: Instructs the optional Y-axis cutting capabilities such as milling head to operate.

ALT____: Axis name and measuring value are entered to instate an additional axis. See Figure 7.11.

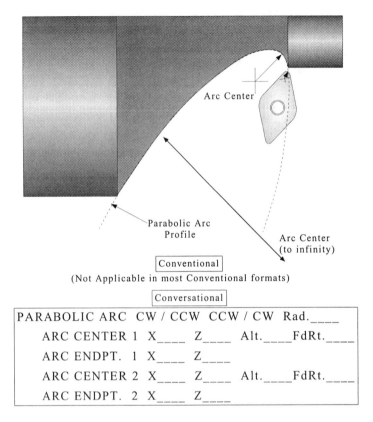

Figure 7.10 *Parabolic-Arc Command—Turning*

Mirror Image

Conventional CNC Format

G05: X AXIS MIRROR IMAGE
G06: Z AXIS MIRROR IMAGE
G07: ALT AXIS MIRROR IMAGE
(ALT[ernate] Axis choice, C, Y, A.)
Each Command instructs the Control to generate a series of movements that
   represents the Mirror Image of a programmed Path or Coordinates.
G09: Cancels Mirror-Image Commands.

Conversational CNC Format

MIRROR AXIS _____ **CL X**___ **Z**___ **ALT**___: Each Command instructs
   the Control to generate a series of movements that represents the Mirror

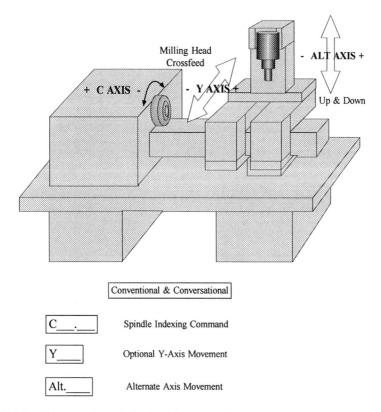

Figure 7.11 *Alternate-Axis Selection Command*

Image of a programmed Path or Coordinates; with a Mirroring Center Line specified by Axis Coordinates. See Figure 7.12.

Canned Turning

Conventional CNC Format

G81 X___ Z1___ Z2___ Fd___: Instructs the machine axis to move (after a positioning block) the cutting tool using a subroutine that Turns a finished surface at the X (value), from Z1 (value) to Z2(value) at the specified Feedrate.

Conversational CNC Format

AUTO TURN 1 / 2 Pass X___ Z1___ Z2___ Fd___: Instructs the machine

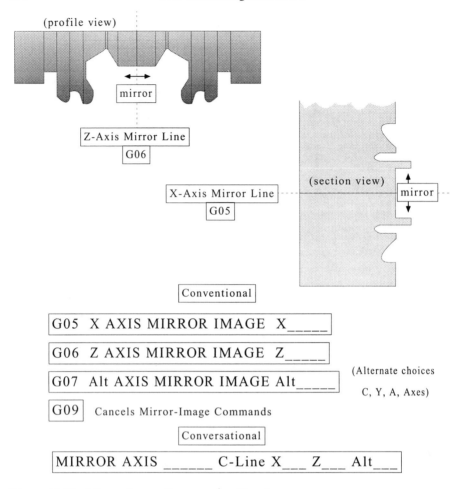

Figure 7.12 *Mirror-Image Commands—Turning*

axis to move (after a positioning block) the cutting tool using a subroutine that Turns a finished surface using a single/double pass at the X (value), from Z1 (value) to Z2(value) at the specified Feedrate. If 2 Pass is selected, the tool will return for a second pass; the finishing amounts are set in Tool Library memory. See Figure 7.13.

Canned Facing

Conventional CNC Format

G82 X1___ X2___ Z___ Fd___: Instructs the machine axis to move the cutting tool (after a positioning block) using a subroutine that Faces a finished surface at the Z (value), from X1 (value) to X2(value) at the specified Feedrate.

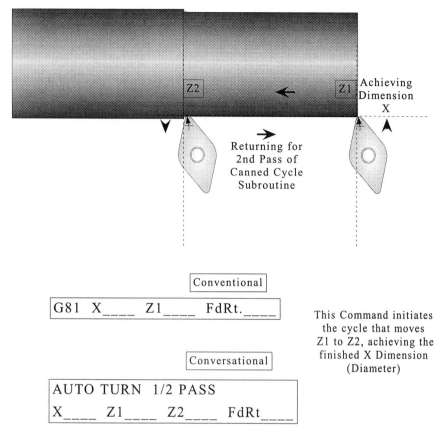

Figure 7.13 Canned Turning Command

Conversational CNC Format

AUTO FACE 1 / 2 Pass X1___ X2___ Z___ Fd___: Instructs the machine axis to move the cutting tool (after a positioning block) using a subroutine that Faces a finished surface using a single/double pass at the Z (value), from X1 (value) to X2(value) at the specified Feedrate. If 2 Pass is selected, the tool will return for a second pass; the finishing amounts are set in Tool Library memory. See Figure 7.14.

Canned Tapering

Conventional CNC Format

G83 X1___ Z1___ X2___ Z2___ Fd___: Instructs the machine axis to move the cutting tool (after a positioning block) using a subroutine that turns a

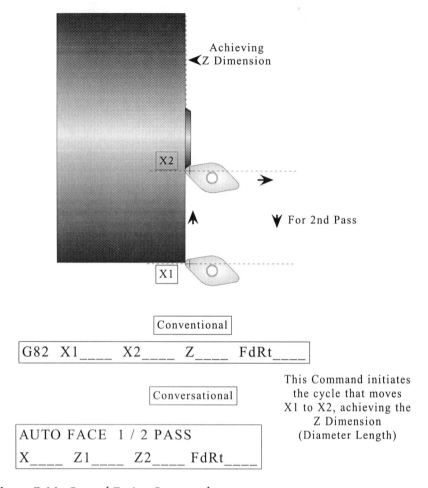

Achieving
◀Z Dimension

X2

→

▼ For 2nd Pass

▲

X1

Conventional

G82 X1____ X2____ Z____ FdRt____

Conversational

AUTO FACE 1 / 2 PASS

X____ Z1____ Z2____ FdRt____

This Command initiates
the cycle that moves
X1 to X2, achieving the
Z Dimension
(Diameter Length)

Figure 7.14 *Canned Facing Command*

Taper, a finished surface from the X1 (value) and Z1 (value) to X2 (value) and Z2 (value) at the specified Feedrate.

Conversational CNC Format

AUTO TAPER 1 / 2 Pass X1___ Z1___ X2___ Z2___ Fd___: Instructs the machine axis to move the cutting tool (after a positioning block) using a subroutine that turns a Taper, a finished surface using a single/double pass from the X1 (value) and Z1 (value) to X2 (value) and Z2 (value) at the specified Feedrate. If 2 Pass is selected, the tool will return for a second pass; the finishing amounts are set in Tool Library memory. See Figure 7.15.

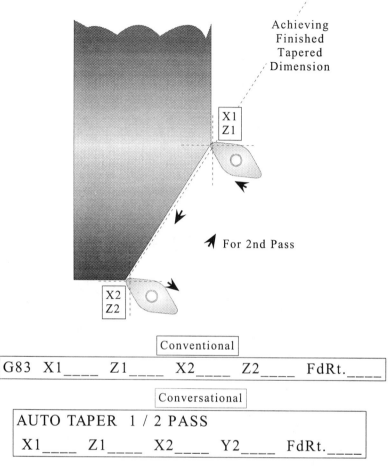

Figure 7.15 *Canned Tapering Command*

Canned Grooving

Conventional CNC Format

Not applicable in most Conventional formats.

Conversational CNC Format

GROOVE : X1___ Z1___ X2___ Z2___ Fd___: Causes the Axis Selected and dimensioned to execute a Single/Double Pass routine that cuts a Groove into the workpiece. This routine can be used for other small areas where

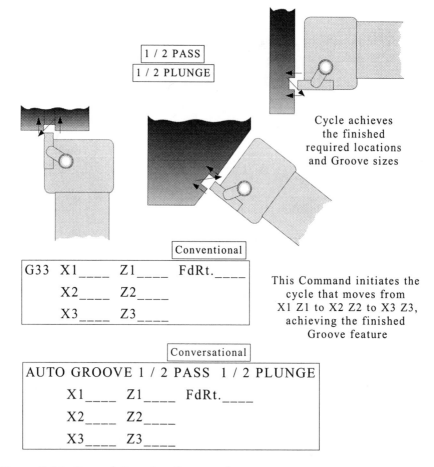

Figure 7.16 *Canned Grooving Command*

box-type toolpaths are needed, saving program space and coordinates entered. See Figure 7.16.

Thread Cutting

Conventional CNC Format

G33 X____ E____: Instructs the machine axis to begin and complete a series of movements: Tool Approach, Feed and RPM synchronization, Tool Exit after completion.

E____: Denotes Thread Pitch followed by the specific accuracy (four-place accuracy in most Controls).

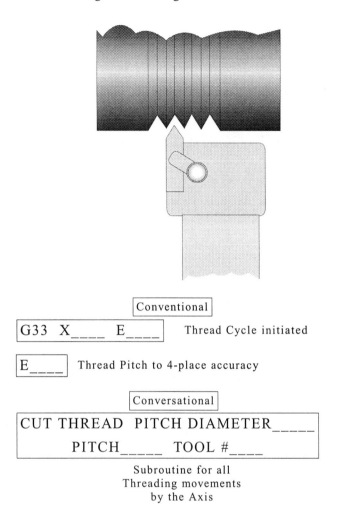

Figure 7.17 *Thread-Cutting Command*

Conversational CNC Format

CUT THREAD P. DIA___ PITCH___ TOOL #___: Instructs the machine axis to begin and complete a series of movements: Tool Approach, Feed and RPM synchronization, Tool Exit after completion. See Figure 7.17.

Thread Interpolation

Conventional CNC Format

G32 X___ E___

G34 X___ E___ (Variable Pitch): Used for special Threads (i.e., Acme, Spherical), where special internal and external thread characteristics need to be entered as geometric values critical to the machine motions.

Conversational CNC Format

INTERP. THREAD P. DIA___ PITCH___ TOOL #___ PASS #___: Used for special Threads (i.e., Acme, Spherical), where special internal and external thread characteristics need to be entered as geometric values critical to the machine motions. The "Pass #" value allows the operation to be divided into partial passes. A programmable finish-feed amount is specified on most Controls.

PROGRAMMING CNC GRINDING MOTIONS (MOVES)

The application of CNC capability to Grinding operations is a rapidly expanding area of technology. This section documents the common and popular machine configurations, and the standard and advanced CNC Grinding Commands for operations and subroutines offered in today's Controls.

Machine-Axis Configurations: Four-Axis CNC Internal Grinding Machine

The 4-Axis CNC Internal Grinder is a very versatile machine that is capable of multiple operations: Bore or Outside-Diameter grinding; Cylindrical or Tapered grinding by Interpolation; Blending Chamfers and Radius capabilities; Front or Back Faces; Vector grinding of Diameters and Faces, all with Negative or Positive Feeds. A common Axis Configuration designates the main axes as X and Z, with B, C, D, and U as Auxiliary Axes. See Figure 7.18.

Grinding Wheel Profiles can also be "Dressed" on these grinders by CNC axes dedicated specifically for this. By using Linear and Circular Interpolation wheel-dressing control, advanced profiles can be dressed: Cylindrical; Tapered; Tapered with Blending Chamfers or Radius at Left/Right; Concave or Convex; Cylindrical with two steps as well as front and/or back Faces.

Four-Axis Contouring CNC Cylindrical Grinding Machines

Four-Axis Cylindrical Grinders are capable of a variety of operations, all under CNC guidance. Plunge Grinding, Traverse Grinding, Tapers, Faces, Contours, Forms, and Profile Dressing are among some of the operations that can be accomplished using 4-Axis CNC Cylindrical Grinders. Combined with available Auxiliary Axes, the possible configurations offer a great flexibility for a variety of grinding operations. See Figure 7.19.

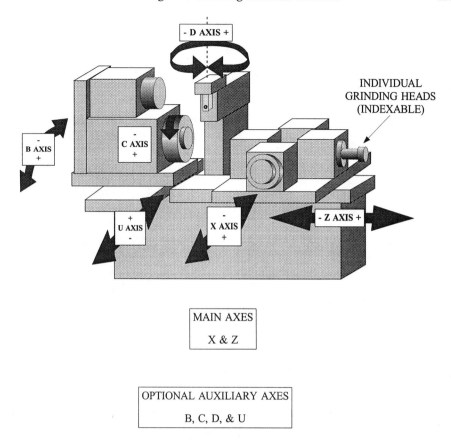

Figure 7.18 *Four-Axis CNC Internal Grinding Machine*

Flexible CNC Grinding Machines for ID, ID/Face, and OD Operations

Conventional CNC Format

Some CNC Grinding machines allow the versatility of using a certain axis to grind ODs for one configuration, change axis location under power, and then face and grind IDs using the same axis. See Figure 7.20.

For special grinding (inner-cone grinding), the B-axis can be instated and controlled for machining (Figure 7.20(a)).

While X- and Z-Axes are ready for grinding, the W-Axis has been rotated 90° CW and now can be instated as the U-Axis for Tangential grinding. Both the U- and W-Axes can be programmed and controlled (Figure 7.20(b)).

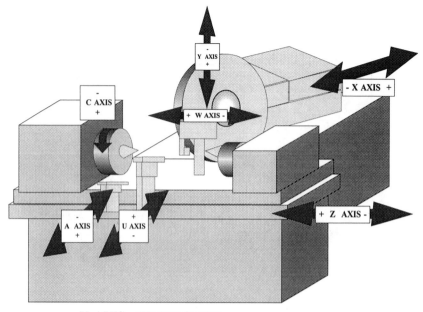

X AXIS : WHEELSLIDE

Z AXIS : WORKSLIDE

C AXIS : WORKHEAD SPINDLE

A AXIS : MULTIRANGE STEADY REST

U AXIS : POSITIONING GUIDE

W AXIS : MEASURING HEAD

Figure 7.19   *Four-Axis Contouring CNC Cylindrical Grinding Machine*

Programmable CNC Grinding Cycles

Most Multiaxis CNC Grinders with contouring Controls have allowed significant advancements in the methods of grinding technology. Ease of programming through the use of grinding-cycle subroutines, combined with the multiaxis flexibility, has made the application of CNC to this area of precision machining very successful.

Many of the common Subroutines are included in this section. *All* are in the *Conversational Format*, but are applicable to Conventional Formats that use the same Subroutines under generic command names. Some Controls may apply alternate names to these same operations. All material amounts removed for roughing and finishing passes are variables entered in each program.

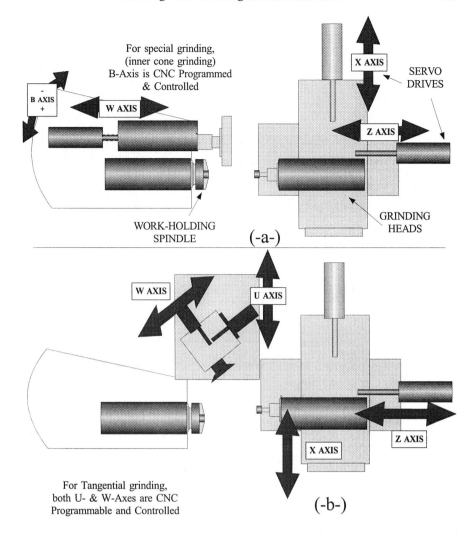

For special grinding,
(inner cone grinding)
B-Axis is CNC Programmed
& Controlled

B AXIS

W AXIS

WORK-HOLDING
SPINDLE

(-a-)

X AXIS

SERVO
DRIVES

Z AXIS

GRINDING
HEADS

W AXIS

U AXIS

Z AXIS

X AXIS

For Tangential grinding,
both U- & W-Axes are CNC
Programmable and Controlled

(-b-)

Figure 7.20 *Flexible CNC Grinding Machines for ID, ID/Face, and OD Operations*

External Cylindrical Subroutines

PLUNGE GRIND STRAIGHT Axis: ( ) . ( ) . ( ) . F_____: A six-step cycle that moves the wheel into the workpiece in 2- or 3-axis directions, each separately: Air Grinding; Roughing; a Stress-Relief backoff; Fine-Finish Pass; Final Sizing and Zero Reset; and Rapid Return to the initial position or next programmed position. See Figure 7.21.

PLUNGE GRIND ANGULAR Axis: ( ) . ( ) . ( ) . F_____: Plunges the wheel into a workpiece surface intersection in a two-axis direction, *simulta-*

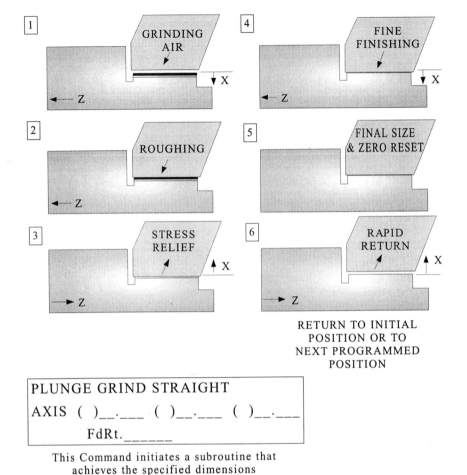

PLUNGE GRIND STRAIGHT
AXIS ( )__.___ ( )__.___ ( )__.___
    FdRt._____

This Command initiates a subroutine that
achieves the specified dimensions
by causing the Grinding-Machine Axes
to sequence through the above Motions

Figure 7.21 *Plunge Grind—Straight Cycle Command*

neously, in an Angular axis-movement direction. All moves in this six-step cycle are in two-axis Angular directions. See Figure 7.22.

TRAVERSE GRIND Axis: ( ) . ( ) . ( ) . F_____ #Passes____: This six-step cycle moves the wheel down a step cut, Traverses the workpiece surface, moves in a step cut, Traverses the surface by the # of Passes specified, finishes, and Resets Zero. See Figure 7.23.

FACE GRIND Axis: ( ) . ( ) . ( ) . F_____ #Passes____: A six-step cycle that moves in and Face-grinds with selected axis movements. The moves

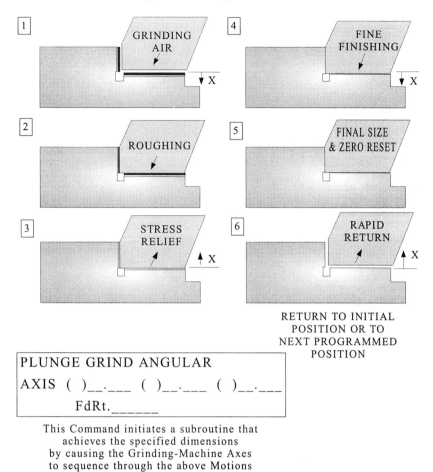

RETURN TO INITIAL
POSITION OR TO
NEXT PROGRAMMED
POSITION

PLUNGE GRIND ANGULAR
AXIS ( )__.___ ( )__.___ ( )__.___
        FdRt._____

This Command initiates a subroutine that
achieves the specified dimensions
by causing the Grinding-Machine Axes
to sequence through the above Motions

Figure 7.22 *Plunge Grind—Angular Cycle Command*

include: Air Grind; Roughing; Stress Relief; Fine Finishing; Final Sizing and
Zero Reset; and Rapid Return. See Figure 7.24.

TAPER GRIND

CONTOUR CONTROL Axis: ( )___ ( )___ ( )___ F____ #Passes____: The six-
step cycle includes 3-axis selection that moves in the chosen # of passes.
Passes step-feed in or out at the beginning and end of each grind. Final Sizing
and Reset with a Rapid Retraction rounds out this cycle. See Figure 7.25.

CONTOUR GRIND Rad 1____ Rad 2____ Rad 3____

CONTOUR CONTROL Axis: ( ) . ( ) . ( ) . F____ #Passes____: An eight-
step cycle that includes the Radii specified for the Contour and the Radius
ground into the wheel corner. See Figure 7.26.

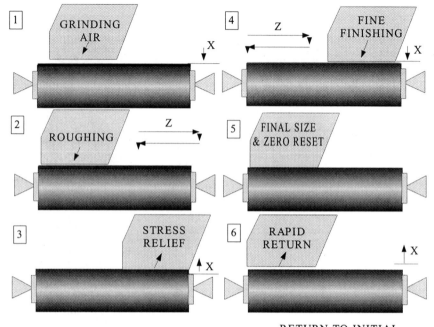

RETURN TO INITIAL
POSITION OR TO
NEXT PROGRAMMED
POSITION

TRAVERSE GRIND

AXIS ( )__.___ ( )__.___ ( )__.___

     FdRt._____

This Command initiates a subroutine that
achieves the specified dimensions
by causing the Grinding-Machine Axes
to sequence through the above Motions

Figure 7.23 *Traverse Grind-Cycle Command*

Multiaxis CNC Internal Grinding Cycles

INSIDE DIAMETER Axis: ( ) . ( ) . ( ) . F___ #Passes____: Grind IDs
(Inside Diameters) with a continuous or pick-feed, using Plunge or Reciprocating
cycles. Notice that Feedrates and # of Passes are selected. See Figure 7.27.

OUTSIDE DIAMETER Axis: ( ) . ( ) . ( ) . F___ #Passes____: Enter
proper Workhead Direction and Speed, Grind ODs with a continuous or pick-
feed, using Plunge or Reciprocating cycles. Notice that Feedrates and # of
Passes are selected. See Figure 7.28.

FACE Axis: ( ) . ( ) . ( ) . F_____ #Passes____: Reciprocate (moves) or
Plunge grind Internal or adapt to External Faces. See Figure 7.29.

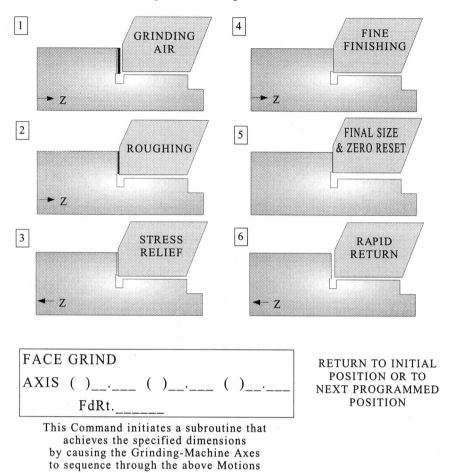

This Command initiates a subroutine that
achieves the specified dimensions
by causing the Grinding-Machine Axes
to sequence through the above Motions

Figure 7.24 *Face-Grind-Cycle Command*

ANGULAR RECIPROCATE Axis: ( ) . ( ) . ( ) . F___ #Passes____: Perform Angular wheel Reciprocation moves and matching wheel In/Out Feed automatically. See Figure 7.30.

VECTOR PLUNGE Axis: ( ) . ( ) . ( ) . F_____ #Passes____: Simultaneously grind External- or Internal-Diameter surfaces and adjacent Face. See Figure 7.31.

REVERSE VECTOR PLUNGE Axis: ( ) . ( ) . ( ) . F_____ #Passes____: Perform a Vector Plunge on surfaces of the workpiece oriented toward the chuck or workhead. See Figure 7.32.

CONTOUR PLUNGE Axis: ( ) . ( ) . ( ) . F___ #Passes____: Transfers shapes "Dressed" onto the grinding wheel to the workpiece. See Figure 7.33.

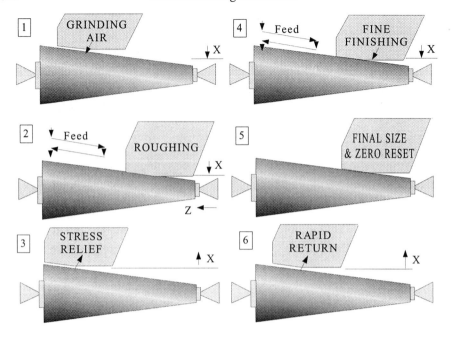

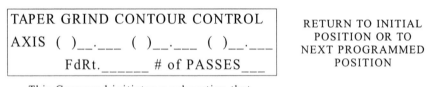

RETURN TO INITIAL
POSITION OR TO
NEXT PROGRAMMED
POSITION

This Command initiates a subroutine that
achieves the specified dimensions
by causing the Grinding-Machine Axes
to sequence through the above Motions

Figure 7.25   *Taper Grind—Contour Control Cycle Command*

CONTOUR GENERATION Axis: (_) . (_) . (_) . F___ #Passes____: Generate Chamfers, Radii, and Compound Curves directly in a workpiece. See
Figure 7.34.

CNC Contoured Grinding-Wheel Dresser

CNC Profile Dressers accurately move a diamond tool in a preprogrammed
toolpath, enabling the placement of complex forms directly onto grinding
wheels for machining into workpiece surfaces. Precision contour wheel dressing
allows the pivoting axis of the dresser to form the smallest, deep Contours into
the wheel as the angle of inclination of the tool (in relation to the curves) is

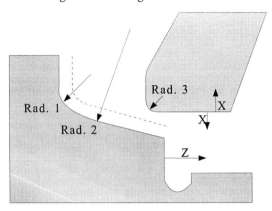

```
CONTOUR GRIND
RAD.1____   RAD.2____   RAD.3____
CONTROL AXIS ( )__.___   ( )__.___   ( )__.___
     FdRt.____   # of Passes_____
```

Figure 7.26 *Contour Grind—Controlled Cycle Command*

determined by the programmer. Figure 7.35 shows the 2-axis configuration for a CNC wheel dresser.

Two-Axis Wheel Profiling

The 2-axis dresser is suitable for uses where the extended life of the diamond tool is required. Many diamond wheels can be selected with Radii starting from .5 mm. Depending on the geometry, the diamond layer varies from 10–30 carats. The drive system of the wheel is direct and designed with integrated spindle bearings and a conical precision head for the diamond wheel. See Figure 7.36. (A common Subroutine used for 2-axis Wheel Dresser)

CONTOUR DRESS Axis: ( ) . ( ) . ( ) . F_____ #Passes____ CONTOUR Rad 1____ Rad 2____ Rad 3____: This eight-step Subroutine dresses shapes into the grinding wheel by moving the Axis selected at the specified Feedrate achieving the Rad. entered. Wheel Radii are entered in memory in the Tool Library. See Figure 7.37.

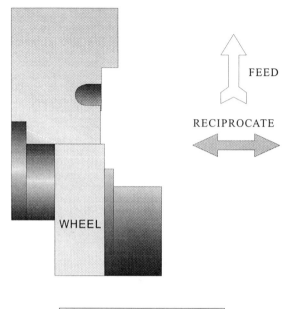

CYCLE for GRINDING
INSIDE DIAMETERS

INSIDE DIAMETER
AXIS ( )__.___ ( )__.___ ( )__.___
    FdRt.____ # of Passes
    Feed__ Reciprocate__

This Command initiates
a cycle that Grinds IDs
with Continuous or Pick
feeds, using Plunge or
Reciprocating motions

Figure 7.27 *Inside-Diameter Cycle Command*

Three-Axis Wheel Profiling

The 3-Axis Profiler has more movement and can dress much more complex
Contours into the wheel surfaces. A single-point dressing diamond is normally
mounted in a precision holder similar to a boring bar, with incremental adjustment capability. See Figure 7.38.

(A common Subroutine for the 3-Axis Control)
CONTOUR DRESS Axis: ( ) . ( ) . (Alt) . F____ #Passes____ CONTOUR
  Rad 1___ Rad 2___ Rad 3___: This Subroutine causes the 3-Axis movement of the wheel dresser to follow the specified toolpath, cutting the Form
  into the wheel. The (Alt) selection available on this command enables the
  third axis to move simultaneously, whereas the 2-axis subroutine does not

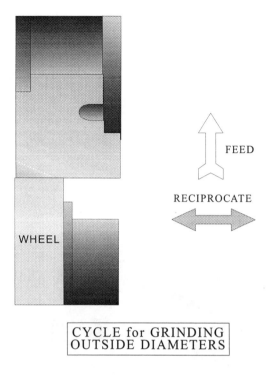

FEED

RECIPROCATE

WHEEL

CYCLE for GRINDING
OUTSIDE DIAMETERS

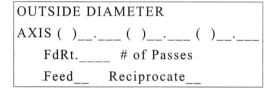

OUTSIDE DIAMETER
AXIS ( )__.___ ( )__.___ ( )__.___
    FdRt.____   # of Passes
    .Feed__   Reciprocate__

This Command initiates
a cycle that Grinds ODs
with Continuous or Pick
feeds, using Plunge or
Reciprocating motions

Figure 7.28 *Outside-Diameter Cycle Command*

move more than two axes at once. The same programming formats used for
CNC milling centers can also control the toolpath movements for the dresser
(see Chapter 6). See Figure 7.39.

Many CNC Profiler Controls use Graphical Selection for subroutines in their
memory. By "selecting" the type of Form to be ground from the Form Profile
Library, a subroutine screen comes up and "asks" for data to be entered. Some
common Form Subroutines are shown in Figure 7.40.

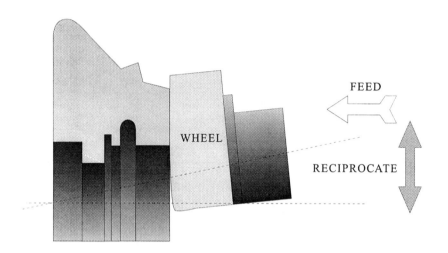

FEED

WHEEL

RECIPROCATE

CYCLE for GRINDING
INTERNAL & EXTERNAL
FACES

FACE GRIND

AXIS ( )__.___ ( )__.___ ( )__.___

    FdRt.____ # of Passes

    Feed__ Reciprocate__

This Command initiates
a cycle that Grinds Faces
with Continuous or Pick
feeds, using Plunge or
Reciprocating motions

Figure 7.29 *Internal/External Facing-Cycle Command*

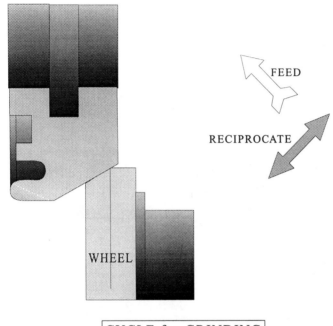

CYCLE for GRINDING
ANGULAR SURFACES

ANGULAR RECIPROCATE

AXIS ( )__.___ ( )__.___ ( )__.___

    FdRt.____   # of Passes

    Feed__   Reciprocate__

This Command initiates
a cycle that performs
Angular Reciprocation
with Continuous or Pick
feeds, using Plunge or
Reciprocating motions

Figure 7.30 *Angular Reciprocation-Cycle Command*

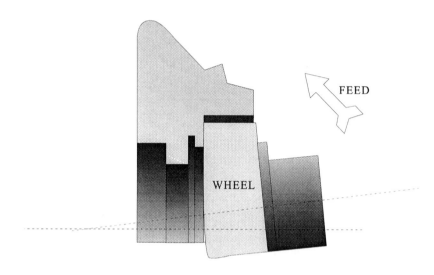

FEED

WHEEL

CYCLE for GRINDING
INTERNAL or EXTERNAL
DIAMETERS & ADJACENT
FACES

VECTOR PLUNGE

AXIS ( )__.___ ( )__.___ ( )__.___

    FdRt.____ # of Passes___

    Feed__   Reciprocate__

This Command initiates
a cycle that simultaneously
Grinds Internal or External
Surfaces & Adjacent Faces
with Continuous or Pick
feeds, using Plunge or
Reciprocating motions

Figure 7.31 *Vector Plunge-Grinding-Cycle Command*

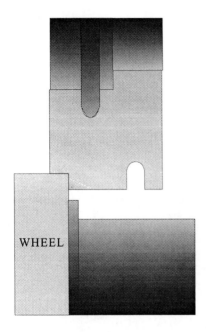

FEED

This Command initiates
a cycle that simultaneously
Grinds Internal or External
Surfaces & Adjacent Faces
on surfaces oriented toward
the Chuck with Continuous
or Pick feeds, using Plunge or
Reciprocating motions

CYCLE for GRINDING
REVERSE VECTOR PLUNGES
on DIAMETERS & ADJACENT
FACES

REVERSE VECTOR PLUNGE

AXIS ( )__.___ ( )__.___ ( )__.___

    FdRt.____ # of Passes___

    Feed__ Reciprocate__

Figure 7.32 *Reverse Vector Plunge-Grinding-Cycle Command*

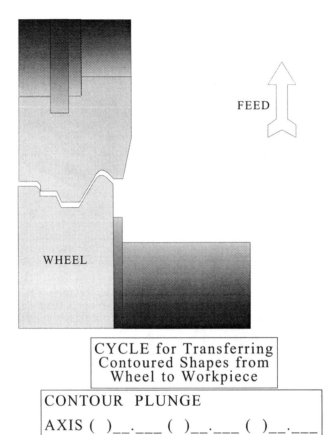

FEED

WHEEL

CYCLE for Transferring
Contoured Shapes from
Wheel to Workpiece

CONTOUR PLUNGE

AXIS ( )__.___ ( )__.___ ( )__.___

FdRt.____   # of Passes___

Feed__   Reciprocate__

This Command initiates
a cycle that transfers "Dressed"
shapes from the Grinding Wheel
to the workpiece surfaces with
Continuous or Pick feeds, using
Plunge or Reciprocating motions

Figure 7.33 *Contour Plunge-Cycle Command*

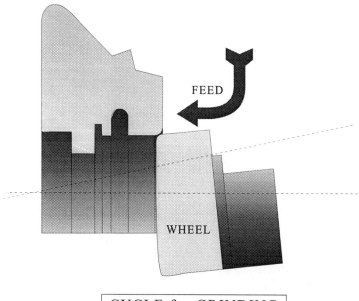

FEED

WHEEL

CYCLE for GRINDING
GENERATED SURFACE
FACES

CONTOUR GENERATION

AXIS ( )__.___ ( )__.___ ( )__.___

    FdRt.____   # of Passes

    Feed__   Reciprocate__

This Command initiates
a cycle that Generates
Contours through simultaneous
Axis Movement with
Continuous feeds

Figure 7.34 *Contour-Generation-Cycle Command*

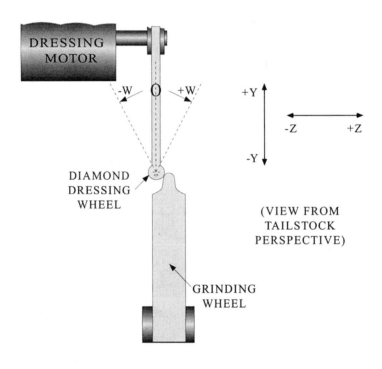

Figure 7.35 *CNC Contoured Grinding-Wheel Dresser: Two-Axis Orientation*

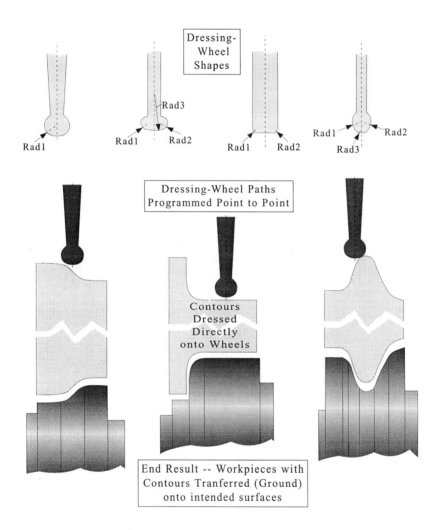

Figure 7.36 *Diamond Dressing-Wheel Shapes and Applications*

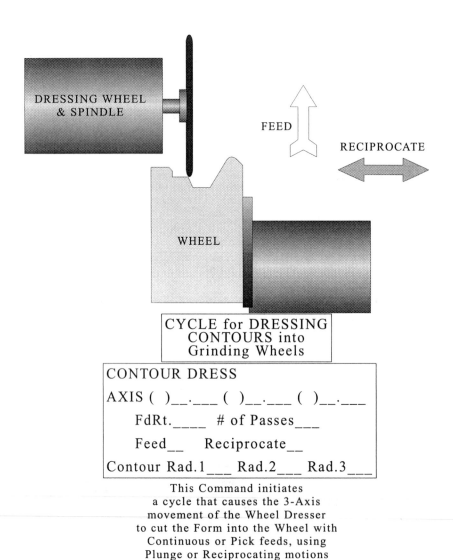

CYCLE for DRESSING
CONTOURS into
Grinding Wheels

CONTOUR DRESS
AXIS ( )__.___ ( )__.___ ( )__.___
    FdRt.____ # of Passes___
    Feed__ Reciprocate__
Contour Rad.1___ Rad.2___ Rad.3___

This Command initiates
a cycle that causes the 3-Axis
movement of the Wheel Dresser
to cut the Form into the Wheel with
Continuous or Pick feeds, using
Plunge or Reciprocating motions

Figure 7.37 *Contour Wheel-Dressing Command*

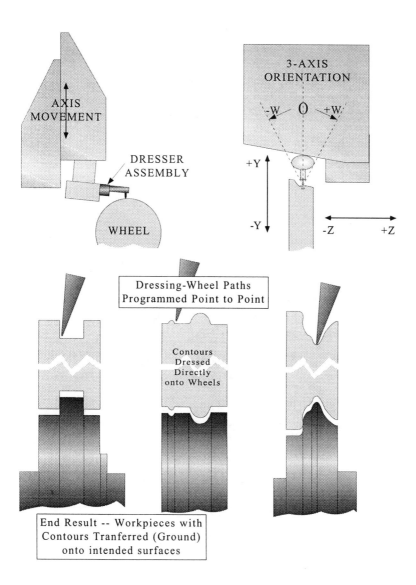

Figure 7.38 *CNC Contoured Grinding-Wheel Dresser: Three-Axis Orientation*

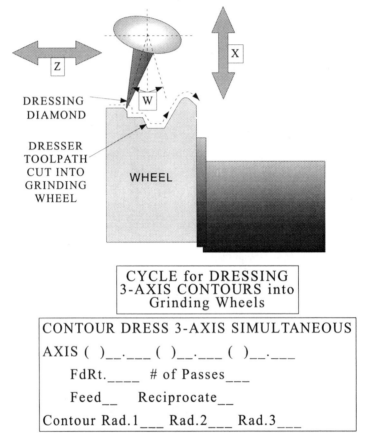

DRESSING
DIAMOND

DRESSER
TOOLPATH
CUT INTO
GRINDING
WHEEL

WHEEL

**CYCLE for DRESSING
3-AXIS CONTOURS into
Grinding Wheels**

CONTOUR DRESS 3-AXIS SIMULTANEOUS

AXIS ( )__.___ ( )__.___ ( )__.___

   FdRt.____   # of Passes___

   Feed__   Reciprocate__

Contour Rad.1___ Rad.2___ Rad.3___

This Command initiates
a cycle that causes the 3-Axis
movement of the Wheel Dresser
to cut the Form into the Wheel
with simultaneous motion, using
Plunge or Reciprocating feeds

Figure 7.39 *Three-Axis Profile Dressing Command*

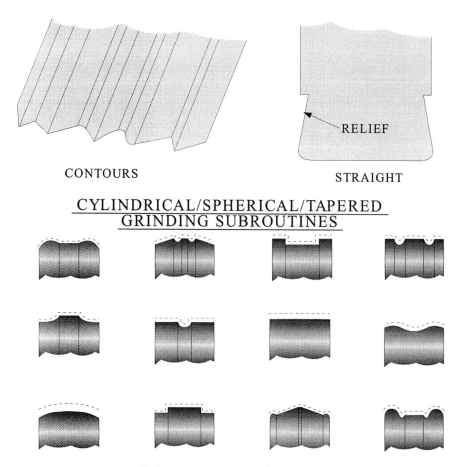

CONTOURS   STRAIGHT

CYLINDRICAL/SPHERICAL/TAPERED
GRINDING SUBROUTINES

Subroutines can be selected
by their Shapes and Combinations
of Shapes. After selection from
Program Groups, Data Windows
appear and wait for required
Dimensional Data to be entered
for individual Workpiece Sizes

Figure 7.40 *Graphical Profile-Selection Library in Memory*

Chapter 8

SUBROUTINES AND COMPENSATION

Subroutines and Canned Cycles and Cutter and Tool Compensation are control-resident miniprograms and powerful work-saving features. When chosen properly, these features can produce maximum machine movement with a minimum of data computation and entry. Subroutines and Compensation can be selected to work in combinations, gleaning the full potential from today's CNC machines.

PROGRAMMING USING SUBROUTINES and CANNED CYCLES

Subroutines and Canned Cycles are essentially the same for discussion purposes. Canned Cycles were offered first as self-contained cycles in conventional CNC Controls and performed specific redundant operations (hole drilling, boring, tapping) under the instruction of a single command line.

Along with the computer revolution, the Subroutine evolved as a more adaptable instrument based upon the original principle. Subroutines in today's computer Controls have the ability to be modified extensively, used in combination with each other, and "inside" each other. One Subroutine can multiply the other Subroutine's power if used in proper sequence. An example is a Loop and Repeat Drilling Subroutine, selected within another Loop and Repeat Subroutine, the end result being 10,000 or more hole locations using only three or four Blocks of program space.

This section gives examples of Subroutines available on many CNC Milling and Boring Centers and Turning Centers.

Pocket

Conversational CNC Format

MILL POCKET 1 / 2 Pass: (X)__. (Y)__. (Z)__. Rad.____ Inside/Outside
XLength_____ YWidth_____ F___ Spiral / ZigZag Cleanout: Instructs the
machine axis to mill a Rectangular Pocket at a (Axes) location to a specified
depth; usually, the lower left-hand absolute corner of a Pocket defines its
location, cleaning-out the center by one of three cutting methods: spiral/in-
side-out, outside-in, or ZigZag at an angle (with Boss avoidance of up to 100
specific island locations); finishing the length and width entered. One or two
passes and the Radius specified, which generates radii in four corners, are
other programmable parameters of this useful feature. See Figure 8.1.

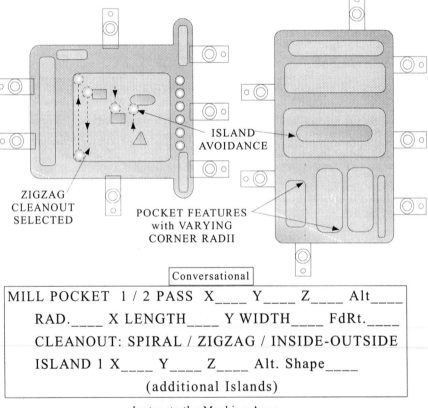

ISLAND AVOIDANCE

ZIGZAG CLEANOUT SELECTED

POCKET FEATURES
with VARYING
CORNER RADII

Conversational

MILL POCKET 1 / 2 PASS X____ Y____ Z____ Alt____
    RAD.____ X LENGTH____ Y WIDTH____ FdRt.____
    CLEANOUT: SPIRAL / ZIGZAG / INSIDE-OUTSIDE
    ISLAND 1 X____ Y____ Z____ Alt. Shape____
              (additional Islands)

Instructs the Machine Axes
to initiate a cycle, Locating
a Pocket feature, Sizing
specified Length/Width/Depth,
Corner Radii, Island Avoidance,
and Cleanout Toolpath

Figure 8.1 *Mill Pocket Subroutine*

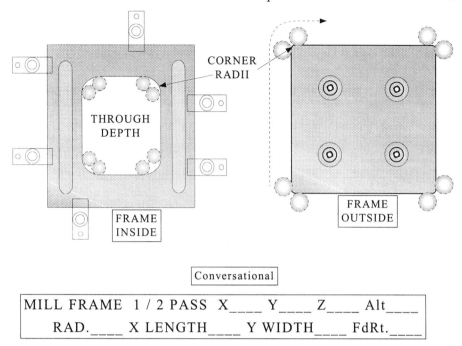

Conversational

MILL FRAME 1 / 2 PASS X____ Y____ Z____ Alt____

RAD.____ X LENGTH____ Y WIDTH____ FdRt.____

Instructs the Machine Axes
to initiate a cycle, Locating
a Frame feature, Sizing
specified Length/Width/Depth,
& Corner Radii

Figure 8.2 *Mill Frame Subroutine*

Frame

Conversational CNC Format

MILL FRAME 1 / 2 Pass: (X)____ (Y)____ (Z)____Rad._____
XLength_____ YWidth_____ F_____ Inside / Outside: Same as the Pocket
feature with no center clean-out; can be selected to cut an inside or outside
Frame. See Figure 8.2.

Circle

Conversational CNC Format

MILL CIRCLE 1 / 2 Pass: (X)_._(Y)_._(Z)_._Inside / Outside
CW / CCW Rad._____ F_____ Spiral / ZigZag Cleanout: Instructs the ma-
chine axis to move around the coordinate location selected at a specified
Radius forming a Circle feature. One or two passes can be chosen as well as

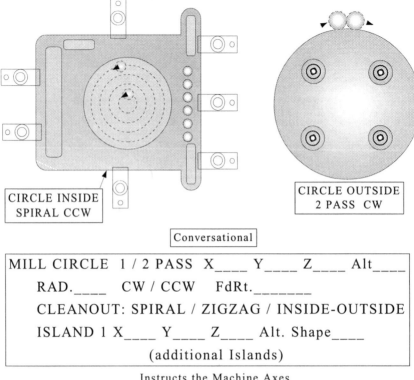

CIRCLE INSIDE
SPIRAL CCW

CIRCLE OUTSIDE
2 PASS CW

Conversational

MILL CIRCLE 1 / 2 PASS X____ Y____ Z____ Alt____
      RAD.____   CW / CCW   FdRt._____
      CLEANOUT: SPIRAL / ZIGZAG / INSIDE-OUTSIDE
      ISLAND 1 X____ Y____ Z____ Alt. Shape____
                    (additional Islands)

Instructs the Machine Axes
to initiate a cycle, Locating
a Circle feature, Sizing specified
Depth, Radii, Island Avoidance,
and Cleanout Toolpath

Figure 8.3 *Mill Circle Subroutine*

Spiral Cleanout of the Center Section. Outside can be chosen to mill the outside of circular features such as Bosses. See Figure 8.3.

Ellipse

Conversational CNC Format
MILL ELLIPSE 1 / 2 Pass : (X) . **(Y)** . **(Z)** . **Inside / Outside**
Rad 1___Rad 2___ XLength_____ YWidth_____ F_____
Spiral / ZigZag Cleanout CW / CCW: Instructs the machine to move around the Axis location selected at specified Radii, forming an Ellipse feature. Typically, the "lower-left low-point" coordinates define location; the Length and Width cause the Control to divide up the available spaces with four Arc Cen-

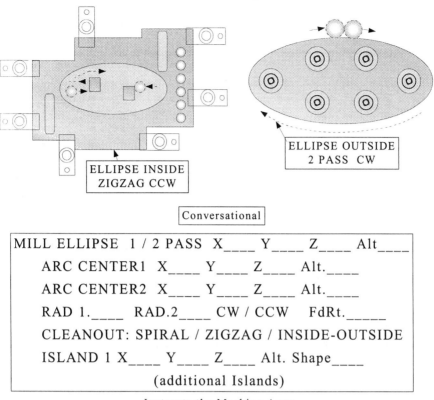

Figure 8.4 *Mill Ellipse Subroutine*

ters and blend the Tool Radius automatically. One or two passes can be chosen as well as Spiral Cleanout of the Center Section. Outside can be chosen to mill the outside of circular features such as Bosses. See Figure 8.4.

Triangle

Conversational CNC Format

MILL TRIANGLE 1 / 2 Pass: (X)_ . (Y)_ . (Z)_ . __Inside / Outside

Rad 1__ Rad 2__ Rad 3__ X1__ Y1__ X2__ Y2__ X3__ Y3__ F__

Spiral / ZigZag CW / CCW: Instructs the machine to move around the Axis location selected at a specified location, forming a Triangle feature. Typically, the "Center" coordinates define location; the X1-3, Y1-3 coordinates cause

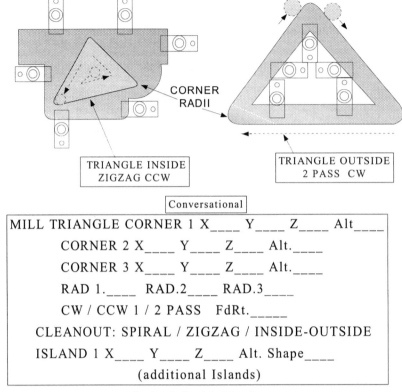

TRIANGLE INSIDE
ZIGZAG CCW

TRIANGLE OUTSIDE
2 PASS CW

Conversational

MILL TRIANGLE CORNER 1 X____ Y____ Z____ Alt____

          CORNER 2 X____ Y____ Z____ Alt.____

          CORNER 3 X____ Y____ Z____ Alt.____

          RAD 1.____ RAD.2____ RAD.3____

          CW / CCW 1 / 2 PASS FdRt._____

CLEANOUT: SPIRAL / ZIGZAG / INSIDE-OUTSIDE

ISLAND 1 X____ Y____ Z____ Alt. Shape____

                    (additional Islands)

Instructs the Machine Axes
to initiate a cycle, Locating
a Triangle feature, Sizing specified
Depth, Radii, Island Avoidance,
Geometry and Cleanout Toolpath

Figure 8.5 *Mill Triangle Subroutine*

the Control to generate the Radii specified around the Arc Centers and blend the Tool Radius automatically. One or two passes can be chosen as well as Spiral Cleanout of the Center Section. Outside can be chosen to mill the outside of Triangular features such as Bosses. See Figure 8.5.

Surface of Revolution

Conversational CNC Format

REV SURF 1 / 2 Pass: (X)__(Y)__(Z)__Rad 1___ Rad 2____ Rad 3___
X1___ Y1___ X2____ Y2____ X3___ Y3___ F___ Revolution ___.____°:
Programs a concave or convex 3-D Surface after an edge of surface is defined.

Swept Surface

Conversational CNC Format

SWEPT SURF 1 / 2 Pass: (X)___(Y)___(Z)___Rad 1___ Rad 2____ Rad 3____
X1____ Y1____ X2____ Y2____ X3____ Y3____ F____: Programs a 3-D surface
defined by two or more 3-D contours.

Ruled Surface

Conversational CNC Format

RULED SURF 1 / 2 Pass: (X)___(Y)___(Z)___ Rad 1___ Rad 2____ Rad 3____
X1____ Y1____ X2____ Y2____ X3____ Y3____ F____: Programs a Ruled Surface (a linear cross-section/blended surface) defined by multiple (i.e., up to
100) 3-D contours.

Lofted Surface

Conversational CNC Format

LOFTED SURF 1 / 2 Pass: (X)___(Y)___(Z)___ Rad 1___ Rad 2___ Rad 3____
X1____ Y1____ X2____ Y2____ X3____ Y3____ F____: Programs a Linear or
Parabolic 3-D Surface defined by multiple cross-sections. Cross-sections may
consist of any combination of Points, Lines, Arcs, and Splines.

Coons Surface

Conversational CNC Format

COONS SURF 1 / 2 Pass: (X)___(Y)___(Z)___ Rad 1___ Rad 2____ Rad 3____
X1____ Y1____ X2____ Y2____ X3____ Y3____ F____: Programs a Linear or
Parabolic 3-D Surface defined by multiple "patches." Patch Boundaries may
consist of any combination of Points, Lines, Arcs, and Splines.

Filleted Surface

Conversational CNC Format

FILLETED SURF 1 / 2 Pass: (X)_._(Y)_._(Z)_._Rad 1___ Rad 2____ X1____
Y1____ X2____ Y2____ X3____ Y3____ F____: Programs a constant or vari-
able Filleted Toolpath between two Swept, Ruled, Lofted, or Coons Surfaces.
The two surfaces are scanned for a "best-fit" Fillet at each intersection point.
The end result is a smooth tangential transition between surfaces.

Project Operation

Conversational CNC Format

PROJECT OPERATION 1 / 2 Pass: (X)___(Y)___(Z)___ Rad 1____ Rad 2____ X1____ Y1____ X2____ Y2____ X3____ Y3____ F___: Programs any "Projected" operation (except Drilling and Surface of Revolution) onto a Tilted Plane, Cylinder, Cone, Sphere, Cross-section, or 3-D Plane.

Drill

Conversational CNC Format

DRILL / PLUNGE : (X)___(Y)___(R)___(Zdn)___(Zup)___Tool#____F___: Programs or initializes a Subroutine or generates the Z moves for Drilling, Counterboring, Peck Drilling, Tapping, and Boring relative to user-defined 3-D points or absolute dimensional coordinates. Also, it is a prerequisite of many Subroutines to start the tool in a machining sequence (i.e., Pocket, Circle, Ellipse, Loop and Repeat, and others).

Loop and Repeat

Conversational CNC Format

LOOP & REPEAT (Operation) : (X)___(Y)___(Alt)____(Z)___ # of Repeats (X)___ (Y)___ (Z)____ (Alt)____ F_____: Establishes a Subroutine, or Canned Cycle, that performs a Drill, CounterBore, Peck Drill, Tap, or Bore operation, and moves an incremental move from the first absolute location. Then the Control repeats the move a specified # of times. This cycle is excellent for symmetrical hole patterns with a great # of hole features.

In Conventional Format, the **"L" Word** followed by # of times to repeat also starts a similar but less adaptable operational sequence.

Peck

Conventional CNC Format

G73 (# of Times)

Conversational CNC Format

PECK # of Times CHIP BREAK / FULL RETRACT: Instructs the machine spindle to use a Chip-Breaking cycle that slightly retracts the tool (or Full Retract if selected) during the Spindle machining cycles (Drill, CounterBore, Bore). It is during the back-out motion that the chip breaks and removes itself. The amount and # of times are variables set by parameter.

Tap

Conventional CNC Format

G74 (Left-Hand Tapping Cycle) (R)
G84 (Right-Hand Tapping Cycle) (R)

Conversational CNC Format

TAP RIGHT-HAND / LEFT-HAND Zup (R) Zdn: Instructs the machine to begin a cycle to machine thread into a preexisting holes. Once the Tap enters the hole and reaches the bottom, the spindle reverses and the tap feeds back out of the hole. Speeds and Feeds are recorded in the Tool Library. (R) is the height defined for some controls, as a "Reference Level."

Bore

Conventional CNC Format

G86: (Standard G86, see Chapter 9)

Conversational CNC Format

BORE: (X)___.(Y)___.(Zdn)___.(Zup)___. Tool#___ F___: Instructs the machine spindle to feed into the hole; the spindle then Stops and Retracts by Rapid Motion. Other Boring cycles are available; this is a commonly used one.

Back Spot-Facing

Conversational CNC Format

PLUNGE—BACK FACE: (X)___.(Y)___.(R)___(Zdn)___.(Zup)___. Tool#___
F1___F2___: Instructs the spindle to rotate CW; the Z-Axis to plunge to the Z down level specified at F1___; Spindle rotation Stops, Reverses rotation, CCW (which "kicks-out" the Reverse Spot-facing "dog"*); Z-Axis moves upward to perform the actual machining to the Zup position at F2___; back downward to the Z down position again; Spindle Stops rotation and Reverses to CW ("dog" retracts); Z-Axis Spindle retracts.

*This operation requires special tooling be used, in this case, a Back Spot-facing Tool that only enables the cutting edge to extend to a cutting position when its rotation is reversed to a Counterclockwise direction.

Back Counterboring

Conversational CNC Format

PLUNGE—COUNTER-BORE: (X)___.(Y)___.(R)___(Zdn)___.(Zup)___. Tool #___
F1___F2___: Instructs the spindle to rotate CW; the Z-Axis to plunge to the Z down level specified at F1___; Spindle rotation Stops, Reverses rotation,

CCW (which "kicks-out" the Reverse Counterboring "dogs"*); Z-Axis moves upward to perform the actual machining to the Zup position at F2____; back downward to the Z down position again; Spindle Stops rotation and Reverses to CW ("dogs" retract); Z-axis Spindle retracts.

*This operation requires special tooling be used, in this case, a Back Counterboring Tool that only enables the cutting edges to extend to a cutting position when its rotation is reversed to a Counterclockwise direction.

Copy

Conversational CNC Format
COPY from BLOCK #_____ to BLOCK #_____
Change: (X)_._(Y)_._(Z)_._(Alt)____ F____ Tool #____: Instructs the Control to Copy a selected segment of the current program, changing any specified Axis Offsets, Feeds, Tool #'s, and so on. This is a very useful Subroutine feature to change Z levels, Tools, and Part Offsets on multiple fixtures, saving time on redundant data input.

Mirror

Conversational CNC Format
MIRROR: (X)___(Y)___(Z)____(Alt)___ Block#____ to Block#____
Mirror Center X____ Y____ Z_____ (Alt)____: Instructs the Control to generate a series of coordinate movements that represent the Mirror Image of a preprogrammed path. This is very useful to create mating parts, avoiding reentering all the data with new axis reversal signs (positive and negative). See Figure 8.6.

Rough Face/Turn

Conversational CNC Format
ROUGH FACE/TURN: X1____ Z1____ F____ IN/MIN RPM_____
X2____ Z2____ # of Passes____ Tool#____ Coolant____: Instructs a Subroutine to be activated, to Rough Face/Turn (selection required) that divides the X1 or Z1 from X2 or Z2 by the # of Rough passes to be taken; the tool moves, cuts, retracts, and ends the Subroutine after completion.

Finish Face/Turn

Conversational CNC Format
FINISH FACE/TURN: X1____ Z1____ F____ IN/MIN RPM____
X2____ Z2____ # of Passes____ Tool#____ Coolant____: Instructs a Subrou-

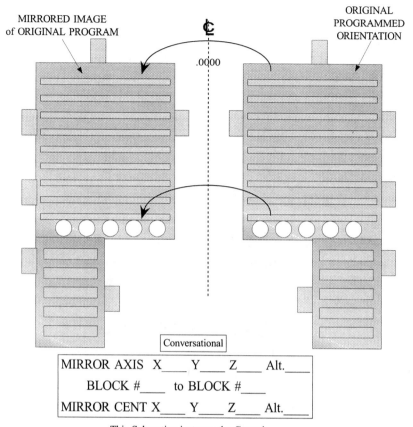

MIRRORED IMAGE
of ORIGINAL PROGRAM

ORIGINAL
PROGRAMMED
ORIENTATION

.0000

Conversational

MIRROR AXIS X____ Y____ Z____ Alt.____

BLOCK #____ to BLOCK #____

MIRROR CENT X____ Y____ Z____ Alt.____

This Subroutine instructs the Control
to Generate a series of coordinate
movements that represent the
Mirror Image of a Preprogrammed Path

Figure 8.6 *Mirror-Image Subroutine*

tine to be activated, to Finish Face/Turn (selection required) that divides the
X1 or Z1 from X2 or Z2 by the # of Rough passes to be taken; the tool moves,
cuts, retracts, and ends the Subroutine after completion. See Figure 8.7.

Groove

Conversational CNC Format

GROOVE 1/2 Pass: (X)__ . (Y)__ . (Z)__ . Rad 1___ Rad 2___ X1___ Y1___
X2___ Y2___ X3___ Y3___ F___: Instructs a Subroutine to be activated
that machines a "U"-shaped or Multiple-Plunge toolpath; XZX or ZXZ, de-

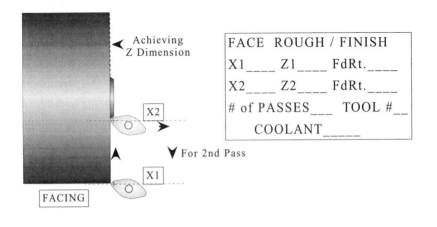

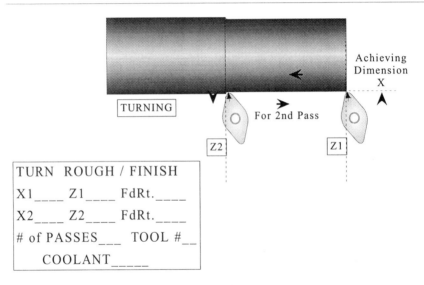

Figure 8.7 *Rough/Finish—Face/Turn Subroutine*

pending on orientation; generates Radii in the corners, if specified; cutting
single pass or the # of passes specified. See Figure 8.8.

Point

Conversational CNC Format

POINT 1 / 2 Pass: (X)__ . (Y)__ . (Z)__ . Rad 1____ Rad 2____
    X1____ Y1____ X2____ Y2____ X3____ Y3____ F____: Instructs a Subroutine
    to be activated that machines a "V"-shaped toolpath; XZX or ZXZ, depending

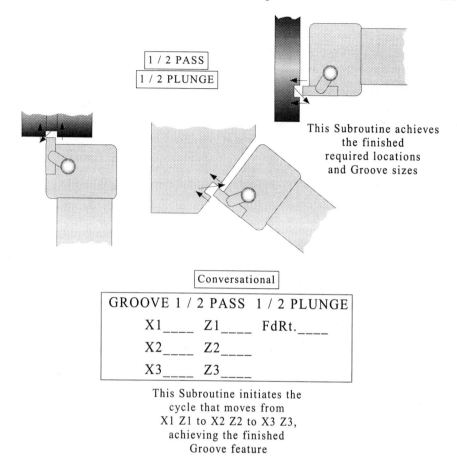

Figure 8.8 *Groove Subroutine*

on orientation; generates Radii at the point, shoulders, if specified; cutting one or the # of passes specified.

Drill

Conversational CNC Format

DRILL: X1____ Z1____ F____ IN/MIN RPM____ Tool#____

Coolant____ X2____ Z2____ (Peck#): Instructs the **Tool** (Z-Axis) to **feed into** the hole location at a **specified Feedrate**; then a **Rapid-out Retraction** from the hole feature takes place. If a number is entered into the **Peck # Box**, the Control will divide up the Z drilling distance by the # of Pecks specified.

Bore/Ream

Conversational CNC Format

BORE: X1____ Z1____ F____ IN/MIN RPM____ X2____ Z2____ Tool#____
Coolant____: Instructs axis (Z) to feed into the hole at a specified feedrate;
then the axis will **Stop** and axis will **Rapid feed out** of the hole.

REAM: X1____ Z1____ F____ IN/MIN RPM____ Tool#____ Coolant____
X2____ Z2____: Instructs axis (Z) to feed into the hole at a specified feedrate;
then the axis will **Stop and Reverse** its feed at the **same Feedrate out** of
the hole.

Thread

Conversational CNC Format

THREAD: X1____ Z1____ F____ IN/MIN RPM____ X2____ Z2____ E____
Tool#____ Coolant____: Instructs the machine axis to begin and complete a
series of movements: Tool Approach, Feed and RPM synchronization, and
Tool Exit after completion.

E____: Denotes Thread Pitch followed by the specific accuracy (four-place accuracy in most Controls).

Canned Turning

Conventional CNC Format

G81 X____ Z1____ Z2____ Fd____: Instructs the machine axis to move (after a
positioning block) the cutting tool using a subroutine that Turns a finished
surface at X (value), from Z1 (value) to Z2 (value) at the specified Feedrate.

Conversational CNC Format

AUTO TURN 1/2 Pass X____ Z1____ Z2____ Fd____: Instructs the machine
axis to move (after a positioning block) the cutting tool using a subroutine
that Turns a finished surface using a single/double pass at X (value), from
Z1 (value) to Z2 (value) at the specified Feedrate. If 2 Pass is selected, the
tool will return for a second pass; the finishing amounts are set in Tool
Library memory.

Canned Facing

Conventional CNC Format

G82 X1____ X2____ Z____ Fd____: Instructs the machine axis to move (after
a positioning block) the cutting tool using a Subroutine that Faces a finished
surface at Z (value), from X1 (value) to X2 (value) at the specified Feedrate.

Conversational CNC Format

AUTO FACE 1 / 2 Pass X1____ X2____ Z____ Fd____: Instructs the machine axis to move (after a positioning block) the cutting tool using a Subroutine that Faces a finished surface using a single/double pass at Z (value), from X1 (value) to X2 (value) at the specified Feedrate. If 2 Pass is selected, the tool will return for a second pass; the finishing amounts are set in Tool Library memory.

Canned Tapering

Conventional CNC Format

G83 X1____ Z1____ X2____ Z2____ Fd____: Instructs the machine axis to move (after a positioning block) the cutting tool using a Subroutine that turns a Taper, a finished surface from X1 (value) and Z1 (value) to X2 (value) and Z2 (value) at the specified Feedrate.

Conversational CNC Format

AUTO TAPER 1 / 2 Pass X1____ Z1____ X2____ Z2____ Fd____: Instructs the machine axis to move (after a positioning block) the cutting tool using a Subroutine that turns a Taper, a finished surface using a single/double pass from X1 (value) and Z1 (value) to X2 (value) and Z2 (value) at the specified Feedrate. If 2 Pass is selected, the tool will return for a second pass; the finishing amounts are set in Tool Library memory.

Arc Clockwise–Counterclockwise

Conventional CNC Format

G02: Instructs machine axes to move in a **CLOCKWISE** direction around a specified **ARC CENTER** maintaining a set **RADIUS** (cutting a standard 2-Axis **ARC** in a Clockwise direction a set distance, or **Radius**, away from a fixed **Arc Center**).

G03: Instructs machine axes to move in a **COUNTERCLOCKWISE** direction around a specified **ARC CENTER** maintaining a set **RADIUS** (cutting a standard 2-axis **ARC** in a Counterclockwise direction a set distance, or **Radius**, away from a fixed **Arc Center**).

Certain Turning-Center Controls reverse these two commands [M02, M03]. Check the manuals.

Conversational CNC Format

TURN ARC CW: Instructs machine axes to move in a **CLOCKWISE** direction around a specified **ARC CENTER** maintaining a set **RADIUS** (cutting a standard 2-axis **ARC** in a Clockwise direction a set distance, or **Radius**, away from a fixed **Arc Center**).

TURN ARC CCW: Instructs machine axes to move in a **COUNTER-CLOCKWISE** direction around a specified **ARC CENTER** maintaining a set **RADIUS** (cutting a standard 2-Axis **ARC** in a Counterclockwise direction a set distance, or **Radius**, away from a fixed **Arc Center**).

Combinations of Subroutines

The canned exponential power of Subroutines can be exploited to the maximum by studying which ones are usable in combination with each other using a minimum of program space. Envision a full selection of miniprograms that reside in orderly directories always present in the Control's memory. By selecting the subroutines that can accomplish the machining operations at hand, only the program space is needed to call on these miniprograms, fill in their blanks, and use them to execute machining operations; the task of programming can be reduced to a minimum. Consider the programming power, exhibited by the following two examples, of using Subroutines in combination.

Combination of Milling-Center Subroutines

DRILL/PLUNGE X .500 Y 1.325 Z–.625 F 2.0 TOOL 3
MILL POCKET 2 Pass XL 2.000 YW 1.500 F 3.5 IPM Spiral In/Out
LOOP & REPEAT X 3.250 Y 2.6882 X# 18 Y# 4: This combination uses the MILL POCKET Subroutine and the LOOP & REPEAT in combination. The Pocket, 2 Pass operation Roughs from the center out with a Spiral toolpath, recutting the full operation with a Finish Pass. The Loop and Repeat Subroutine repeats the Pocket feature 18 times in the +X direction and 4 times in the +Y direction. The end result is a section of program only 3 Blocks long, creating 72 finished pocket features in a workpiece. See Figure 8.9.

Combination of Turning-Center Subroutines

GROOVE 1 / 2 Pass: (X) 1.2561 (Z) .5502 Rad 1 .020 Rad 2 .020 X1 .000 Z1 .000 X2–.125 Y2 .000 X3 –.125 Y3 –.125 F 1.8 ipm
TRANSLATE: (X) 1.3562 (Z) .6875 Degree –4.500 Rad __.___
REPEAT: (#X) 8 (#Z)___ (# Alt Axis)_ : This sequence uses the GROOVE, TRANSLATE, and REPEAT Subroutines in combination. The Groove Subroutine Locates the feature on the workpiece by the specified XZ location; Groove Width and Depth are also specified. Next, Translate orients the Groove toolpath at a specified angle (–4.5°). Then, Repeat remachines the Groove toolpath the number of specified times entered in the Repeat Subroutine. This sequence, also, occupies only three Blocks of program space. It could machine an almost unlimited # of features in this combination of Subroutines. See Figure 8.10.

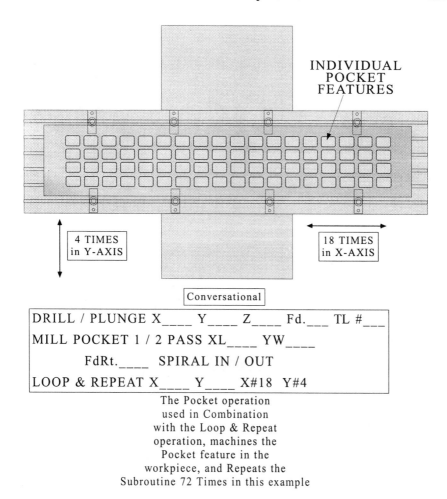

INDIVIDUAL
POCKET
FEATURES

| 4 TIMES |
| in Y-AXIS |

| 18 TIMES |
| in X-AXIS |

Conversational

| DRILL / PLUNGE X____ Y____ Z____ Fd.___ TL #___ |
| MILL POCKET 1 / 2 PASS XL____ YW____ |
| FdRt.____ SPIRAL IN / OUT |
| LOOP & REPEAT X____ Y____ X#18 Y#4 |

The Pocket operation
used in Combination
with the Loop & Repeat
operation, machines the
Pocket feature in the
workpiece, and Repeats the
Subroutine 72 Times in this example

Figure 8.9 *Combination of Milling-Center Subroutines*

CNC COMPENSATION

Compensation serves numerous uses on many types of CNC Machines. In most situations, compensation allows the programmer to concentrate on optimum toolpaths, instead of continuously calculating hard-to-find Tool-Center coordinates. Every form of compensation for every kind of CNC Control operates on the basis of Offsets. Offsets instruct the Control what numerical value must be compensated for on future machine moves.

CNC machine Offsets are similar to values supplied in an algebraic equation. Offsets are packaged values, or a value, that the program can access for use when called on. Offsets are simply measurements that stand for a tool size,

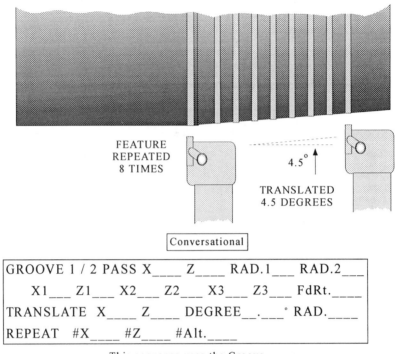

FEATURE
REPEATED
8 TIMES

4.5°

TRANSLATED
4.5 DEGREES

Conversational

GROOVE 1 / 2 PASS X____ Z____ RAD.1___ RAD.2___

   X1___ Z1___ X2___ Z2___ X3___ Z3___ FdRt.____

TRANSLATE X____ Z____ DEGREE__.___° RAD.____

REPEAT #X____ #Z____ #Alt.____

This sequence uses the Groove,
Translate, & Repeat Subroutines
in Combination. The Groove Subroutine
locates the feature on the workpiece
by the specified XZ Location, Groove Width,
& Depth. Translate orients the Groove
Toolpath at the Angle required, 4.5°. Repeat
remachines the Groove Toolpath the number
of times entered in the Repeat Subroutine

Figure 8.10 *Combination of Turning-Center Subroutines*

fixture size, tooling location, or other axis point to be referenced by the program. Today's CNC Controls have multiple Offsets from as few as 10 to as many as 200 in number. The Offset Table in the Control's memory, the Tool Library, and other electronic residences can be accessed and changed at any time by the programmer/operator.

The Offset value is called on or instated by an Offset Number in the program. For some CNC Controls, a single Offset Number can reference multiple values. Each Turning-Center Offset normally carries two or more values, the X Offset and the Z Offset. Both the X Offset and the Z Offset are accessed in programming by one Offset Number. Various CNC Controls arrange the Tool Offsets in the same specific sequence they are called in the program. Some dedicate directories of Offsets for cutter radii or diameters, and additional directories of Offsets are specifically for tool lengths. It is easy to locate certain Offsets using a system designated like this.

For Machining Centers, this text covers *Tool-Length Compensation, Cutter-Length Compensation,* and *Fixture Offsets.*

For Turning Centers, this text covers *Dimensional Tool Offsets* and *Tool-Nose-Radius Compensation.*

COMPENSATION FOR MACHINING CENTERS

Tool-Length Compensation

This type of compensation is popular in CNC Machining Centers and other CNC Machine Tools, CNC Jig Borers, CNC Drilling Machines, and so on. Tool-Length Compensation enables a programmer to concentrate on the program as it is being prepared and to not be overly concerned with each tool's length. The primary objective of Tool-Length Compensation is to keep the length of the tools as an independent variable separate from the program itself. (In this book, "Compensation" is sometimes referred to as "Comp.")

It is important to recognize that tool length is measured from the tip of the cutting tool to the nose or face of the spindle. Depending on the style, certain machining centers may vary on which nose surface the measurement originates. However, the length of the tool must be measured from the tip of the cutting tool to the face of the movable spindle housing. See Figure 8.11.

Conventional CNC Format

The industry standard for CNC Controls uses three CNC "words" associated with Tool-Length Comp.

G43: Is the G Code that initializes or instates Tool-Length Comp. Normally, this is the tool's primary Z-Axis motion command for a tool named. Only one G43 command exists for a single Tool # in a program.

Combined with the G43 command is an "H" word (always present) instructing the Control which Offset Number is being accessed as the tool's Length. The "H" word stands for the Height of the tool. The "H" word is normally in direct correlation with the Tool Station (i.e., Tool Station #6 will use H code 6 (H06) or Tool Station 3 will use H Code 3 (H03)).

Along with the G43 commands is a Z-Axis departure. This value represents the coordinate on the Z-Axis where the tool point is to Stop. It is an absolute measurement from Program Zero. If the tool is to stop at a distance of .625" above Program Zero, the Z-Axis would be instructed by a command such as **Z.625**. Also related to Tool-Length Comp in CNC Machining Centers is another "word"—a G49 command.

G49: Is the command for Tool-Length Comp Cancelation.

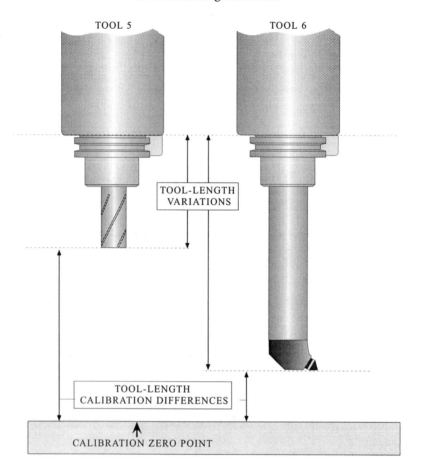

Figure 8.11 *Tool-Length Compensation*

Conversational CNC Format

TOOL CAL(ibration) **00.0000**: This value is stored in the Tool Calibration section of the Tool Library in CNC memory. By calibrating all tools on a recorded Reference point, the actual Tool-Length Comp for each tool is an internal value not exposed (or of concern) to the programmer. When a Tool # is called in a program block, its Zero Reference point, 00.0000, originates from the surface of calibration.

Cutter-Diameter Compensation

Many versions of CNC Machining Centers use Control-resident features called Cutter-Diameter Compensation, or "Cutter Comp" (sometimes called "Cutcom" or Cutter Radius Offset). All these names apply to the function that is a designed Control feature that, when activated, transforms the Toolpath by a value entered in the Cutter Comp memory for that offset. The value in the memory is calculated by the programmer when the job is being prepared.

The cycle enables the programmer to set aside concern about the cutting tool's radius or diameter, and Tool-Center coordinates during programming. It virtually makes programming easier, as with all forms of Compensation, because the programmer can focus on proper Toolpath movement while the program is being prepared. Cutter Comp also allows the radius of the cutting tool to vary, within the feature's limitations, without changes to the program coordinates. Cutter Comp cannot be used with all forms of cutters though. Only tools that have the characteristics of cutting on the periphery of the cutter can be used with Cutter Comp. Certain Face Mills, Shell Mills, and Endmills have the characteristics that work with Cutter Comp.

Entering the center-line coordinates of the Toolpath is a proven and accepted method of programming; it has many advantages, but some limitations. In certain situations, Cutter Comp can relieve many programming predicaments. The programmer and operator are not bound to use only a set or predetermined cutter diameter in a program. The principal difference is the entering into the Control only the actual finished surface dimensions—and the Cutter Diameter (Offset)—allowing the computer to mathematically calculate the tool centers as the workpiece is being machined. There are some limitations regarding the smallest and largest usable cutter sizes, but a full range of diameters is possible. Therefore, no program revision is necessary if a cutter size must be changed; a new Cutter Diameter (Offset) is entered and the finished sizes are achieved. See Figure 8.12.

Cutter deflection can also throw the most precisely calculated toolpath out of tolerance due to Tool Pressure during machining. Despite following the very best tooling procedure, some tool deflection occurs. Although the smallest deflection may not be enough to cause dimensional tolerance problems, there are times when the accuracy of the part is so demanding that small adjustments must be made. If fixed center-line coordinates were used, the cutter toolpath would have to be reprogrammed to allow for deflection. With Cutter Comp, an adjustment can be made to the Offset, one entry vs. hundreds of Tool-Center modifications.

As cutters dull, deflection also increases. This change in deflection during the machining life of the cutting tool can be a real problem if fixed center-line coordinates are used in the program. This adjustability with Offsets is a tremendous advantage in these instances. When faced with the problems presented by programming complex contours, calculating the center-line coordinates for the path of the Endmill can also be complicated. When Angular Surfaces intersect or blend into Arcs (especially with changing Arc Centers), locating cut-

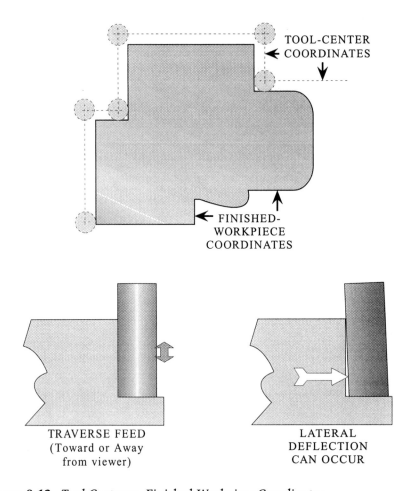

Figure 8.12 *Tool-Center vs. Finished-Workpiece Coordinates*

ting-tool center lines can involve more trigonometry than many programmers are willing or able to tackle. Cutter Comp, in this instance, can save hundreds of hours of programming, especially where complex contouring may need adjustments during machining.

Directly related to machining complex contours is the ability to Rough with Cutter Comp. The complication of making an allowance for a consistent amount of finishing stock over all surfaces being machined during roughing can be alleviated. Normally, the programmer not only must calculate the center-line coordinates of the cutter during finishing, but must first calculate the center-line coordinates during the roughing operation. By using Cutter Comp, the same series of coordinates used for the finishing pass can be used for roughing. Only the Offset value is changed, keeping the cutting edge away an even amount on all surfaces.

Commands Related to Cutter Compensation

Cutter Comp commands do vary from Control builder to builder. Also, early versions of Cutter Comp were more difficult to program than today's. Three standard G Codes are used with Cutter Comp. Two of these G Codes are used for calling up or instating Cutter Comp. There is a programming word also used along with these three G Codes to specify the Offset Number when using Cuter Comp. Normally, a "D" word (sometimes an "H" word, depending on Control model) is used to specify the Offset #.

In Machine Shop language and Word Address, Cutter Comp is activated/de-activated through the use of G Codes: **G41, G42, and G40**.

G41: Cutter Diameter Compensation Left. When the G41 command is given, the tool compensates to the LEFT of the programmed surface by the Offset amount assigned to that Tool #. The tool moves to a compensated position on the next X-, Y-, or Z-Axis move *after* the G41 is read by the Control.

G42: Cutter Diameter Compensation Right. When the G42 command is given, the tool compensates to the RIGHT of the programmed surface by the Offset amount assigned to that Tool #. The tool moves to a compensated position on the next X-, Y-, or Z-Axis move *after* the G42 is read by the Control.

G40: Cancels Cutter Diameter Compensation. When the command G40 is given, Cutter Comp is turned off. The tool transforms from a compensated position on the *next* X-, Y-, or Z-Axis move to a Tool-Center coordinate position.

In this Word Address format, Comp can be activated for any axis; a G Code is given to specify in which axis combination to compensate. If the part is to be machined using the X- and Y-Axes, compensate in the X/Y Plane; if using the X- and Z-Axes, compensate in the X/Z Plane; if using the Y- and Z-Axes, compensate in the Y/Z Plane. Normally, the X/Y Plane is most commonly used.

The G Codes to specify the desired work plane in Word Address are as follows:

G17: X/Y PLANE
G18: X/Z PLANE
G19: Y/Z PLANE

The command Cutter Comp is also initialized in the "Ramp On" and "Ramp Off" moves. See Figure 8.13.

After a G41 command is given, the tool (shown in the figure) moves from the prior coordinate to the next coordinate and Cutter Comp is instated. Notice that when Comp is "Ramped On," it takes a full coordinate to allow the Comp

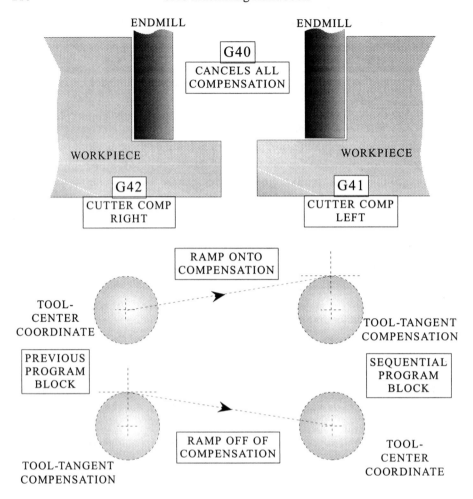

Figure 8.13   *Cutter-Compensation Orientation*

to take effect. As with Ramp On, Ramp Off takes an entire move to complete its switching Off of Compensation. Note that precautions should be taken to allow the Ramp On and Ramp Off to take place away from cutting material on finished surfaces to avoid interference and gouging into unintended surfaces.

Fixture Offsets

Fixture Offsets are a type of Compensation used on Laser Cutting equipment, Wire EDM Machines, Turret Presses, and Machining Centers. Fixture Offsets enable the programmer and operator to work with several coordinate measuring systems directly inside the same program.

It is advantageous when more than one workpiece has to be machined in a single setup. Many different operations on the same workpiece can be machined while several workpieces are being held at different locations and orientations in the setup. The option of being able to reference one set of workpiece coordinates and move to the next workpiece with little more than an Offset reference # is a true advantage.

Fixture Offsets allow the programmer to also assign one Program Zero point to each side of a preprogrammed workpiece. This is especially useful when a workpiece must be machined in a rotary device of some kind, typically, in horizontal machining centers. Fixture Offsets are also very useful at times when workpiece job lots are run very often; programs are reentered and dedicated fixtures are mounted, spacing workpieces at known intervals. Offsets can be recalled and CNC machines, in turn, suffer minimal downtime.

Programming using Fixture Offsets, as with many forms of compensation, makes machining easier. Normally, a series of G Codes are in Memory, one for each Fixture Offset. One typical CNC Control design programs 6 to 12 Fixture Offsets. Therefore, 6 to 12 G Codes are designated. The common configuration that uses 6 G Codes, from G54 through G59, designates the various Fixture Offsets in use. G54 logically represents Fixture Offset #1, G55 for #2, in sequence through Fixture Offset #6, G59. See Figure 8.14.

COMPENSATION FOR TURNING CENTERS
Using Dimensional Tool Offsets

All Turning Centers use Dimensional Tool Offsets. The Offsets make the programmer much more productive and therefore make programming easier. Dimensional Tool Offsets (also referred to as "Tool Offsets" in many shops) are required for all the following operations in CNC Turning Centers: Rough Facing, Finish Facing; Rough Turning, Finish Turning; Rough Boring, Finish Boring; Drilling; Threading; and Grooving.

Typically, some miscalibration or misalignment of cutting tools can create setup problems. Dimensional Tool Offsets enable the programmer/operator to precisely calibrate the positions of all tools without physically reorienting the tools in their holders. See Figure 8.15.

Often, each tool experiences wear. Dimensional Tool Offsets allow the setup person/operator to compensate in precision adjustments for individual cutting edges.

The terminology used with Dimensional Tool Offsets remains universal between most Turning-Center Controls. A "T" word is included in the program to determine which Offset # is to be used. The "T" word performs a dual function on most CNC Turning-Center Controls. A four-digit number accompanies it; the first two digits locate the Tool Station # of the turret in operation and

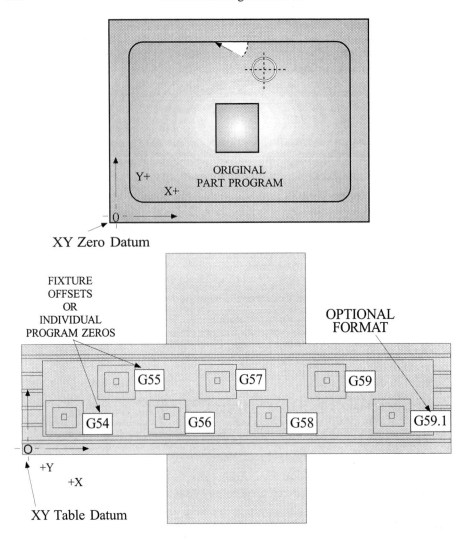

Figure 8.14 *Fixture Offsets*

actually initiates the turret to orient to the commanded tool station. The "T" word's second two digits represent the Offset # recorded for the tool and instate the offset. It is recommenced to use the identical Offset # as the Tool Station #. This creates a universal communication throughout the shop.

The following is an example of a Turret Command:

N040 G00 T0101

In Program Line # 040, the T0101 instructs the Control to index to Station #1 and simultaneously instate Offset #1. It is recommended to include the G00,

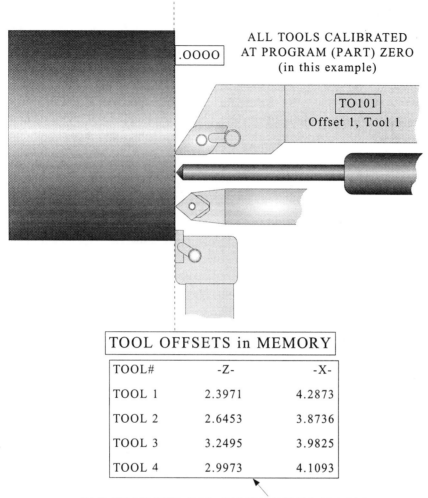

ALL TOOLS CALIBRATED
AT PROGRAM (PART) ZERO
(in this example)

.0000

TO101
Offset 1, Tool 1

TOOL OFFSETS in MEMORY		
TOOL#	-Z-	-X-
TOOL 1	2.3971	4.2873
TOOL 2	2.6453	3.8736
TOOL 3	3.2495	3.9825
TOOL 4	2.9973	4.1093

CAN BE EDITED FOR CALIBRATION ADJUSTMENT
IN ANY DIRECTION AFTER SETTING

Figure 8.15 *Dimensional Tool Offsets*

as shown, along with the Turret Command to make this movement at a Rapid Feedrate. Many CNC Controls no longer require the G00. Most Dimensional Tool Offsets use two values in the (graphic) Offset Table. A single value represents the X-Axis Offset and the remaining value the Z-Axis offset. This enables the operator/programmer to precisely adjust for mismatches and recalibrations on both the X- and the Z-Axes.

Tool-Nose-Radius Compensation

Every type of Turning and Boring tools classified as "single-point" tools incorporate a Radius of some size where the two cutting edges intersect. Standard sizes include 1/16 (.0625"); 3/64 (.046"); 1/32 (.0316"); 1/64 (.0156"), and for a sharp corner, .0025". Even though the Radii range down to the microscopic (sharp corner), the smallest Nose Radius can cause variations in the workpiece surface if compensation is not initiated for Toolpath assistance. See Figure 8.16.

During Toolpath Plotting, the peripheral surface of the tool on the X- and/or Z-Axis is the edge being programmed as the tangent contact point. Tool-Nose-

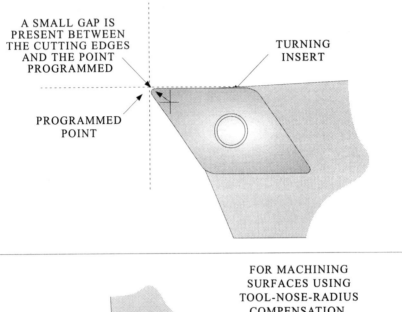

A SMALL GAP IS
PRESENT BETWEEN
THE CUTTING EDGES
AND THE POINT
PROGRAMMED

TURNING
INSERT

PROGRAMMED
POINT

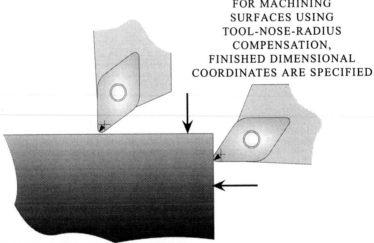

FOR MACHINING
SURFACES USING
TOOL-NOSE-RADIUS
COMPENSATION,
FINISHED DIMENSIONAL
COORDINATES ARE SPECIFIED

Figure 8.16 *Tool-Nose-Radius Compensation*

Radius Comp enables the programmer to positively maintain constant cutting-tool-radius edge contact with the intended workpiece surface.

Instating Tool-Nose Compensation

G41: If the tool is on the Left side of the surface to be machined, a G41 must be used to instate or initialize Tool-Nose-Radius Comp.

G42: If the tool is on the Right side of the surface to be machined, a G42 must be used to instate or initialize Tool-Nose-Radius Comp. See Figure 8.17.

G40: A G40 word is used to Cancel Tool-Nose-Radius Comp. The G40 can be included in the tool's command to retract the tool to the normal position for a tool change.

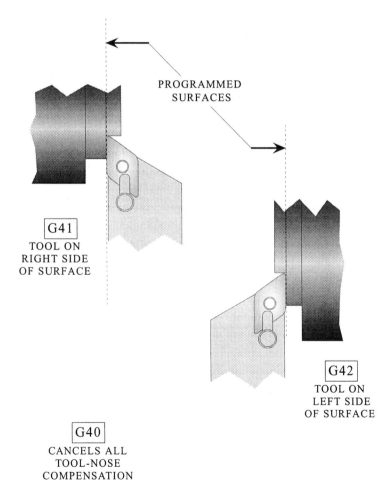

Figure 8.17 *Instating Tool-Nose-Radius Compensation*

Caution must be taken when programming to machine narrow recesses. The width of a recess must be at least wide enough to allow double the tool Radius (X and Z Radius) into the recess. Tool-Nose-Radius Comp requires an Offset to instruct the Control of the tool Radius, as with all forms of Comp. The method used to assign Offsets varies from CNC machine to CNC machine. Most use the same Tool Offset, where dimensional offset values are stored—two storage positions in the same offset—one for X and one for Z. If Tool-Nose-Radius-Comp is used, a third position in the Offset is utilized. The letter address "R" is designated with it, allowing the programmer to record the Radius of the tool in use into memory.

The four general choices of the Radius of the Turning Tool are .0156" (1/64); .0316" (1/32); .0456" (3/64); and .0625" (1/16). When using Tool-Nose-Radius Comp, a "T" in the Offset Table is also required in most Turning-Center Controls. The Control "knows" the type of tool being used by associating it with a code number. The Control, therefore, can make decisions during motion commands to know which way to compensate the tool. The Control also must know if the tool is designed to machine outside diameters (turning tool) or inside diameters (boring bar) in order to make compensations correctly. Tool orientation is filed in the Graphical Tool Library.

CHAPTER 9

USEFUL PROGRAMMING FORMULAS, COMMANDS, AND TABLES

This chapter contains Tables, Formulas, Definitions, and Reference material necessary to solve programming problems encountered in the CNC field. Conversion Tables are provided to calculate Speeds and Feeds, change English measurements to Metric, and Decimals to Fractions. Toolpath Blend Formulas are illustrated for fast cross-referencing with specific Toolpath configurations.

Formats for various machine languages require the programmer to have access to definitions. G- and M-Code tables are listed, detailing complete Word Address definitions and individual applications to various machine Controls. Trigonometric Formula Tables provided can be used in combination with Geometric Cutting-Tool-Tangent Tables in this chapter to calculate any complex contour coordinates.

Datum References and Material Condition Symbols on CNC prints can cause confusion during programming. Provided are clear, concise Tables and illustrations of the CNC-relevant references and symbols for any programming task that may be encountered.

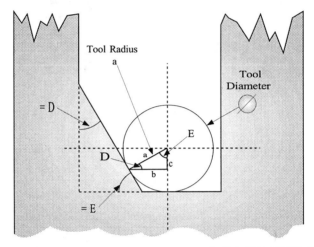

$b = a \sin E$	$b = a \cos D$
(or)	(or)
$\dfrac{a}{\csc E}$	$\dfrac{a}{\sec D}$
$c = a \cos E$	$c = a \sin D$
(or)	(or)
$\dfrac{a}{\sec E}$	$\dfrac{a}{\csc D}$

A requirement to understand Tool-Tangent principles is necessary
for Arc End Points to be properly calculated. This allows the programmer
to "know" where and when the tool edge becomes tangent to surfaces that
the arc is blending into, intersecting with, and matching radii to. Some
helpful formulas are given.

Figure 9.1 *Tool-Tangent Formulas*

$$E = D(1 + \tan B) \qquad X = N - E$$

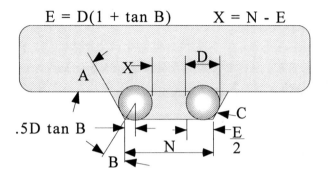

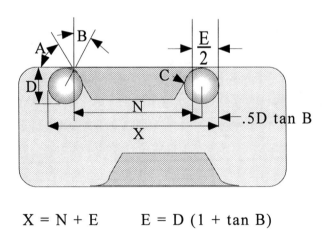

$$X = N + E \qquad E = D(1 + \tan B)$$

Figure 9.2 *Tool-Tangent Formulas (continued on p. 220)*

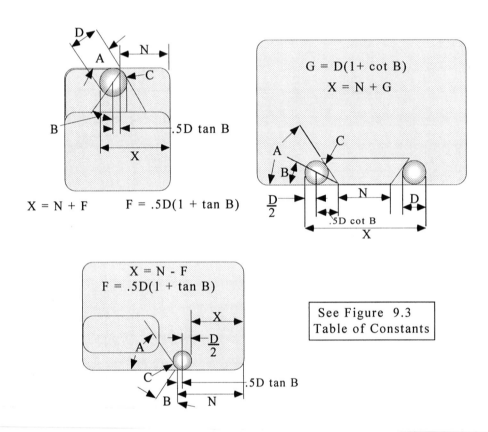

Figure 9.2 *Continued*

STD. TOOL DIA.		E		F		G	
FRACTION	DECIMAL	A = 45°	60°	A = 45°	60°	A = 45°	60°
3/64	.04688	.06629	.07394	.03315	.0369	.16004	.12806
1/16	.0625	.08839	.09858	.04419	.04929	.21339	.17075
5/64	.07813	.11048	.12323	.05524	.06162	.26673	.21344
3/32	.09375	.13258	.14788	.06629	.07381	.32082	.25613
1/8	.125	.17678	.19717	.08839	.09858	.42677	.34150
5/32	.15625	.22097	.24646	.11048	.12323	.53347	.42688
3/16	.1875	.26516	.29575	.13258	.14763	.64016	.51226
1/4	.250	.35355	.39434	.17678	.19717	.85355	.68301
5/16	.3125	.44194	.49292	.22097	.24646	1.0669	.85376
3/8	.375	.53033	.59151	.26516	.29575	1.2803	1.0245
7/16	.4375	.61872	.69009	.30936	.34504	1.4937	1.1953
1/2	.500	.70710	.78867	.35355	.39434	1.7071	1.3660
5/8	.625	.88388	.98584	.44194	.49292	2.1339	1.7075
3/4	.750	1.0607	1.1830	.53033	.59151	2.5607	2.0490
1	1.000	1.4142	1.5774	.70711	.78867	3.4142	2.7321
1 1/4	1.250	1.7678	1.9717	.88388	.98584	4.2678	3.4141
1 1/2	1.500	2.1213	2.3660	1.0607	1.1830	5.1213	4.0981
2	2.000	2.8284	3.1547	1.4142	1.5774	6.8284	5.4641

Machining prints contain an assortment of odd and common sizes & angles.
When calculating Tool Tangents, Standard Tool Diameters should be chosen if
possible. This reduces the calculating complexity when working with long formulas.
The chart lists precalculated Tool Tangents using Standard Tool Diameters
and Common Angles of 45° and 60°. Notations in columns "E", "F", & "G" apply to
Formulas both on this page and in Figure 9.2 (previous page).

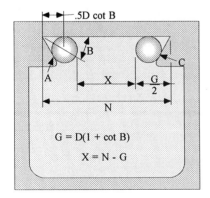

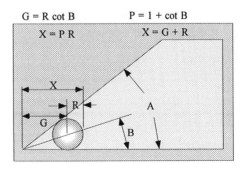

Figure 9.3 *Constants for Calculating Tool Tangents with Common Angles and Standard Tool Diameters*

Radius $1 = \sin a = \cos a = \sin a \csc a = \cos a \sec a = \tan a \cot a$

$$\sin a = \frac{\cos a}{\cot a} = \frac{1}{\csc a} = \cos a \tan a = \sqrt{1 - \cos^2 a}$$

$$\cos a = \frac{\sin a}{\tan a} = \frac{1}{\sec a} = \sin a \cot a = \sqrt{1 - \sin^2 a}$$

$$\tan a = \frac{\sin a}{\cos a} = \frac{1}{\cot a} = \sin a \sec a$$

$$\cot a = \frac{\cos a}{\sin a} = \frac{1}{\tan a} = \cos a \csc a$$

$$\sec a = \frac{\tan a}{\sin a} = \frac{1}{\cos a}$$

$$\csc a = \frac{\cot a}{\cos a} = \frac{1}{\sin a}$$

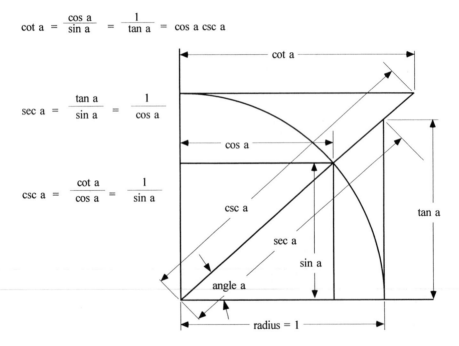

Figure 9.4 *Cutting-Tool-Related Trigonometric Formulas*

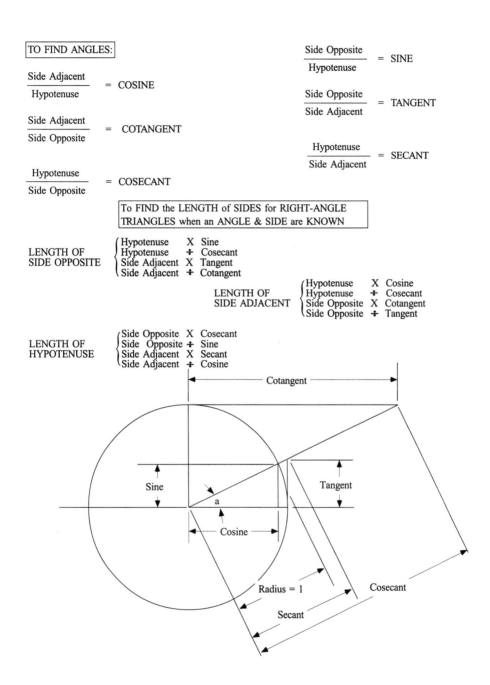

$$\boxed{\text{TO FIND ANGLES:}}$$

$$\frac{\text{Side Opposite}}{\text{Hypotenuse}} = \text{SINE}$$

$$\frac{\text{Side Adjacent}}{\text{Hypotenuse}} = \text{COSINE}$$

$$\frac{\text{Side Opposite}}{\text{Side Adjacent}} = \text{TANGENT}$$

$$\frac{\text{Side Adjacent}}{\text{Side Opposite}} = \text{COTANGENT}$$

$$\frac{\text{Hypotenuse}}{\text{Side Adjacent}} = \text{SECANT}$$

$$\frac{\text{Hypotenuse}}{\text{Side Opposite}} = \text{COSECANT}$$

$$\boxed{\begin{array}{l}\text{To FIND the LENGTH of SIDES for RIGHT-ANGLE}\\ \text{TRIANGLES when an ANGLE \& SIDE are KNOWN}\end{array}}$$

LENGTH OF
SIDE OPPOSITE
{
Hypotenuse   X   Sine
Hypotenuse   ÷   Cosecant
Side Adjacent   X   Tangent
Side Adjacent   ÷   Cotangent
}

LENGTH OF
SIDE ADJACENT
{
Hypotenuse   X   Cosine
Hypotenuse   ÷   Cosecant
Side Opposite   X   Cotangent
Side Opposite   ÷   Tangent
}

LENGTH OF
HYPOTENUSE
{
Side Opposite   X   Cosecant
Side Opposite   ÷   Sine
Side Adjacent   X   Secant
Side Adjacent   ÷   Cosine
}

Figure 9.5 *Formulas for Finding Tool-Tangent Triangles for Programming*

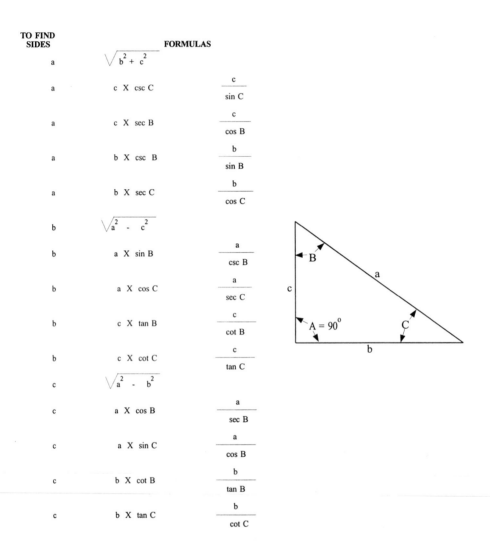

TO FIND SIDES   **FORMULAS**

TO FIND SIDES	FORMULAS	
a	$\sqrt{b^2 + c^2}$	
a	$c \times \csc C$	$\dfrac{c}{\sin C}$
a	$c \times \sec B$	$\dfrac{c}{\cos B}$
a	$b \times \csc B$	$\dfrac{b}{\sin B}$
a	$b \times \sec C$	$\dfrac{b}{\cos C}$
b	$\sqrt{a^2 - c^2}$	
b	$a \times \sin B$	$\dfrac{a}{\csc B}$
b	$a \times \cos C$	$\dfrac{a}{\sec C}$
b	$c \times \tan B$	$\dfrac{c}{\cot B}$
b	$c \times \cot C$	$\dfrac{c}{\tan C}$
c	$\sqrt{a^2 - b^2}$	
c	$a \times \cos B$	$\dfrac{a}{\sec B}$
c	$a \times \sin C$	$\dfrac{a}{\cos B}$
c	$b \times \cot B$	$\dfrac{b}{\tan B}$
c	$b \times \tan C$	$\dfrac{b}{\cot C}$

Figure 9.6 *Right-Triangle Tool-Tangent Segments*

TO FIND ANGLES	FORMULAS		
C	$\dfrac{c}{a} = \sin C$	$90^{o} - B$	
C	$\dfrac{b}{a} = \cos C$	$90^{o} - B$	
C	$\dfrac{c}{b} = \tan C$	$90^{o} - B$	
C	$\dfrac{b}{c} = \cot C$	$90^{o} - B$	
C	$\dfrac{a}{b} = \sec C$	$90^{o} - B$	
C	$\dfrac{a}{c} = \csc C$	$90^{o} - B$	
B	$\dfrac{b}{a} = \sin B$	$90^{o} - C$	
B	$\dfrac{c}{a} = \cos B$	$90^{o} - C$	
B	$\dfrac{b}{c} = \tan B$	$90^{o} - C$	
B	$\dfrac{c}{b} = \cot B$	$90^{o} - C$	
B	$\dfrac{a}{c} = \sec B$	$90^{o} - C$	
B	$\dfrac{a}{b} = \csc B$	$90^{o} - C$	

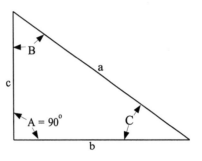

Figure 9.7 *Right-Triangle Tool-Tangent Segments*

TO FIND	KNOWN	SOLUTION
C	A, B	$180^\circ - (A + B)$
b	a, B, A	$\dfrac{a \sin B}{\sin A}$
c	a, A, C	$\dfrac{a \sin C}{\sin A}$
tan A	a, C, b	$\dfrac{a \sin C}{b - (a \cos C)}$
B	A, C	$180^\circ - (A + C)$
sin B	b, A, a	$\dfrac{b \sin A}{a}$
A	B, C	$180^\circ - (B + C)$
cos A	a, b, c	$\dfrac{b + c - a}{2bc}$
sin C	c, A, a	$\dfrac{c \sin A}{a}$
cot B	a, C, b	$\dfrac{a \csc C}{b} - \cot C$
c	b, C, B	$b \sin C \csc B$

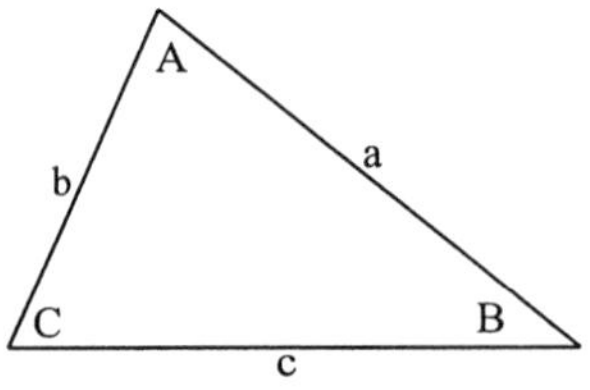

Figure 9.8 *Oblique-Triangle Tool-Tangent Segments*

SINGLE BLEND

(Offset for) $Y = CR \left[\tan \left(\angle^{\circ}/2\right)\right]$

CR: cutter radius

$Y = .3004$

(Offset for) $X = CR \left[\tan \left(\angle^{\circ}/2\right)\right]$

CR: cutter radius

$X = .1246$

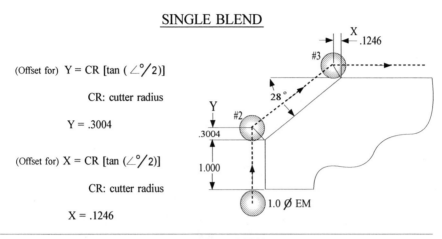

DOUBLE BLEND

(Offset for) $Y = CR \left[\tan \left(\angle^{\circ}/2\right)\right]$

(for location # 6)   CR: cutter radius

$Y = .369$

(Offset for) $X = CR \dfrac{\left[\sin \left(\frac{\angle_1 + \angle_2}{2}\right)\right]}{\left[\cos \left(\frac{\angle_1 - \angle_2}{2}\right)\right]}$

(for location # 7)   CR: cutter radius

$X = .2475$

(Offset for) $Y = CR \dfrac{\left[\cos \left(\frac{\angle_1 + \angle_2}{2}\right)\right]}{\left[\cos \left(\frac{\angle_1 - \angle_2}{2}\right)\right]}$

(for location # 7)   CR: cutter radius

$Y = .4558$

(Offset for) $X = CR \left[\tan \left(\angle_2/2\right)\right]$

(for location # 8)   CR: cutter radius

$X = .2226$

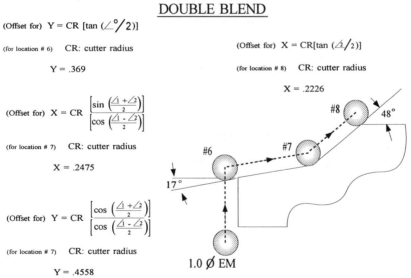

Figure 9.9 *Tool-Tangent Formulas for Toolpaths with Angled-Surface Blends*

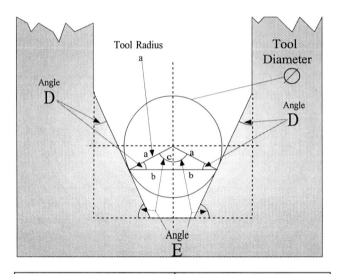

b = a sin E	b = a cos D
(or)	(or)
$\dfrac{a}{\text{csc } E}$	$\dfrac{a}{\text{sec } D}$
c = a cos E	c = a sin D
(or)	(or)
$\dfrac{a}{\text{sec } E}$	$\dfrac{a}{\text{csc } D}$

Figure 9.10 *Tool-Tangent Formulas*

			CHARACTERISTIC	FORM
INDIVIDUAL FEATURE SYMBOLS	**T O L E R A N C E**	**FORM**	STRAIGHTNESS	—
			FLATNESS	▱
			CIRCULARITY	○
			CYLINDRICITY	⌭
INDIVIDUAL & RELATION SYMBOLS	**C A T E G O R Y**	**PROFILE SYMBOLS**	PROFILE of LINE	⌒
			SURFACE PROFILE	⌓
FEATURE RELATION SYMBOLS		**ORIENTATION SYMBOLS**	ANGULARITY	∠
			PERPENDICULARITY	⊥
			PARALLELISM	//
		LOCATION SYMBOLS	POSITION	⊕
			CONCENTRICITY	◎
		RUNOUT SYMBOLS	**CIRCULAR RUNOUT**	↗
			TOTAL RUNOUT	↗↗

Figure 9.11   *CNC-Related Print-Feature Symbols: Geometric Characters*

The relationship between the controlled feature of a workpiece and the Datum, or Datums, is governed by the Datum Reference Letter. Typically, Datums are specified by letter; they represent surfaces, lines, planes, or selected features that act as precision dimensional reference points. All alphabetical letter can be used (with the exception of I, O, and Q), preferably in order starting with A. On a print or drawing, the Datum feature symbol appears in a box, or "Frame," having a dash on each side. A Datum Target Symbol is used in specific Datum locations instead of a Datum Feature Symbol.

Datum Feature   Datum Target
Symbol   Symbol

A Single Datum and Multiple Datums can represent Datum References. If only a single letter appears in the Feature Control Frame, the workpiece feature has a relationship to one (1) Datum. If more than one Datum is related to a workpiece feature, Multiple Datums appear in the frame and are sequenced by dimensional priority. The Primary appears first, the Secondary Datum is shown to the right of the first, and the Tertiary appears last, farthest to the right. If two (2) surfaces are referenced as Datums, a Dual Primary Datum can be used, which is noted by a dash between the Datum reference letters. CNC prints use these very often to tie in hole patterns or diameters to close-tolerance surfaces.

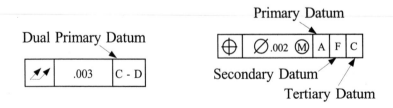

Figure 9.12 *CNC Datum References*

Prints drawn for CNC machining require interpretation beyond axis coordinates for input into the Control. Specific workpiece features labeled by geometric characteristic symbols are exactly located by the information in the feature control frame. Modifiers are associated with selected conditions and tolerance specs. Maximum Material Condition (MMC), Least Material Condition (LMC), and Regardless of Feature Size (RFS) are all modifiers that are positioned after the tolerance value or the Datum reference, or after both.

(M) (MMC) Maximum Material Condition

(L) (LMC) Least Material Condition

(S) (RFS) Regardless of Feature Size

CNC has adapted different versions to accommodate unique dimensional layouts and complexities. Shown below are some examples of the variances that exist.

Composite-Feature
Control Frame

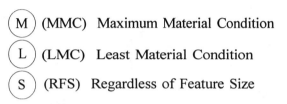

Combined-Feature
Control Frame

Projected Tolerance Zone

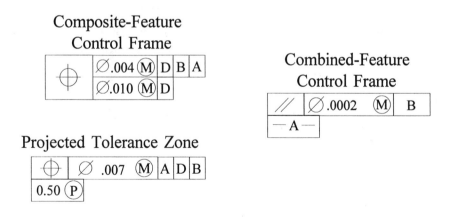

Figure 9.13 Material Conditions and Feature Sizes

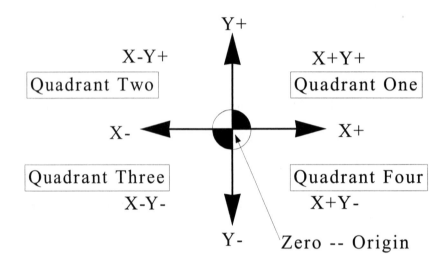

Program Zero and Part Zero are designated on many CNC-related drawings and prints using the Four-Axis Coordinate System divided into four (4) main Quadrants. If any of the Quadrant Lines are crossed, the sign (plus or minus) will change.

Shown above is an example of how this applies to the XY Coordinate Plane. Notice how crossing the Quadrant Line "inverts" the signs: positive to negative, negative to positive. This applies to all Axis orientations.

Figure 9.14 *Two-Axis Rectangular Coordinate System: The Four Quadrants*

TO FIND	KNOWN VALUES	FORMULAS
Surface(orPeriphery) Speed in Feet per Minute = SFM	Diameter of Tool in Inches = D Revolutions per Minute = RPM	$SFM = \dfrac{D \times 3.1416 \times RPM}{12}$
Revolutions per Minute = RPM	Surface Feet per Minute = SFM Tool Diameter in Inches = D	$RPM = \dfrac{SFM \times 12}{D \times 3.1416}$
Feed amount per Revolution Inches = FR	Feed in Inches per Minute = IPM Revolutions per Minute = RPM	$FR = \dfrac{IPM}{RPM}$
Feed in Inches per Minute = IPM	Feed per Revolution in Inches = FR Revolutions per Minute = RPM	$IPM = FR \times RPM$
Number of Cutting Teeth per Minute = TM	Number of Teeth in Tool = T Revolutions per Minute = RPM	$TM = T \times RPM$
Feed per Tooth = FT	Number of Teeth in Tool = T Feed per Revolution in Inches = FR	$FT = \dfrac{FR}{T}$
Feed per Tooth = FT	Number of Teeth in Tool = T Feed in Inches per Minute = IPM Speed in Rev. per Minute = RPM	$FT = \dfrac{IPM}{T \times RPM}$

Figure 9.15 *CNC-Related Speed and Feed Formulas for Milling Cutters and Other Related Tools*

TO FIND	KNOWN VALUES	FORMULAS
Surface (or Periphery) Speed in Meters per Minute = S (m/min)	Diameter of Tool in Millimeters = D Revolutions per Minute = RPM	S = D x .00314 x RPM
Revolutions per Minute = RPM	Surface Speed in Meters per Minute = S Tool Diameter in Inches = D	$RPM = \dfrac{S}{D \ x \ .00314}$
Feed amount per Revolution Millimeters = FR	Feed in Millimeters per Minute = FMM Revolutions per Minute = RPM	$FR = \dfrac{FMM}{RPM}$
Feed in Millimeters per Minute = FMM	Feed per Revolution in Millimeters = FR Revolutions per Minute = RPM	FMM = FR x RPM
Number of Cutting Teeth per Minute = TM	Number of Teeth in Tool = T Revolutions per Minute = RPM	TM = T x RPM
Feed per Tooth = FT	Number of Teeth in Tool = T Feed per Revolution in Millimeters = FR	$FT = \dfrac{FR}{T}$
Feed per Tooth = FT	Number of Teeth in Tool = T Feed in Millimeters per Minute = FM Speed in Rev. per Minutes = RPM	$FT = \dfrac{FM}{T \ x \ RPM}$

Figure 9.16 *Metric CNC-Related Speed and Feed Formulas for Milling Cutters and Other Related Tools*

The rate that a given point on the Circumference of the workpiece passes the cutting tool in a minute is referred to as the Cutting Speed (-CS-). Cutting Speed can be in Feet per Minute (ft/min.) or Meters per Minute (m/min.)

Cutting Speed varies for different materials. Cutting Tool and metal manufacturers have determined some benchmark Cutting Speeds favorable to tool life and production outputs. The Diameter of the work and Cutting Speed of the material should be known to formulate Revolutions per Minute (RPM). Many Turning Centers provide an unlimited number of speed settings, but special turning operations still require that the RPM be calculated precisely. The following formulas can be used to calculate Cutting Speeds.

INCH CUTTING-SPEED FORMULAS

$$RPM = \frac{CS\ (ft)\ \times\ 12}{\pi\ \times\ work\ dia.\ (in.)} = \frac{CS\ \times\ 12}{3.1416\ \times\ D} \qquad RPM = \frac{CS\ \times\ 4}{D\ (in.)}$$

METRIC CUTTING-SPEED FORMULAS

For calculation of RPM when using the Metric measurement system, the following formulas are used.

$$RPM = \frac{CS\ (m)\ \times\ 1000}{\pi\ \times\ work\ dia.\ (mm)} = \frac{CS\ \times\ 1000}{3.1416\ \times\ D} \qquad RPM = \frac{CS\ \times\ 320}{D\ (mm)}$$

Figure 9.17 *Turning-Center Cutting Speeds*

Knowing a primary Cutting Speed to enter while programming is beneficial. The type of material being machined, the depth of cut, and the grade of insert or tool bit used are all factors that can cause Cutting Speeds to vary. The table of Cutting Speeds that follows works well for baseline values to enter while programming. Once machining operations are started, Feedrate Overrides can fine-tune the optimum Cutting Speeds, harmonizing all factors to achieve the perfect machining speeds and feeds.

CNC CUTTING SPEEDS — SURFACE FEET per MINUTE			
MATERIAL	ROUGHING	FINISHING	THREADING
Tool-Steel, Annealed	80	110	40
Machine Steel	110	130	50
Cast Iron	90	120	45
Bronze	110	130	50
Brass	200	280	95
Aluminum	300	400	100
Monel	80	100	40
Copper	170	200	80
Magnesium	300	400	100
Plastics	500	600	300
Stainless	150	180	60
(All cuts taken using Carbide Inserts)			

Figure 9.18 *CNC Turning-Center Speeds and Feeds*

CNC Speeds and Feeds affect overall job time and good or scrap workpieces. The cutting edges of a tap can break down quickly from excessive RPM and Feedrate, which build up a great amount of heat. Tapping speeds also prevent efficient lubrication in the cutting zone, in turn, welding small particles of material to the cutting edges. This causes loading up and Tap breakage.

Attention must be given to several factors when Tapping by CNC. Accurate trial Speeds & Feeds; Hole specification; Type of Material; Tap Holders (use only CNC-dedicated Tap Holders); and Tapping Lubricant, cutting fluids formulated for automatic thread cutting.

CNC TAPPING SPEEDS & FEEDS

MATERIAL	SURFACE FEET per MINUTE	M / MIN. (METRIC)
Aluminum	90-120	27-36
Brass	90-110	27-33
Bronze	40-70	12-21
Tool Steel	25-40	8-13
Machine Steel	40-70	12-21
Cast Steel	20-30	6-9
Stainless Steel	15-25	5-8
Nickel Alloys	20-30	6-9
Malleable Iron	35-60	11-18
Cast Iron	70-80	21-24

(All Speeds and Feeds are given for High-Speed Taps)

Figure 9.19 *CNC Tapping Speeds*

Expressions on most CNC-related part prints are either Decimal Equivalents and Fractions in Inches or Meters.

If it is desired to Convert a Fraction to a Decimal Equivalent :

DIVIDE the NUMERATOR by the DENOMINATOR

$$\frac{\text{NUMERATOR}}{\text{DENOMINATOR}} = \text{NUMERATOR} \div \text{DENOMINATOR} = .(\text{DECIMAL})$$

Example : $\frac{5}{8}$ = 5.0 ÷ 8.0 = .6250

COMMONLY-USED DECIMAL EQUIVALENTS

16	32	64	DECIMAL	16	32	64	DECIMAL	
		1/64	.015625			33/64	.515625	
	1/32	2/64	.03150		17/32	34/64	.531250	
		3/64	.046875			35/64	.546875	
1/16	2/32	4/64	.06250	9/16	18/32	36/64	.56250	
		5/64	.078125			37/64	.578125	
	3/32	6/64	.093750		19/32	38/64	.593750	
		7/64	.109375			39/64	.609375	
(1/8)	4/32	8/64	.12500		20/32	40/64	.62500	(5/8)
		9/64	.140625			41/64	.640625	
	5/32	10/64	.15625		21/32	42/64	.656250	
		11/64	.171875			43/64	.671875	
3/16	6/32	12/64	.18750	11/16	22/32	44/64	.68750	
		13/64	.203125			45/64	.703125	
	7/32	14/64	.218750		23/32	46/64	.71875	
		15/64	.234375			47/64	.734375	
(1/4)	8/32	16/64	.25000		24/32	48/64	.75000	(3/4)
		17/64	.265625			49/64	.765625	
	9/32	18/64	.281250		25/32	50/64	.781250	
		19/64	.296875			51/64	.796875	
5/16	10/32	20/64	.31250	13/16	26/32	52/64	.812500	
		21/64	.328125			53/64	.828125	
	11/32	22/64	.34375		27/32	54/64	.843750	
		23/64	.359375			55/64	.859375	
(3/8)	12/32	24/64	.37500		28/32	56/64	.87500	(7/8)
		25/64	.390625			57/64	.890625	
	13/32	26/64	.406250		29/32	58/64	.906250	
		27/64	.421875			59/64	.921875	
	7/16	14/32	28/64	.43750	15/16	30/32	60/64	.937500	
		29/64	.453125			61/64	.953125	
	15/32	30/64	.46875		31/32	62/64	.968750	
		31/64	.484375			63/64	.984375	
(1/2)	16/32	32/64	.50000	16/16	32/32	64/64	1.0000	

Figure 9.20 *Decimal Equivalents—Inches*

Metric Measurements appearing on CNC prints can be converted to Inch measurements by using the methods approved by the American Standards Association.

1.000 Inch	=	25.4 Millimeter (mm)
39.37 Inches	=	1.0 Meter
1.0 Foot	=	.3048 Meters
.3937 Inch	=	1.0 Centimeter
.03937 Inch	=	1.0 Millimeter

For Subdivisions and Multiples, Prefixes are used:

Kilo	=	1000
Hecto	=	100
Deca	=	10
Deci	=	1/10
Centi	=	1/100
Milli	=	1/1000

COMMON NOMINAL METRIC CONVERSIONS

INCH	=	METRIC
1/64 (.015625)		.396875
1/32 (.031250)		.793750
1/16 (.06250)		1.58750
1/8 (.1250)		3.1750
1/4 (.2500)		6.3500
3/8 (.3750)		9.5250
1/2 (.500)		12.7000

Figure 9.21 *Metric Conversion*

A

Milling Center: Rotary Axis Designation. Typically, A-Axis is given as the name for a Rotary Table.
5-Axis Milling Center: Angular pivoting Axis of a milling head, parallel to the Y-Axis.
Turning Center:
Grinding Center: A-Axis controls a multirange steady rest for contour controlled grinding.

B

Milling Center: Rotary Axis Designation. Typically, B-Axis is the name assigned for a Rotary Indexer.
5-Axis Milling Center: Angular pivoting Axis of a milling head, parallel to the X-Axis.
Turning Center:
Grinding Center:

C

Milling Center: Spindle Axis Orientation. Automatic Tool Changers require the spindle to be in positive orientation to align toolholder drive keys.
Turning Center: Multiaxis Turning Centers require C-Axis or Spindle (headstock) orientation for alternate axis operations, a C+, C- direction of rotation, Clockwise—Counterclockwise.
Grinding Center: Workhead Spindle Orientation, contour controlled.

D   Usually reserved in most Controls for Offset purposes.

E

Turning Center: Used in many Controls to specify the Thread Pitch when executing a Threading Operation. Six decimal places of accuracy may be given after an "E."

F   Used in all Controls to specify the desired Feedrate in a motion command. Rates vary from machine to machine, Milling, Boring: IMP; Turning: SFM, etc.

G   Preparatory Functions. See full list of G Codes in this chapter.

H   Usually reserved in all Controls for Offset purposes; Tool-Length Compensation

I   Defines the X-Axis Arc Center. Depending on the Control, "I" can designate the Absolute X coordinate of an Arc Center, or the Incremental measurement from the current cutter location to the Arc Center.

J   Defines the Y-Axis Arc Center. Depending on the Control, "I" can designate the Absolute Y coordinate of an Arc Center, or the Incremental measurement from the current cutter location to the Arc Center.

K   As with I and J, "K" defines the Z-Axis Arc Center when using circular interpolation in the XZ plane or the YZ plane.

L   Normally reserved in Controls for Subroutines and special programming features, such as its use in multiaxis Grinding and Turning.

M   Miscellaneous Functions. Typically, "M" words turn On and Off machine switches, such as the spindle, coolants, etc. See the complete list of "M" word functions in this chapter.

N   A Sequence Number. Most conventional CNC formats use sequence numbers for program command identification, each program line assigned a number.

O   Program Number. The "O" word is used at the beginning of a program. The assignment of a number, normally between 0001 and 9999, identifies an individual program.

P   Period of Dwell time, or Pause. All Axes affected by a dwell command, in Conventional format, are instructed of the length of dwell time by "P" followed by 3, 4, or 5 digits. Example: 2 1/4 seconds = P2250 (No decimal used).

R   Arc Radius. Some Controls require that the circular motion command includes the Radius measurement for Arcs being machine.

S   Spindle Speed. By entering into the Control an "S" word followed by the RPM of SFM, the spindle (or Headstock spindle) rotates at the specified rate. Some Controls require a "+" or "-" before the rotation rate to identify Clockwise or Counterclockwise rotation of the spindle.

T   Tool Station. For CNC Controls instructing Automatic Tool Changers & Turrets, the "T" word designates which Tool is desired.

U

Grinding Machines: Designates the U-Axis, an axial positioning gage for probing diameters of the work face. Target dimensional positioning is used on most U-Axis system components.

V

Turning & Grinding Centers: V-Axis capabilities enable the Tailstock to move perpendicular to the Spindle Plane for correction of cylindricity errors under Control command.

W

Grinding Center: W-Axis movement enables the longitudinal positioning of the Absolute Diameter Measuring head using target positioning.

X

Milling Center: X-Axis designation, typically, the longest "table axis" perpendicular to the Y- & Z-axes.
Turning Center: X-Axis designation, typically, the longest "cross-slide axis," perpendicular to Spindle Plane and Z-Axis movement. It is normally the axis used to control diameters machined.
Grinding Center: X-Axis designation, typically, controlling the wheelslide angling into & away from work, and controlling ground diameters.

Y

Milling Center: Y-Axis designation, typically, the "saddle" or cross-axis perpendicular to the X-Axis with shorter travel.
Grinding Center: Y-Axis designation, typically, controlling the Absolute Diameter Measuring head opening and closing movements.

Z

Milling Center: Z-Axis designation, typically, controlling movement of the spindle perpendicular to the X- and Y-Axes.
Turning Center: Z-Axis designation, typically controlling movement of the Turret or Tailstock in or away.
Grinding Center : Z-Axis designation, typically, controlling movement of the entire workslide in toward and away from the workhead spindle, under contour controlled power.

Figure 9.22 *Word Address Format*

G Words are Preparatory Functions that vary from CNC Control to Control. The following is a list of G codes that are commonly defined for Turning-Center and Milling-Center Formats.

G00   Rapid Positioning Command.

G01   Linear Interpolation; Straight-line cutting motion, F____ Feedrate to be specified.

G02   Circular Cutting Motion, Clockwise (CW); Helical Interpolation, additional Axis required.

G03   Circular cutting motion, Counterclockwise (CCW); Helical Interpolation, additional Axis required.

G04   Dwell Command (followed by P____, specifies Pause length in seconds)

G05   X Mirror Image

G06   Y Mirror Image

G07   XY-Axis Exchange; Imaginary Axis Interpolation

G09   Cancels Mirror Image and XY Exchange; Exact Stop

G10   Programmable Work Coordinate System Offset

G17   X-Y Plane Selection

G18   X-Z Plane Selection

G19   Y-Z Plane Selection

G20   Inch Mode

G21   Metric Mode

G22   Stroke Check before Axis Feed

G25   Subroutine Program Call

G27   Reference Point Verify; Jump Instruction

G28   Reference Point Return Command; Machine Zero Return; 1st Reference Point

G30   2nd/3rd/4th Reference Point Return

G31   Skip Function

G32   Threading Command

G38   Tool-Diameter Offset

G39   Tool-Diameter Offset

G40   Cutter-Radius-Compensation Cancel

G41   Cutter-Radius-Compensation LEFT

G42   Cutter-Radius-Compensation RIGHT

G43   Tool-Length-Compensation; Tool Offset

G44   Tool Offset

G45   Tool-Offset-Expansion Command; Tool-Length Offset

G46   Tool-Length Offset

G48   Tool-Length Offset

G49   Cancel Tool-Length Compensation

G50   Program Zero Designation

G51   Alternate Mirror Image

G52   Local Coordinate System

G53   Automatic Coordinate System Setting; Machine Coordinate System Setting

G54   Fixture Offsets; Work Coordinate System Offsets.

G60   Unidirectional Positioning

G61   Exact Stop Mode

G62   Automatic Corner Override

G63   Tapping Mode

G64   Cutting Mode

G65   Magnetic-Tape/Floppy-Disk Operation

G66   Activation of RS 232 Interface

G68   Coordinate Rotation

G69   Coordinate Rotation

G73 through G79   Subroutines (individualized per Control)

G80 through G89   Hole-machining Subroutines (individualized per Control)

G90   Absolute Positioning Mode

G91   Incremental Positioning Mode

G92   Program Zero Designator; Coordinate System Setting

G94   Feedrate, Inches per Minute; Feed per Minute

G95   Feedrate, Revolutions per Minute

G96   Constant Surface Speed, Spindle Mode

G97   RPM Spindle Mode

Figure 9.23   *G Words—G Codes*

The Letter Address "M" represents a succession of Miscellaneous Functions. "M" words can vary from Control to Control; some manufacturers assign standardized "M" words mixed with their own selection. Also check machine manuals.

M00 Program Stop

M01 Optional Stop

M02 End of Program

M03 Spindle ON in Clockwise Direction

M04 Spindle ON in Counterclockwise Direction

M05 Spindle Stop

M06 Tool-Change Command

M07 Mist Coolant ON

M08 Flood Coolant ON

M09 Coolants OFF (all)

M17 Return to Main Program

M19 Spindle Orient Command, Automatic Tool-Changer Requirement

M21 Mirror Image X-Axis

M22 Mirror Image Y-Axis

M23 Mirror Image OFF

Figure 9.24 *M Words*

CHAPTER 10

CNC TOOLING

The crucial link between the precision CNC Machine Tool and the machined workpiece is Tooling. Tooling consists of all precision work-alignment/holding components and all Cutting Toolholders and Cutting tools.

CNC Tooling is designed specifically for use with CNC Machines and their machining characteristics. CNC Workholding devices can enable multiple-workpiece fixturing for prototype job lots, and provide durability for high-production part runs. The Workholding components are adaptable, versatile, and designed for strength and wear resistance. CNC Cutting Tools and Toolholding systems are specifically manufactured and dedicated to the application of automated machining. CNC cutting tools withstand higher cutting temperatures, greater cutting pressures, and are generally tougher and more wear-resistant. CNC Toolholders enable automatic tool changing, positive tool-length measurements, and strength.

The following time-tested and proven Tooling components function ideally in CNC applications.

TOOLING for MILLING/BORING CENTERS

Modular Tooling for Tables and Pallets

Modular Fixturing is very popular and is an effective time-saving method to build precision Workholding setups for CNC Tables and Pallets. By securing "subplates" or "base plates" onto tables/pallets covered with tapped holes and alignment keyways, the availability of clamping holes for setups is greatly increased. Also, precision-ground keyways spaced between the tapped holes enables the setup to be aligned quickly and positively.

Modular setup blocks of various sizes are included with modular tooling sets. Hole-pattern spacings match (universally) between components, along with key-

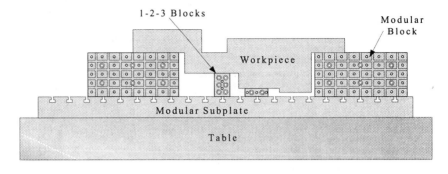

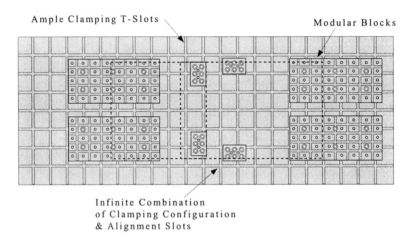

Figure 10.1 *Modular Tooling for Tables and Pallets*

way spacing. Each block and plate surface is ground flat and square within .0003", in most sets. This inspected and certified accuracy allows blocks to be indexed, flipped, and clamped on any surface for versatility and adaptability to many setup configurations without question of flatness, squareness, or perpendicularity. See Figure 10.1.

Blocks, Cubes, and 1–2–3's

Precision modular "Cubes" or large modular "Blocks" have certified accuracy, typically attached with documentation. For close-tolerance operations on surfaces that require precision machining, Cube sets or Block sets can be used. Similar to those used in Inspection departments, "banking against" surfaces known to be flat and perpendicular to the base or table surface can help to assure that sufficient setup preparation is made for the closest-tolerance operations and rigid machining strength. Certification of squareness over all six sides of cubes can be attained to .000050 over 12" (cubed). Using tooling that has inherent accuracies as close as this helps to achieve very tight dimensional requirements on precision workpieces.

Smaller 1–2–3 Blocks are very handy setup components that are also certified for accuracy. These blocks are ground and lapped to nominal inch sizes, so specific setup dimensions can be designed.

All of these components are complete with tapped holes and clearance holes for stacking and modular fixture "building." See Figure 10.2.

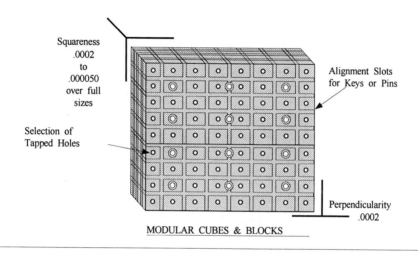

MODULAR CUBES & BLOCKS

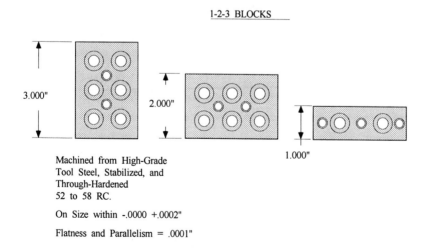

1-2-3 BLOCKS

Machined from High-Grade
Tool Steel, Stabilized, and
Through-Hardened
52 to 58 RC.

On Size within -.0000 +.0002"

Flatness and Parallelism = .0001"

Figure 10.2 *Certified Accuracy of Modular Components*

ANGLE PLATES

Angle Plates provide the same type of perpendicular machine surface (to the table or pallet) that "Cubes" do. Angle Plates, however, are lighter and occupy much less space in the working environment. Usually gusseted for strength, Angle Plates are a less expensive component than a cube or block, and sometimes are not hardened and therefore machineable. Setups can be custom designed with Angle Plates by machining locating holes directly into the Angle Plate that correspond with workpiece hole centers of fixture-locating holes.

Angle Plates also provide ample patterns of tapped holes for clamping. Usually, tapped holes are spaced at set distances that line up with other modular component hole patterns. See Figure 10.3.

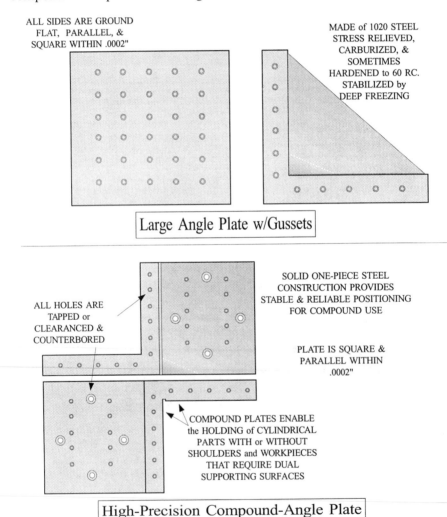

Figure 10.3 CNC Angle Plates

CNC VISES

Stability and precision design are the two most important features in a CNC Vise. The new Pull-Type Vises can minimize deflection, holding the workpiece in the most immobile state possible during machining. The overall external uniformity enables the vises to be used in multiples of 2, 3, 4, and more to maximize production in today's high-speed, high-precision Machining Centers.

Features to look for in a CNC Vise include the following (see Figure 10.4):

- All sides having finished flatness to .0003" guaranteed for precise mounting in three modes: Upright, Left, and Right side.
- A vise that minimizes deflection up to 80%.
- Vise pulls and exerts pressure only against the stationary jaw.
- Pull-type action reduces stationary jaw deflection.
- Up to 20,000 lb precision clamping force.
- CNC style allows side-by-side mounting, both sides being ground square to within .0003" with base and top.
- 80,000-lb ductile iron body.

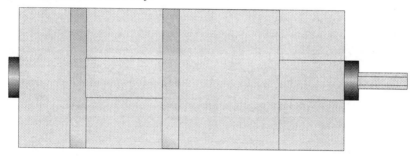

ALL SIDES HAVE FLATNESS
to .0003" for PRECISION MOUNTING
in UPRIGHT, LEFT- & RIGHT-SIDE
MOUNTING POSITIONS

CLAMPING ACTION REDUCES
DEFLECTION by up to 80%

ALL PULL-DOWN EXERTION PRESSURE
is AGAINST the
STATIONARY VISE JAW

UP TO 20,000 LB of PRECISION
CLAMPING FORCE

80,000-LB DUCTILE IRON BODY

Figure 10.4   *CNC Machine Vise*

The CNC Double-Vise

The CNC Double-Vise offers two clamping stations designed to pull in toward the same stationary jaw. The innovative design features one screw and transmits equal and opposite forces against the single stationary jaw. It eliminates multiple setups and secondary operations.

Features unique to the CNC Double-Vise are as follows (see Figure 10.5):

- Clamping with equalization eliminates 99.99% of jaw deflection.
- Antitilt spherical mechanism within moveable jaws provides alignment to workpieces without jaw tilt.
- Vise is designed to hold different-sized parts in each individual station.

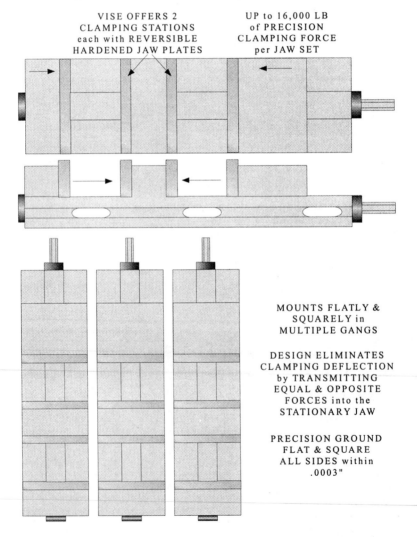

VISE OFFERS 2
CLAMPING STATIONS
each with REVERSIBLE
HARDENED JAW PLATES

UP to 16,000 LB
of PRECISION
CLAMPING FORCE
per JAW SET

MOUNTS FLATLY &
SQUARELY in
MULTIPLE GANGS

DESIGN ELIMINATES
CLAMPING DEFLECTION
by TRANSMITTING
EQUAL & OPPOSITE
FORCES into the
STATIONARY JAW

PRECISION GROUND
FLAT & SQUARE
ALL SIDES within
.0003"

Figure 10.5 *CNC Double-Lock Vise*

- Slim-line models allows closer center-to-center distances between multiple vises, precision-ground on all three sides.
- Bed parallelism .0003".
- Bed height matched .0003".
- Perpendicularity for the fixed jaw to the bed within .0001" per inch.
- Center line of the keyway to the center line of the fixed jaw within .0004".

Soft Jaws

Many parts requiring machining are shaped in such a way that they are not able to be held effectively in standard vise jaws. This is where the use of soft vise jaws is adopted. Soft vise jaws made out of aluminum and other machinable materials are the answer to many unique partholding, clamping, and fixturing problems.

One advantage of soft jaws is the ability to clearance areas where tools might travel. When milling or turning surfaces of parts totally clamped in a vise or three-jaw chuck, the Toolpath can continue into the jaw area, something not even considered with a hardened jaw. Drilling can also be permitted in an area where normally a parallel or support for a piece would not allow a drill to be traveling—close to a part edge, to a jaw, and so on.

One application that is ideal for soft jaws is the nesting ability of round pieces. Certain workpieces require flat surfaces or keyways milled down their entire length and additional operations performed. Normally, round stock is difficult to hold for large cuts or operations that subject the workpieces to lateral tool force. Clamping round stock in normal flat vise jaws causes flats to be pressed onto the outer diameter, and during machining, parts pull up.

Half-nests can be easily machined into soft jaws to accommodate round stock with solid machining capabilities. Then, also, there is top access for milling or drilling without any fear of part movement. Round stock that needs total nesting can be clamped with soft jaws, also with modification. Total encasement can be attained by machining the workpiece nest into the jaws before they are bolted in the vise. See Figure 10.6.

Long and Wide Jaws

Certain parts, although ideal to clamp in a vise for the operations to be performed, do not fit into a standard-width machine vise. Either the parts are too long or too wide for the standard jaw opening. Jaws can be made up to accommodate parts that are too long and unsupported.

When making extra-long jaws, it is a good idea to start with a 6061-T6 Aluminum bar stock that is 1-1/2" to 2" thick. This will provide rigidity, even out to the extreme jaw ends. This added thickness will also be beneficial when

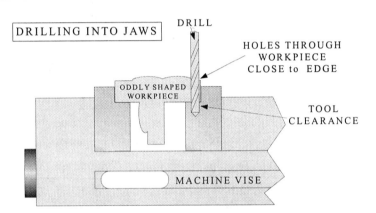

Figure 10.6 *Soft Jaws for CNC*

machining in "parallels," alleviating the search or purchase of items that are expensive in such lengths. See Figure 10.7.

WORKHOLDING DEVICES: CLAMPS

T-Slot Clamps

Safety during CNC machining is priority one. The selection of clamping components that meet a specific criteria is necessary. T-Slot Clamps that incorporate a pull-down arm and cam-locking mechanism provide good clamping capabilities. A one-piece base with a full range of adjustability and 8.000 lb of clamping power are some features this type of clamping system offers.

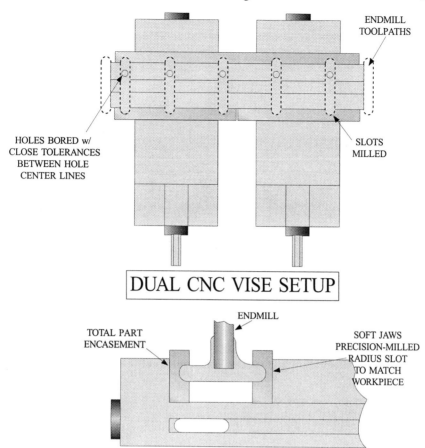

Figure 10.7 *Special Soft Jaws for CNC Applications*

Buttress Clamps

Many setups require low-profile clamps that do not interfere with extended tools, Toolpaths, Tool Changes, and limited space in complex table setups or turning fixtures. Also, the smaller Buttress Clamps have considerably less total mass and therefore eliminate some out-of-balance conditions larger clamps impose on rotating setups in turning and grinding operations. These Workholding clamps are also designed for use on thin workpieces instead of ordinary strap clamps. They feature a self-aligning pivot and jack-heel so that the torque bolt is always vertical and induces no side forces. See Figure 10.8.

Single-Block Clamps

These units all work on the same principle—the worm-and-gear mechanism. Precision worm-and-gear design works by holding the workpiece (with the

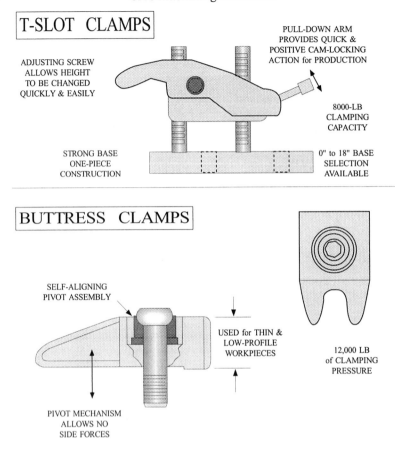

Figure 10.8 *Machining Clamps for Special CNC Setups*

clamping power originating in an enclosed gearbox) by exerting force through a leverage-multiplying device. The worm, attached to the tightening wrench, can turn the gear, but the gear cannot turn the worm. So the clamp cannot loosen through pressure reversals or vibration.

- This system can save up to 80% in setup time and clamps new part heights and surface levels quickly and securely.
- Clamping is safe, all holding forces are preengaged—no variables exist.
- Low overall height provides good tool clearance; can be swiveled or retracted.
- Single-Block Clamps can be used in special fixtures or subplates, and are modular—the clamping device is on top and is built up with riser blocks.
- Single-Block Clamps press with a force of 3200 lb when tightened to a torque of only 58 ft-lb. See Figure 10.9.

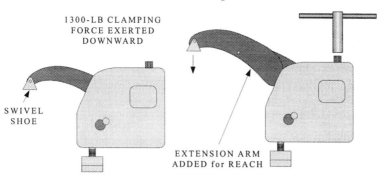

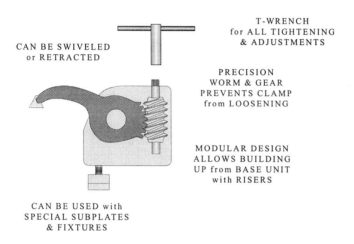

Figure 10.9 *CNC Single-Block Clamps*

CNC Clamping Studs, Straps, Bolts, and Nuts

All CNC clamps, straps, bolts, studs, and nuts should be constructed of stress-proof steel, having a Tensile Strength of 125,000 Min. PSI and an Elongation of 10% in 2″. Machinability should be 80% of B-1112, Rockwell of 25C. Notice the specifications detailed in Figure 10.10.

ROTARY TABLES and ROTARY INDEXERS

A Programmable CNC Precision Rotary Table, equipped with a servo-drive system and interfaced with the machining system's Control, provides a fifth or sixth A- or B-Axis. Its rotary indexing/motion is coordinated with the motion of the other axes to generate complex cams and other complicated shapes.

High-precision bearing surfaces insure ultra-smooth rotation. All tables

TABLE
CLAMPING STUDS

TENSILE STRENGTH
125,000 P.S.I.

BRINELL is 225

MACHINABILITY
is 80% of B-1112

ROCKWELL of 25C

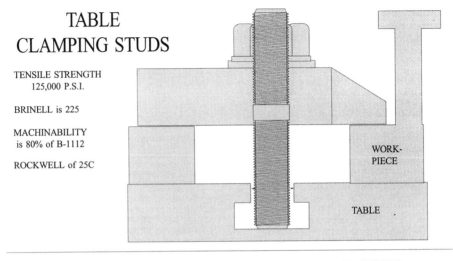

FIXTURE
CLAMPING STUDS

For FIXTURE
CLAMPING, a
HEAVY-DUTY
NUT is used to
LOCK the STUD in
POSITION at the
exact Length Required

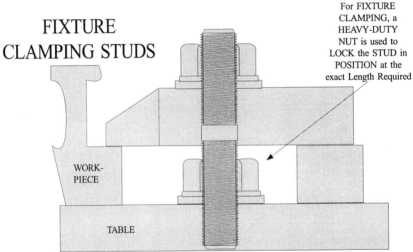

Figure 10.10   *CNC Clamp Requirements*

should be precision-ground and individually supplied with a certificate of inspection. Other features and requirements a CNC Rotary axis should offer are as follows:

- Dual-position action locks
- Clamping Surface Flatness (Concave): .0006"
- Cylindrical Center-bore concentricity: .0008"
- Accuracy: ±2 Arc-Seconds
- Trueness of Rotation (TIR): .0000040
- Programmable Resolution: .0005 Degree. See Figure 10.11.

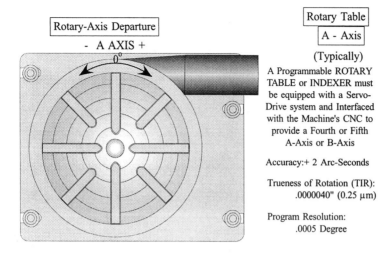

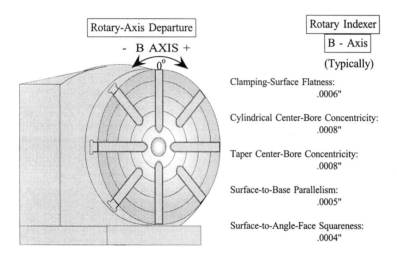

Figure 10.11 *Fourth- and Fifth-Axis Designation*

Fixturing for Rotary Tables and Rotary Indexers

Modular Fixture plates, or Subplates, are available for Rotary Tables and Rotary Indexers. Basically, the modular base plates match the major diameters of the clamping tables on the rotary devices. The Subplates have the same matching hole patterns that the longer rectangular subplates for milling machines have. This enables the interchangeable use of all standard modular blocks, cubes, alignment systems, and clamping sets. See Figure 10.12.

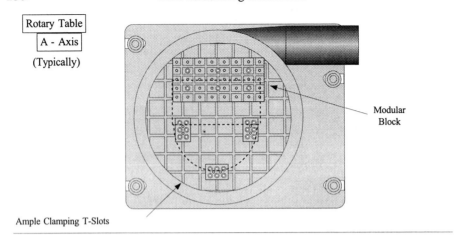

Rotary Table
A - Axis
(Typically)

Modular
Block

Ample Clamping T-Slots

Modular Blocks
Infinite Combination
of Clamping Configuration
& Alignment Slots

Workpiece

1-2-3 Blocks

Modular Subplate

Table

Figure 10.12 *Rotary Table/Indexer: Modular Tooling*

CNC TOOLHOLDERS

Standard CNC machining center tooling systems are universal throughout the industry. Three of four tapers encompass 99% of all CNC spindle configurations in use. All "V"-Flange tooling is interchangeable with Erickson, Universal, Valenite, Carbaloy, Brown & Sharpe, De Vlieg, Burgmaster, Cincinnatti Milacron, Pratt & Whitney, Moog, White Sund Strand, and Excello. The most popular taper sizes in use are #40, #45, and #50.

General CNC practice dictates that positive attention be given to toolholding/clamping procedures and the preservation of concentricity. If possible, always hold cutting tools in a solid precision-ground holder, secured with double set-screws as opposed to collet-type toolholders. Use collet-type toolholder systems only when holding an odd-sized shank or drill size. Collets do not grip as positively or run with precision concentricity as do solid, ground holders. See Figure 10.13.

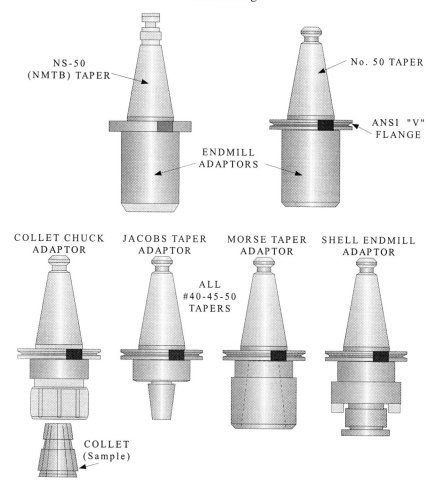

NS-50
(NMTB) TAPER

No. 50 TAPER

ANSI "V"
FLANGE

ENDMILL
ADAPTORS

COLLET CHUCK
ADAPTOR

JACOBS TAPER
ADAPTOR

MORSE TAPER
ADAPTOR

SHELL ENDMILL
ADAPTOR

ALL
#40-45-50
TAPERS

COLLET
(Sample)

Figure 10.13 *CNC Toolholders for Machining Centers*

CNC CUTTING TOOLS

To obtain efficient metal removal by conventional techniques, the cutting operation must be made smoothly, firmly, and cleanly. Cutting efficiency is influenced by the design of machine tools, cutting tools, and the quantity and quality of cutting lubricants.

Because specific cutting forces can be high in the machining of some exotic metals and some super-alloys, the CNC machine must have the following attributes: Ample Power; Low- and High-Speed cutting capabilities; Rigid Construction, including provisions for Tool and Workpiece support; and the Freedom from Backlash.

The requirements that influence the choice of cutting tools are as follows:

- The tools must resist abrasive wear and be capable of supporting and retaining smooth, sharp cutting edges.
- They must be rigid.
- Cutting and clearance angles must be carefully selected to (a) give maximum support to the cutting edge, (b) promote conduction of heat from the cutting edge, and (c) provide ample clearance for swarf removal.

The cutting fluid should have good extreme-pressure characteristics to minimize metal buildup on the cutting edges. It should be supplied to the cutting zone in adequate quantities to dissipate the large amounts of heat generated by the cutting process.

Despite the considerable amount of field research already carried out, machinability is not readily related to measured properties of materials nor are there any standardized methods of assessing machinability in a practical manner. The preferred manner of assessing machinability remains the carefully controlled machining test under conditions closely simulating those of production practice. In the descriptions of specific CNC machining operations, it is possible only to suggest conditions that give good results based on the principles already outlined. If the work is of a repetitive nature, it is worthwhile determining by experiment the optimum conditions for the specific operation involved.

TOOL MATERIALS

In general, high-speed tool steels (HSS) are used only when the hardness of workpieces does not exceed 280 H_V (28R_C) or when the cut is intermittent. In the fully heat-treated condition, many aerospace/alloyed products are normally harder than 280 H_V (28R_C). Therefore, it is usually most economical to employ carbide-tipped tools, which permit higher cutting speeds and feeds. If full advantage is to be taken of the superior cutting qualities of carbide-tipped tools, cutting should be continuous. In addition, careful attention must be given to providing adequate rigidity for the entire machining setup, including the machine itself, the cutting tool, and the workpiece. Use of traveling or fixed steady rests when turning is recommended whenever possible. It is advisable to use a live center in the tailstock to avoid center wear and chatter, where applicable.

CNC MILLING

The essential requirements of milling are high accuracy and a smooth finish. In order to achieve these results, it is imperative to have sharp tools, rigid machines and fixtures, and ample power. The milling cutters should have adequate side and top clearances to facilitate chip removal and should be set in their holders with maximum holding power. Because of interrupted cutting action, milling cutters are usually made of high-speed steel (e.g., M-2, M-10) with the 5% V, 5% Co type (e.g., T-15), with Titanium-Nitrite-coated Endmills increasingly used. However, to cut high-strength alloys like Inconel alloy MA6000, carbide-tipped cutters are recommended for economical machining.

Climb-milling is generally preferred to conventional milling because it causes less harmful cutter deflection, usually pushing the cutter over the work, leaving extra material on the surface being cut as opposed to cutting the surface undersize. It also avoids the rubbing action at the beginning of the cut. In addition, the downward effect of the tool on the workpiece assists rigidity, and consequently avoids chatter. For the same reasons, face milling, which does not involve chips tapering to zero thickness, is generally preferred to slab-milling.

Cobalt Premium Endmills (T-15's) are excellent all-around CNC cutting tools for milling. Made of Cobalt-compounded Super-High-Speed Steel, these tools are designed with a special geometry to match the high demands of CNC machining. They are intended for use on the typical aerospace materials: Aluminum, Magnesium, Stainless Steels. They are also very capable of milling the newer high-strength, thermal-resistant, space-age materials. When used in combination with the coatings available for wear resistance, T-15 Cobalt is quite effective for great abrasive material resistance and materials that require a high red-hardness. In addition, higher surface speeds can be achieved and significantly longer tool life may be expected when machining stainless steels, abrasive plastics and bakelite, cast iron, 30-50 Rockwell "C" hardness range steels, and other related materials.

Some popular cutter types are displayed in Figures 10.14 and 10.15.

CNC DRILLS

CNC operations generally require one of three types of drills. The three types normally used are Low-Helix Twist drills, High-Helix Twist drills, and Coolant-Feeding drills.

Low-Helix twist drills have polished flutes designed to eject chips rapidly and prevent clogging. The slow helix reduces the rake angle at the cutting lips, which makes these drills particularly useful for drilling brasses, phosphor-bronze, hard plastics such as bakelite, hard rubber, and materials made of compressed fibers.

High-Helix twist drills are designed for drilling aluminum alloys, copper, and other soft metals. The fast helix increases the rake angle at the cutting lips. The flutes are wider than standard and are polished to prevent them from becoming choked with chips.

Coolant-Feeding drills are heavy-duty twist drills used largely in vertical drilling applications for tough jobs. They are also used effectively for drilling deep holes in soft materials. The straight-shank drill is tapped at the shank end with a pipe thread for attaching a coolant-feed fitting. However, when held in a CNC toolholder, the coolant line is managed through the machine's integral coolant

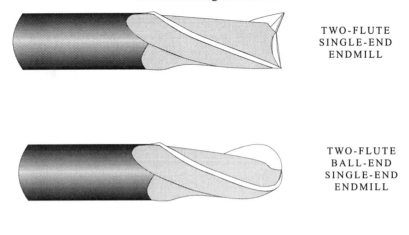

TWO-FLUTE
SINGLE-END
ENDMILL

TWO-FLUTE
BALL-END
SINGLE-END
ENDMILL

FOUR-FLUTE,
SINGLE-END
ENDMILL
(Bottom)

T-15 COBALT
SUPER-HIGH-
SPEED STEEL

DESIGNED with SPECIAL
TOOL GEOMETRY

LONGER TOOL LIFE for
CNC OPERATIONS in
STAINLESS STEELS,
30-50 ROCKWELL
"C" HARDNESS STEELS;
& HIGH-STRENGTH,
THERMAL-RESISTANT,
SPACE AGE METALS

Figure 10.14 *CNC Endmills*

lines. The two coolant holes run through the lands to the cutting lips. The notch-thinned point and ground-shank diameter ensure accurate hole location. A high-helix angle ejects chips rapidly even under varying liquid and mist-coolant pressure settings. The coolant is fed into the coolant fittings, then into the shank and down through the drill to the cutting lips.

Of these three general types of drill design, a full variety of grinds are used, each specialized for individual materials.

Multifacet Drills

To optimize CNC performance, many different variations on the standard twist have been experimented with: the Helical drill, Split-point drill, Racon, and so on, all striving for better performance in certain operations. More than 25 different types of Multifacet drills have proven themselves successful in Low-

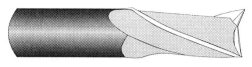

M42 COBALT
COARSE TOOTH &
ROUND TOOTH

DESIGNED TO QUICKLY ROUGH
& REMOVE MATERIALS:
REFRACTORY METALS, ULTRA-
HIGH-STRENGTH STEELS,
NICKEL-BASED ALLOYS,
TITANIUM, & HEAT-RESISTANT
ALLOYS.

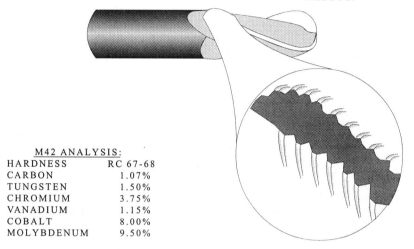

M42 ANALYSIS:

HARDNESS	RC 67-68
CARBON	1.07%
TUNGSTEN	1.50%
CHROMIUM	3.75%
VANADIUM	1.15%
COBALT	8.00%
MOLYBDENUM	9.50%

Figure 10.15 CNC Roughing Endmills

Helix and High-Helix twist-drill varieties under various working conditions and workpiece materials. Functional concerns of the Multifacet drill are hole quality, drill life, tool force, heat transfer, and chip removal. Each of these factors is very predominant in CNC machining.

A common Multifacet drill has six principal facets. See Figure 10.16.

Flanks A, B, and C are shown on both cutting edges (six total). Flank A's form is that of a conventional twist-drill flank. A cylindrical form is ground into Flank A, forming an arc-shaped cutting edge on the inside of the flute (Flank B). Flank C is an additional cylindrical form ground to create the drill center and diminish the length of the chisel point. Detail features are designated as follows:

- EL = chisel edge length
- TH = tip height
- PA = point angle of the inner edge

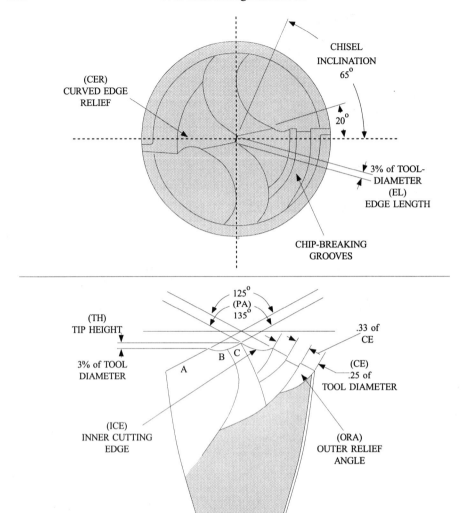

Figure 10.16 *Typical Multifacet Drill*

EL (chisel edge length) is normally about 3%, or .03, of the tool diameter, lessening the tool cutting force, and similar in design to the split drill and drills with thinned webs.

TH (tip height) is designed to be 3% of the tool diameter with PA (point angle of inner edge) being 135°, thereby making the chisel edge length stronger. The tip height is exclusive to the Multifacet drill because of the dual-tipped cutting edge. A sizable dimension is needed for PA to anticipate high-temperature heat dissipation in the reduced chisel edge. Heat causes cutting-edge breakdown and reduced tool life or breakage.

Cutting edge length (CE) and radius of the curved edge (RC), differ from those of a standard drill where the rake angle decreases from the outer edges inward to the tool center. The rake angle is close to zero, .2 times the tool diameter from the tool axis. The cutting edge length (CE) equals .2 to .3 times the tool diameter. The Multifacet drill incorporates an arc cutting edge increasing the rake angle using a radius curved edge equaling .1 diameter. This arc cutting edge greatly improves drill centering and chip-breaking capabilities of the tool.

The inner cutting edge angle varies from 20° to 30°, depending on the length of the inner cutting edge (ICE), in proportion to the chisel edge length and the inner cutting edge rake angle.

The Multifacet drill's outer relief angle (ORA) is generally greater than the conventional drill, corresponding to the increased feedrates of the improved tool. The outer relief angle is from 10° to 15°. From that measurement, the curved edge relief angle (CER) is 2° to 3° greater than the 10° to 15° of the ORA.

The point angle is directly related to the rake angle and the cutting force, heat dissipation (transfer), and chip ejection. This combination of varied cutting angles working together modifies (positively) the machine feed rates and spindle speed parameters (RPM). Because the point angle, rake angle, and thrust force all increase, the torque needed decreases. Chip breaking is greatly improved along with chip ejection. This makes the Multifacet drill a preferred tool choice when setting up CNC machine tools, where increased RPM and feedrates directly reflect greater productivity. The temperature of the outer tool areas increases, however. The standard twist-drill point angle normally measures 118°. The Multifacet drill point angle is specified at 125°.

A unique feature on the flank of the Multifacet drill is a single or dual groove ground into Flank A. Generally, if the diameter is .625 or greater, these grooves provide superior chip-breaking properties for the tool. This is especially effective in soft and stringy steels.

The advantages of using Multifacet drills are the functional improvements during machining. Their design is centered around the following: improved tool centering; extended cutting edge and tool life; reduced forces during machining, allowing higher feedrates without workpiece distortion; improved heat dissipation and transfer; and strengthening of the center of the drill, reducing tool walking and breakage.

Tool centering during machining is improved using Multifacet drills mainly because the thrust force (radially) is reduced. The reduction is due to the arc cutting edge being located in the middle of the cutting lip to increase the rake angle. A conventional twist drill creates great thrust forces because the rake angle decreases toward the drill center. The outer edges produce an even chip, but the inner edges have negative rake measurements.

The Multifacet drill also has a reduced chisel edge length, decreasing thrust forces, and a large point angle of 125°, which increases the rake angle at the outer sections.

Tool centering is attributed to the reduced chisel edge in comparison to the conventional twist drill. Also, the small radius of the arc cutting edge improves centering. In soft materials such as aluminum and copper, where large elongation and low hardness are factors, the design of the tip height of the Multifacet drill is increased to .05 to .06 of the tool diameter, and the angle of the inner edge is reduced to about 110° to enforce the centering capabilities of the tool. To improve machining of titanium and stainless steel, the tip height is increased to .06 to .08 of the tool diameter. The chisel edge length is increased simultaneously to strengthen the center part of the drill.

To decrease the temperature accumulation within a tool when drilling certain materials, such as cast iron, which increases wear at the outer cutting edge, the double-point angle is incorporated to make the outer point angle approximately 70°. To further reduce frictional forces and heat accumulation, the clearance angle of the Multifacet drill is greater than that of a standard twist drill.

Chip removal and ejection can be a real problem for a drill cutting edge. The arc cutting edge is designed and used on a Multifacet drill to divide the chip, allowing easier ejection. The point angle of the Multifacet drill is designed to counter toughness and elongation of a workpiece material. The Multifacet drill for aluminum, for example, is 140° to 170°; titanium, 125° to 140°; stainless steel, 135° to 150°. In addition, the larger Multifacet drill uses the one or two grooves to aid in chip breaking.

Strengthening of the Multifacet drill is accomplished by keeping the chisel edge to a limit of .02 diameter and the point angle of the inner edge enlarged to 135°, with the tip height limited to the range of .02 to .03 of the tool diameter.

Special Multifacet drills are designed and specified for the best cutting properties under various working conditions and operations. Figure 10.17 illustrates the best design for drilling Cast iron. A special second conical surface with the small point angle of the inner edge at 70° reduces the working temperature at the outer tool edges. Cast iron should be cut dry with a vacuum system pulling out the powder produced.

Figure 10.18 illustrates the best design of a Multifacet drill for cutting Plexiglass. Two notable changes are the radiusing of the outer corners and the forming of a modified cutting edge, improving the inner-hole surface quality. High RPM and feedrates are used for plastic cutting, to avoid dwelling or pecking cycles. Also, surface -G- is ground to increase the angle of rake to the outer cutting edge. Surface -H- is formed to minimize friction between the hole and drill margin.

Thin material sheets are best cut with a Multifacet drill ground, as shown in Figure 10.19. Ideal centering is provided by the sharp tip in the center, the two

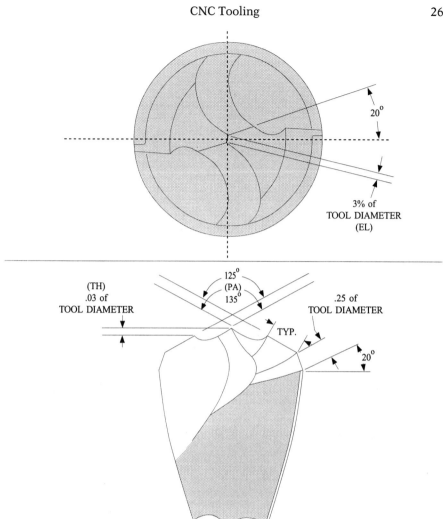

Figure 10.17 *CNC Multifacet Drill for Cutting Cast Iron*

outer cutting edges act as trepanning tools to "bore" the hole edges first, pre-venting elongation and egg-shaped holes.

Flexible Plastics and Rubber are ideally drilled by grinding a Multifacet drill to the specifications shown in Figure 10.20. The two sharp outer edges establish the outer limits of the tool. The grind, as shown, has proven to cleanly cut these difficult-to-machine materials. Tools must be maintained with razor sharpness to avoid ripping and stretching of rubber.

The Multifacet drill designed to *finish workpieces* has a positive angle on its cutting edge, as shown in Figure 10.21. This design will not allow cut chips to touch the machined hole surface, resulting in a better overall surface finish.

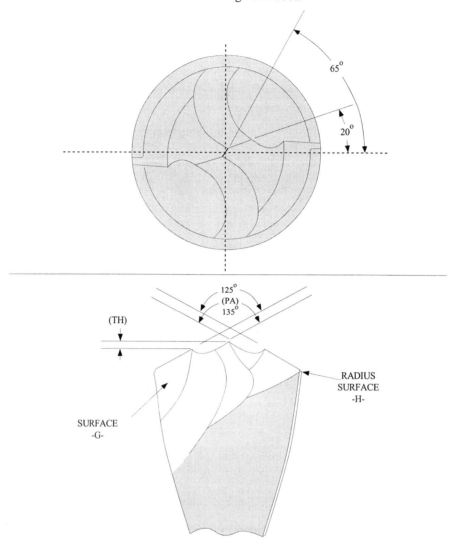

Figure 10.18 *CNC Multifacet Drill for Cutting Plexiglass*

To enlarge previously drilled holes, the Multifacet drill shown in Figure 10.22 has a short drill with two tips of the outer cutting edges centered on the existing hole-walls. This allows the thrust force of the limited cutting areas to be directly over the material to be cut.

When drilling on inclined or irregular surfaces when centering is a problem, a Multifacet drill with a point angle of 110° prevents the drill from drifting away from its intended location. See Figure 10.23.

The Multifacet drill that is designed solely for aluminum, aluminum alloys,

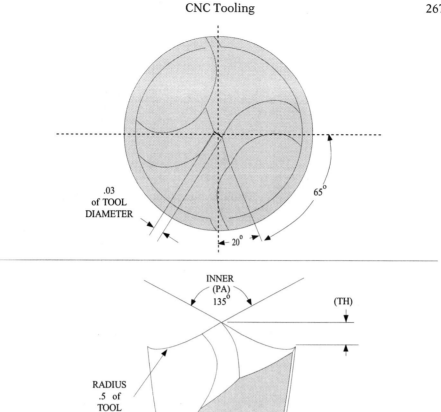

.03
of TOOL
DIAMETER

65°

20°

INNER
(PA)
135°

(TH)

RADIUS
.5 of
TOOL
DIAMETER

Figure 10.19 *CNC Multifacet Drill for Cutting Thin-Material Sheets*

and magnesium has several features: The point angle is as high as 140° to 170° for better chip removal and ejection. An additional ground section is added to the outer cutting edge to reduce the rake angle from 8° to 10°, because the point angle is fairly high in the design of this tool. To increase centering tendency, the center point of the *Aluminum Multifacet drill* is slightly higher. See Figure 10.24. To improve chip ejection even further in aluminum and magnesium, the tip height of one cutting edge is .030", and the other edge is .020". Visually, the tool is not symmetrical.

Composite materials are quickly becoming popular materials for many aerospace components. They are hard materials, brittle to cut, powdering instead

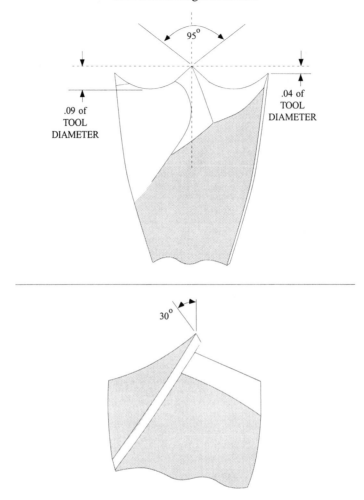

Figure 10.20 *CNC Multifacet Drill for Cutting Flexible Plastics, Rubber*

of cutting into clean chips. The tool shown in Figure 10.25 has proven positive results with lower spindle RPMs, and fast Axis feedrates keep temperatures down. Chip removal is necessary by air or vacuum systems to prevent excessive tool wear.

Multifacet drills find wide use in today's shops, especially those using automatic equipment, CNC milling and turning centers, drilling machines, and screw machines. Long runs of certain materials or particularly difficult operations on specific jobs call for a Multifacet drill to be made or purchased. Noticeable differences in allowable feedrates will be obvious when testing these tools in manual machines. As a general practice, feedrates may be stepped up in 10% increasing increments matched with corresponding RPM increases. This

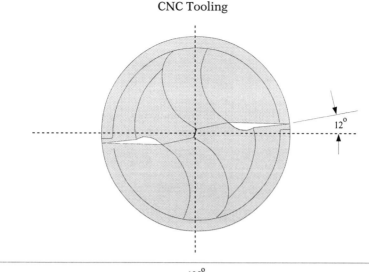

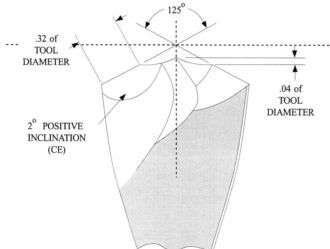

Figure 10.21 *CNC Multifacet Drill for Finishing Surfaces*

can be continued until the tool's limits are reached and a safe margin is then set. Centering tendency and temperature factors alone allow increased feedrates. Chip ejection greatly prolongs tool life. All these factors make the upgrade to Multifacet drills worth the investment of tool-grinding time or tool purchase.

Three-Lip drills are designed with three separate cutting lips and flutes, offering a number of advantages. The three-flute configuration removes more metal per revolution than two-flute tools. The additional flute enables the Three-Lip drill to track straighter while in the hole, vastly reducing runout. The additional land riding in the hole produces reamer-class surface finishes.

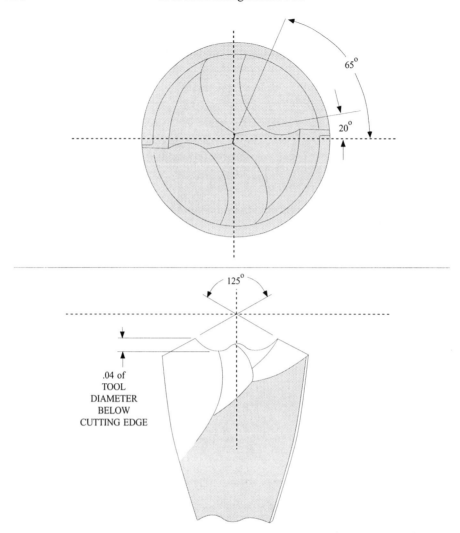

Figure 10.22 *CNC Multifacet Drill for Enlarging Holes*

Normally, Three-Lip drills are made of solid carbide. Carbide is much more durable and dissipates heat much quicker than HSS or HSCO (High-Speed Cobalt). As a result, Three-Lip drills can withstand very high feedrates without sacrificing longevity. The 150° self-centering point is an aggressive point design that eliminates the need for spot drilling. The point is web-thinned extensively. Because the tip makes contact with the workpiece at only one point, the tool's tendency to wander is reduced and the need to spot-drill is eliminated. The Three-Lip drill has a short overall length and a heavy-duty parallel web that

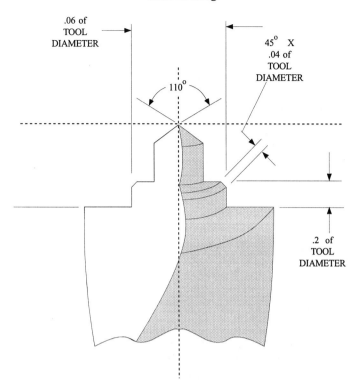

Figure 10.23 *CNC Multifacet Drill for Irregular Surfaces: Pilot Included*

make the tool very sturdy. Because the tool is so rigid, and removes metal so efficiently, the drill cuts well in cast iron, brass, bronze, aluminum alloy, hardened steel, fiber-reinforced plastic, alloyed and nonferrous steel, and titanium alloys.

If selected with a Titanium Nitrite Coating, the microthin coating substantially increases tool hardness and tool life when cutting abrasive materials. The enhanced lubricity reduces the likelihood of tool wear and breakage caused by buildup on the tool's edges when drilling materials prone to cold welding. Hole production can increase by as much as 100% with the addition of TiN Coating. See Figure 10.26.

BORING TOOLS

There are many excellent grades of Carbide on the market for Boring under CNC power. "Micrograin" grades of carbide boring tools are ground out of space-age carbide material developed for machining high-strength, thermal-resistant alloys, and in high-intensity CNC environments. Micrograin carbide bor-

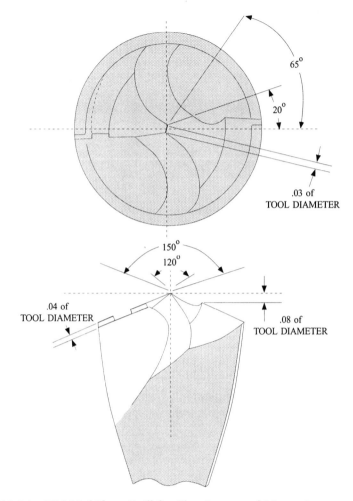

Figure 10.24 *CNC Multifacet Drill for Aluminum and Magnesium*

ing tools work well with the following materials: Aluminum, Brass, Bronze, Cobalt, Hastalloy, High-Speed Steel (HSS), "M" Series HSS, Inconel, Maraging Alloys, Molybdenum, Rene 41, 80, and 95, Super Alloys (Iron and Nickel Base), Tungsten, Titanium, Waspalloy, and Zirconium.

The following suggestions have proven successful when machining with micrograde carbide under CNC power:

To Alleviate Boring Vibration Marks: Grind 5–10° positive top rake onto tool, radius nose .010" to .020", and lightly hone cutting edge.

Box Turning: When turning square or hex stock, grind a "land" across the

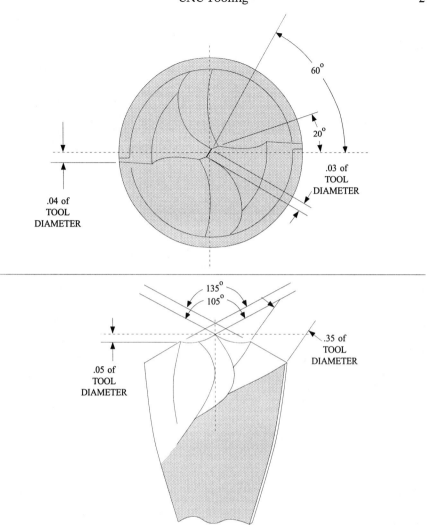

Figure 10.25 *CNC Multifacet Drill for Composite Materials*

entire face of the tool .020" to .025". Be sure to lightly hone cutting edge after grind.

Cutoff: Depending on the material, quite often removing the tool and breaking the chip becomes necessary. The microcarbide chip-breaker recommendations are: land = 1 to 1.5 times the feed per revolution; width = 3 to 4 times the feed per revolution; depth = .010" to .015". Always use as high a feed as possible.

Milling: It is important to select an Endmill not only in the appropriate di-

DETERMINE RPM USING
THE FOLLOWING EQUATION:

$$\frac{SFM \times 3.82}{DRILL\ DIAMETER}$$

DETERMINE CYCLE TIME
IN SECONDS
USING THE FOLLOWING
EQUATION:

$$\frac{HOLE\ DEPTH}{RPM} \times 60$$

SOLID CARBIDE
TIN-COATED

THREE CUTTING-LIP
DESIGN OFFERS
SUPERIOR HOLE
QUALITY, WHILE
REDUCING CYCLE
TIME FROM INCREASED
FEEDRATE CAPACITY

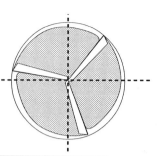

| MATERIAL | CUTTING SPEED SFM | CNC 3-LIP DRILL FEEDRATE (IPR) | | | | | COOLANT |
		.125 (3.17 mm)	.2500 (6.35 mm)	.3750 (9.52 mm)	.6250 (15.87 mm)	.7500 (19.05 mm)	
LOW-ALLOY STEEL	200-325	.0020	.0040	.0055	.0078	.0098	SOLUBLE OIL
HIGH-ALLOY STEEL (-130,000 PSI TENSILE STRENGTH-)	130-260	.0020	.0040	.0055	.0078	.0094	SOLUBLE OIL
CORROSION- & HEAT-RESISTANT STEEL	70-200	.0012	.0024	.0031	.0047	.0063	CUTTING OIL SOLUBLE OIL
GRAY & MALLEABLE CAST IRON	200-325	.0024	.0047	.0071	.0094	.0118	DRY/SOL. OIL
COPPER SHORT CHIPPING	260-400	.0024	.0055	.0071	.0087	.0110	DRY/SOL. OIL
BRASS HARD or TOUGH	325-525	.0031	.0063	.0078	.0094	.0118	SOLUBLE OIL
BRONZE	130-260	.0016	.0040	.0055	.0071	.0098	DRY/SOL. OIL
ALUMINUM	200-525	.0031	.0071	.0094	.0118	.0142	SOLUBLE OIL
MAGNESIUM	325-650	.0031	.0071	.0094	.0118	.0142	DRY (NO WATER)
TITANIUM	70-165	.0012	.0024	.0031	.0047	.0066	SOLUBLE OIL
DURO-PLASTIC	200-325	.0020	.0047	.0063	.0078	.0098	DRY

Figure 10.26 *CNC Three-Lip Drills*

ameter for the job, but to also choose the correct size with the number of flutes most efficient for the milling operations performed. For Carbide in general, the harder the workpiece, the higher the number of flutes that should be selected; the softer the material, the fewer, but wider flutes that are required for better chip clearance. After each resharpening, the feather edge on the flutes should be removed with a fine-grit hone to avoid chipping.

Turning: Rigidity of the setup and starting the cut at the center line is of the utmost importance. A side rake angle of 15° is desirable, and 35° to 40° for side cutting edge angles distribute the cutting force and improve tool life. For heavy interrupted cuts or forgings, use as large a nose radius as possible.

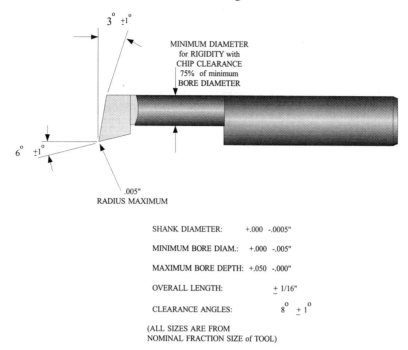

Figure 10.27 *Solid-Carbide CNC Cutting Tools*

For light finishing cuts, grind a 45° land, .010" deep across the nose, of radius .015" to .020". All chip breakers should have a radius equal to the depth at the rear.

Grinding Micrograde Carbide Boring Tools

Use diamond wheels with coolant whenever possible. Hold the tool against the wheel with relatively light pressure and remember to keep the tool in constant motion. Always start with the top face and follow with side-end reliefs, grinding the radius last. By following this sequence, it is possible to obtain a better cutting edge because minute flaking at the cutting edge is avoided. Lightly hone the cutting edge with a hand hone after each grind. Depending on the depth of cut, hone .001 to .003 for light machining cuts and .004 to .006 for heavy machine cuts. Never cool the tool after grinding by quenching in water or oil; let cool naturally.

Brazing: Micrograin carbide, because of its density, should be "sandwich-brazed." This is a procedure that includes the placing of a copper shim between two pieces of silver solder material. This eliminates "stress cracking" due to the coefficient of expansion. See Figures 10.27 and 10.28.

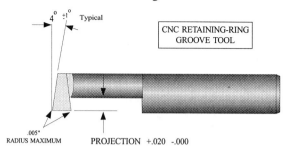

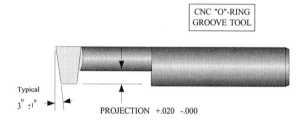

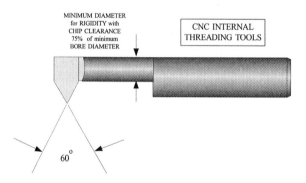

Figure 10.28 *Solid-Carbide CNC Cutting Tools*

Universal Boring-Head Systems

These widely known boring-head systems are readily adapted to many machines. An important feature of these heads is the threaded back, which can be fitted with interchangeable shanks. All universal boring heads have clearly graduated lead screws of heat-treated steel with threads ground from the solid after hardening.

Space is always an important factor in CNC machining, so the overall length of most universal boring heads is held to a minimum. This feature has the

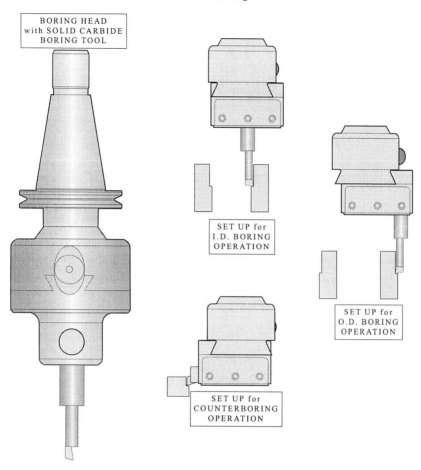

Figure 10.29 *Universal CNC Boring-Head Systems*

additional advantage of contributing to greater tool rigidity that in turn, assures a smoother, more accurately bored hole. The generous bearing surface of these heads makes possible heavy roughing cuts, and more accurate finish cuts. Another important feature is the large adjustment range. This often eliminates offset bars and special setups. Because the graduations are widely spaced and easy to read, adjustments of .0005 and less are easily made. All parts on a quality head (Moore, Criterion, Wahlhauper) that are subject to wear are hardened to guarantee long life and continued accuracy. See Figure 10.29.

To properly operate universal boring heads and adjust for diameter-cutting sizes, a consistent procedure should be followed. The end side-plate screws need to be tightened only enough to hold the bar holder firmly in place. The dial or micrometer screw should be snug but free to turn. The locking, then, is done only with the middle side-plate screw. Once locked securely, no further adjustment should be made with the dial screw. To advance even a ten-thousandth or two, the middle locking-screw should be released and then retightened when the proper position is determined. This practice greatly improves the accuracy attainable and significantly prolongs the life of your boring head.

In Milling or Jig-Boring operations, when precision holes must be located to extreme exactness, the boring head is used in the conventional way. The shank or adaptor is inserted into the machine spindle and the necessary adjustments are made. Then, the stationary work is bored by a consistent down-feed rate. With specially ground boring tools, other operations may now be performed with no further setting change necessary.

The universal boring head can also be of extreme importance when very close diameters are to be held on turret lathes. Here, the boring head can be used as a turning-toolholder, with the cutting edge placed on top of the workpiece. In this manner, any small indexing error in the turret will not alter the dimensions of the turned diameter. For general boring in the turret, the same principle applies. Also, placing the cutting edge at the top of the bore brings the added advantage of allowing greater chip freedom. See Figure 10.30.

USING BORING HEAD
in CNC TURNING TURRET
to CUT DIAMETERS with
CLOSE TOLERANCES

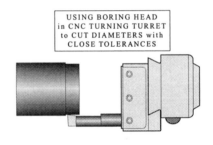

GRINDING PERIPHERAL
CLEARANCE SURFACE
on BORING TOOL
in BORING HEAD

DRESSED
GRINDING
WHEEL

Figure 10.30 *Uses of CNC Universal Boring Head*

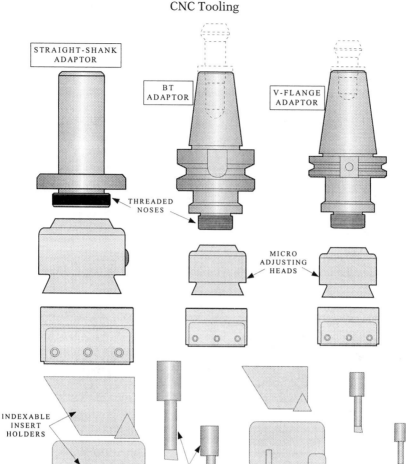

Figure 10.31 *Versatility of Universal Boring Systems*

The use of the universal boring-head system of rotating adjustable boring bars is a practical approach to the field of precision boring. With the use of accessories available with these bars, holes ranging from 1/8" to 5-1/8" diameter can be bored easily. The basic system consists of Insert Holders, Bodies, Dial Screws, Intermediate Adapters, Shanks, Boring Bar Holders, Slotted Toolholders, and Fly Cutters. See Figures 10.31, 10.32, and 10.33.

CNC TAPPING

A very important factor in CNC Tapping is the selection of the proper drill size. Decreasing the thread engagement decreases the torque necessary to drive the

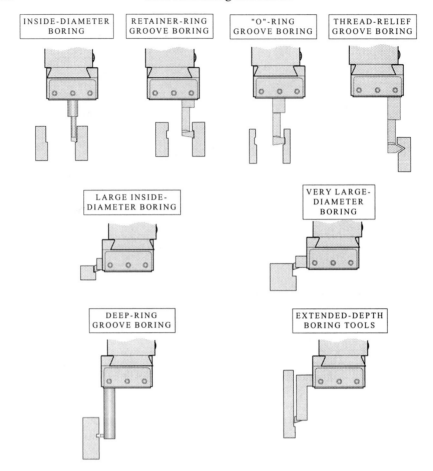

Figure 10.32 *Application to Special CNC Operations*

tap and markedly decreases tap breakage. A thread engagement of 55–60% is recommended. A four-flute tap, where possible, is preferred to a three-flute tap, as it has opposing cutting edges. A minimum lead on all taps of four or five threads is advisable with a rake angle of from 10–15°. As opposed to a simple semicircular cross-section, the flutes are shaped to have a positive rake at the cutting edges to ensure smooth chip flow. This feature is particularly necessary on holes of .2 " (5 mm) in diameter or less. For these smaller-sized taps, additional torsional strength may be obtained by using a three-flute tap. Taps should be adequately backed off, because most of the trouble encountered in CNC machine tapping is in the backing-out process.

It is necessary to keep taps sharp. Because heat-resistant alloys are not good bearing metals against themselves and rough threads are conducive to seizing, threads must be accurately cut and have a smooth finish. Inaccurate and rough

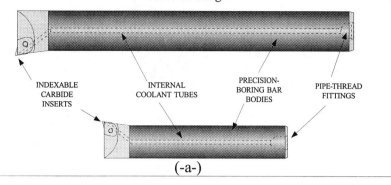

INDEXABLE
CARBIDE
INSERTS

INTERNAL
COOLANT TUBES

PRECISION-
BORING BAR
BODIES

PIPE-THREAD
FITTINGS

(-a-)

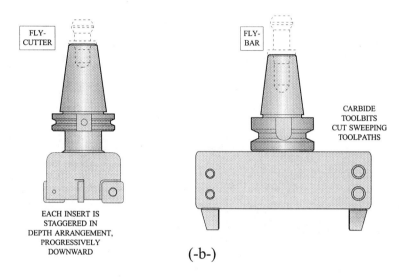

FLY-
CUTTER

FLY-
BAR

CARBIDE
TOOLBITS
CUT SWEEPING
TOOLPATHS

EACH INSERT IS
STAGGERED IN
DEPTH ARRANGEMENT,
PROGRESSIVELY
DOWNWARD

(-b-)

Figure 10.33 *(a) CNC Coolant-Fed Boring Bars and (b) CNC Flycutters and Flybars*

threads prevent a thread gage from fitting properly and cause the parts to fail inspection.

Standard high-speed steel taps with ground and nitrited threads and three or four 7° spiral flutes, or spiral pointed plug taps, are suggested for CNC machine tapping. The drive should be through a clutch mechanism to prevent overload. Tapping speeds should be adjusted according to materials. (See Chapter 9 for full Tapping Chart of speeds and feeds.) Super-alloys like Inconel alloy MA6000 should be machine tapped in the range of 5–10 feet per minute. Inconel may be best threaded with a series of standard taps modified in diameter so that each successive tap increases the thread diameter proportionately. Ample lubricant is essential for CNC Tapping. See Figure 10.34.

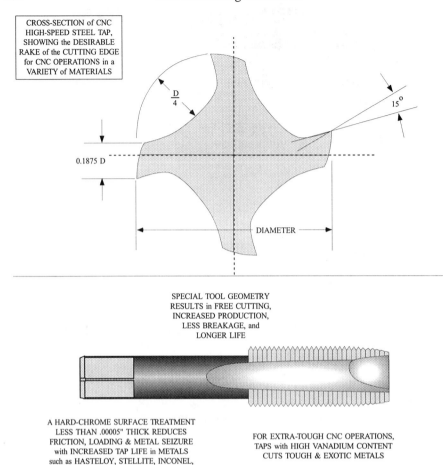

CROSS-SECTION of CNC HIGH-SPEED STEEL TAP, SHOWING the DESIRABLE RAKE of the CUTTING EDGE for CNC OPERATIONS in a VARIETY of MATERIALS

$\frac{D}{4}$

15°

0.1875 D

DIAMETER

SPECIAL TOOL GEOMETRY RESULTS in FREE CUTTING, INCREASED PRODUCTION, LESS BREAKAGE, and LONGER LIFE

A HARD-CHROME SURFACE TREATMENT LESS THAN .00005" THICK REDUCES FRICTION, LOADING & METAL SEIZURE with INCREASED TAP LIFE in METALS such as HASTELOY, STELLITE, INCONEL, WASPALOY, etc.

FOR EXTRA-TOUGH CNC OPERATIONS, TAPS with HIGH VANADIUM CONTENT CUTS TOUGH & EXOTIC METALS

Figure 10.34   *CNC Taps*

CNC ANGLE MILLING HEADS

Angle Milling Heads allow the conversion of axis orientation without tilting the major axes of the Machining or Turning Center. The heads also enable machines to attain an axis orientation not normally possible on 3-axis Machining or Turning Centers.

Also, Angle Milling Heads can be set up to reach deep into cavities and recesses, providing stable, rigid machining capabilities where normally they would not exist. See Figure 10.35.

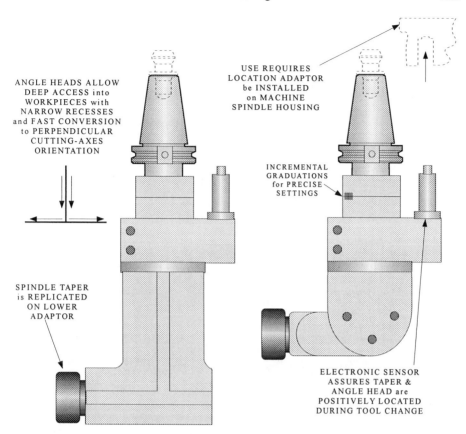

ANGLE HEADS ALLOW
DEEP ACCESS into
WORKPIECES with
NARROW RECESSES
and FAST CONVERSION
to PERPENDICULAR
CUTTING-AXES
ORIENTATION

USE REQUIRES
LOCATION ADAPTOR
be INSTALLED
on MACHINE
SPINDLE HOUSING

INCREMENTAL
GRADUATIONS
for PRECISE
SETTINGS

SPINDLE TAPER
is REPLICATED
ON LOWER
ADAPTOR

ELECTRONIC SENSOR
ASSURES TAPER &
ANGLE HEAD are
POSITIVELY LOCATED
DURING TOOL CHANGE

Figure 10.35 *CNC Angle-Milling Heads*

CNC TOOLING for TURNING CENTERS

Three-Jaw Universal CNC Chucks

The three-jaw universal scroll chuck is a self-centering chuck, that is, all three jaws move in toward the center at the same time. There are many CNC designs on the market: Air, Electric, and Mechanically activated, some being more effective in certain areas than others. Air-actuated chucks are fast, and variable clamping pressure makes them adjustable. For safety, these should have independent air supplies.

All internal components are very similar; one adjusting screw operates a scroll plate to move all jaws at the same time. In addition, each jaw has its own adjusting screw so that each jaw can be fine-adjusted individually.

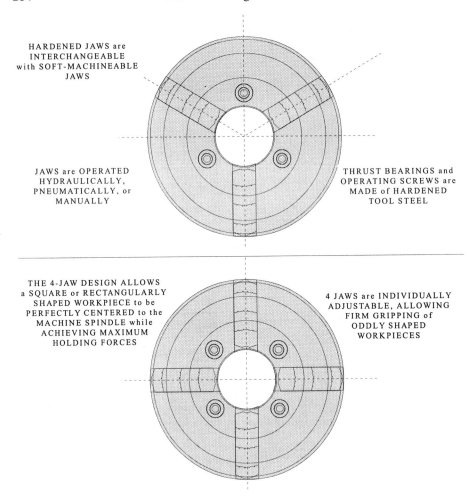

HARDENED JAWS are
INTERCHANGEABLE
with SOFT-MACHINEABLE
JAWS

JAWS are OPERATED
HYDRAULICALLY,
PNEUMATICALLY, or
MANUALLY

THRUST BEARINGS and
OPERATING SCREWS are
MADE of HARDENED
TOOL STEEL

THE 4-JAW DESIGN ALLOWS
a SQUARE or RECTANGULARLY
SHAPED WORKPIECE to be
PERFECTLY CENTERED to the
MACHINE SPINDLE while
ACHIEVING MAXIMUM
HOLDING FORCES

4 JAWS are INDIVIDUALLY
ADJUSTABLE, ALLOWING
FIRM GRIPPING of
ODDLY SHAPED
WORKPIECES

Figure 10.36 *Three-and Four-Jaw Universal CNC Chucks*

Four-Jaw Universal CNC Chucks

The four-jaw CNC chuck is the most versatile chuck for the general clamping of a wide variety of shapes and workpiece configurations. The four-jaw design allows square, rectangular, or odd-shaped workpieces to be precisely centered to the machine's spindle or C-Axis while maintaining maximum holding force. The individual adjustability of each jaw enables a stable, rigid nest or fixture to be created for a workpiece. In addition, each jaw has individual clamping locks to be applied after clamping actions are made. See Figure 10.36.

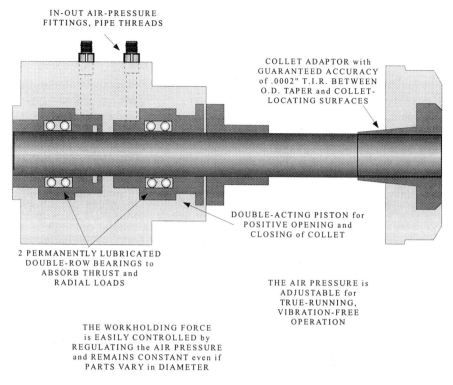

Figure 10.37 *Pneumatic Collet Systems for CNC Turning Centers*

Air-Operated Collet Systems for CNC

Air-operated collet systems for CNC turning machines are fast-actuating workholding systems that require minimum machine or operator involvement (CNC controlled), and result in high-production work output. The workholding force is easily controlled by regulating the air pressure and remains constant even if pieces vary in diameter. The air cylinder is adjustable for true-running, vibration-free operation. See Figure 10.37.

Dead-Length Collet Chucks for CNC Turning Machines

Dead-Length Collet Chucks have tremendous advantages for CNC Turning operations. The machining of the overall lengths of workpieces held in collets can be difficult without this system. Dead-Length collets make it easy to hold length tolerances by using an inner sleeve that pushes to compress the collet. The collet remains stationary so that there is no part retraction due to collet drawback. The maximum closing sleeve runout relative to the

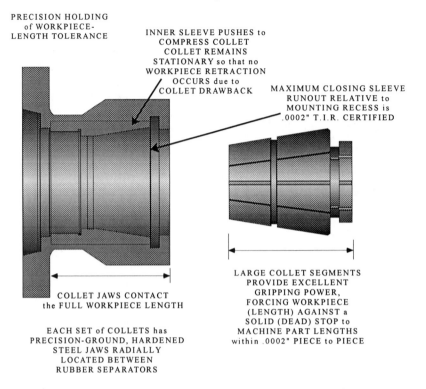

PRECISION HOLDING
of WORKPIECE-
LENGTH TOLERANCE

INNER SLEEVE PUSHES to
COMPRESS COLLET
COLLET REMAINS
STATIONARY so that no
WORKPIECE RETRACTION
OCCURS due to
COLLET DRAWBACK

MAXIMUM CLOSING SLEEVE
RUNOUT RELATIVE to
MOUNTING RECESS is
.0002" T.I.R. CERTIFIED

COLLET JAWS CONTACT
the FULL WORKPIECE LENGTH

EACH SET of COLLETS has
PRECISION-GROUND, HARDENED
STEEL JAWS RADIALLY
LOCATED BETWEEN
RUBBER SEPARATORS

LARGE COLLET SEGMENTS
PROVIDE EXCELLENT
GRIPPING POWER,
FORCING WORKPIECE
(LENGTH) AGAINST a
SOLID (DEAD) STOP to
MACHINE PART LENGTHS
within .0002" PIECE to PIECE

Figure 10.38 *Dead-Length Collet Chucks for CNC Turning Machines*

mounting recess is .0003". Every assembly is inspected and certified to these close tolerances.

Each collet in the system is a set of precision-ground, hardened-steel jaws radially located between synthetic rubber separators. The hardened-steel jaws contact the workpiece over the full length of the collet. This means that oversize or undersize stock (hot-rolled or centerless ground) is gripped over the entire jaw length. The rubber segments provide a seal to help prevent chips and cutting fluid from entering the spindle. The large segments give good gripping power and prevent the jaws from twisting under heavy cutting loads. See Figure 10.38.

CENTERS

All CNC Turning centers require Precision Live Centers as an essential tooling component. Many jobs require Centers be used for specific operations. The necessary features needed when selecting Live Centers are Three-Bearing construction; Accuracy of .0001" T.I.R.; Radial front bearing and Angular bearing

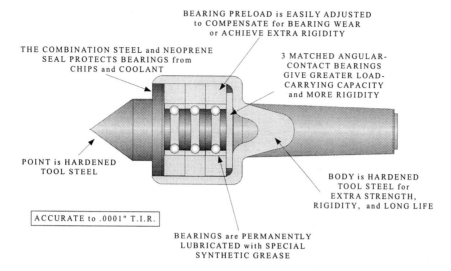

BEARING PRELOAD is EASILY ADJUSTED
to COMPENSATE for BEARING WEAR
or ACHIEVE EXTRA RIGIDITY

THE COMBINATION STEEL and NEOPRENE
SEAL PROTECTS BEARINGS from
CHIPS and COOLANT

3 MATCHED ANGULAR-
CONTACT BEARINGS
GIVE GREATER LOAD-
CARRYING CAPACITY
and MORE RIGIDITY

POINT is HARDENED
TOOL STEEL

BODY is HARDENED
TOOL STEEL for
EXTRA STRENGTH,
RIGIDITY, and LONG LIFE

ACCURATE to .0001" T.I.R.

BEARINGS are PERMANENTLY
LUBRICATED with SPECIAL
SYNTHETIC GREASE

Figure 10.39 *Live Centers for CNC Turning*

in the rear for thrust loads; Chip and coolant slinger on the Point to protect the bearings; hardened tool steel Point; bearings permanently lubricated with special synthetic grease; and a design intended for continuous duty and heavy loads. See Figure 10.39.

FIXTURES

Modular Tooling for Tables and Pallets

Turning centers have adapted Modular Tooling as a method to build workholding fixtures similar to the systems for milling centers. By bolting subplates onto the standard Lathe faceplate, the availability of clamping holes and alignment slots for custom setups is greatly increased.

Modular setup blocks of various sizes are included with modular tooling sets. Hole-pattern spacings match between components, as do with keyway spacing. Each block and plate surface is ground flat and square within .0003" in most sets. This inspected and certified accuracy allows blocks to be indexed, flipped, and clamped on any surface for versatility and adaptability to many setup configurations. See Figure 10.40.

Blocks, Cubes, and 1–2–3's

Turning centers can also use "Cubes," "Blocks," and "1–2–3 Blocks" in setups, especially setups that are built on modular subplates. Similar to inspection components in Inspection Departments, "banking against" surfaces known to

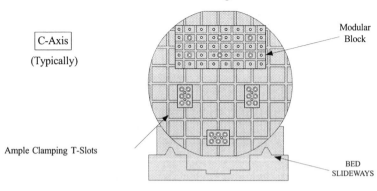

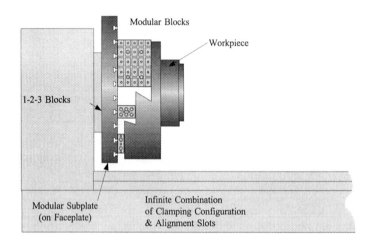

Figure 10.40 *Modular Tooling Applications for CNC Turning Centers*

be flat and perpendicular to the subplate or faceplate surface can assure that the maximum setup preparation is taken for the closest tolerance operations. Certification of squareness over all six sides of cubes can be attained to .000050" over 12" (cubed).

Smaller 1–2–3 Blocks are very handy setup components that are also certified for accuracy. Because these blocks are ground and lapped to nominal inch sizes, specific setup dimensions can be easily achieved. All of these components are complete with tapped holes and clearance holes for stacking and modular fixture "building." Highest priority must be paid, however, to the balancing and counterbalancing of setups on Turning machines where blocks and cubes are added to "spinning configurations." Out-of-balance conditions severe enough to throw machine balancing into a dangerous operating state must be guarded

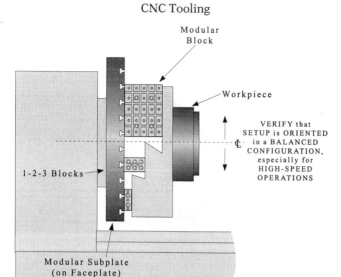

Figure 10.41 *Use of Modular Blocks and Cubes for CNC Turning Centers*

against. If large blocks or cubes are used in a setup, be sure to add counter-weights where they are needed. See Figure 10.41.

CUTTING TOOLS for CNC TURNING

Tool Nomenclature

There are many similarities in nomenclature between high-speed steel (HSS) and carbide tools. The body of the tool that is held in the machine and supports the cutting edge is known as the shank. The cutting material that may be clamped or brazed to the shank is called the insert or tip. CNC Carbide-Tool nomenclature is illustrated in Figure 10.42.

Basic Tool Types

There are two basic tool types used in carbide cutting. They are indexable insert tools and standard brazed tools.

Indexable insert tools are the most economical for practically all types of metal-cutting operations, especially CNC machining operations. The inserts pro-

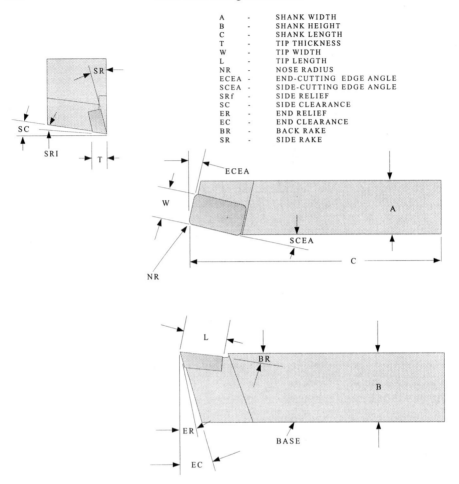

A	-	SHANK WIDTH
B	-	SHANK HEIGHT
C	-	SHANK LENGTH
T	-	TIP THICKNESS
W	-	TIP WIDTH
L	-	TIP LENGTH
NR	-	NOSE RADIUS
ECEA	-	END-CUTTING EDGE ANGLE
SCEA	-	SIDE-CUTTING EDGE ANGLE
SRf	-	SIDE RELIEF
SC	-	SIDE CLEARANCE
ER	-	END RELIEF
EC	-	END CLEARANCE
BR	-	BACK RAKE
SR	-	SIDE RAKE

Figure 10.42 *CNC Turning-Tool Nomenclature*

vide a number of low-cost indexable cutting edges. After all the edges are used, it is more economical for industry in general to replace the insert than it is to pay a machinist to regrind a brazed tool. Various devices are used to lock the insert in position. A cam-type lock pin, a clamp, or a combination of lock pin and clamp are some of the successful devices used.

Most carbide tool companies conform to industry standards in styles and sizes of cutting tools for general types of machining operations. Indexable insert tools use flat, multiple-edge inserts in triangular, square, round, and diamond shapes. Inserts are clamped in heat-treated holders at negative, positive, or neutral rake angles.

Negative rake tools permit inserts to be turned over, thereby doubling the number of cutting points available. Inserts used with positive rake tools are

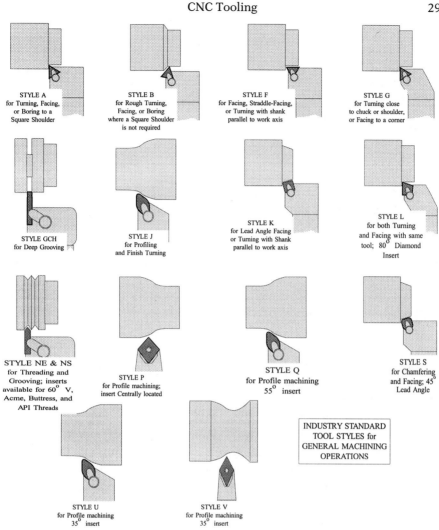

Figure 10.43 *CNC Turning-Tool Styles*

indexable, but cutting edges are provided on one face only. Up to eight new cutting edges are available by loosening the clamp and rotating the insert, or by turning it over. Insert seats or shims provide hard, flat, backup surfaces for the insert to sit on. Shims also provide positive protection to the holder.

Effective chip control is provided by solid carbide, chip-breaker plates that have exceptional strength and resistance to material "pickup." Some inserts also have preformed chip grooves that provide constant chip control over a wide range of feeds.

Use negative rake tools for general-purpose machining of most materials, especially for rough or interrupted cuts. They are also used for hard materials on rigid setups.

Use positive rake tools for machining softer steels and nonferrous metals; for gummy, work-hardening alloys; for thin parts or thin-wall tubing that will not stand high cutting forces; and on low-powered machines or setups that lack rigidity. See Figure 10.43.

Toolholder Selection

In selecting toolholders and inserts, the following suggestions are common for carbide cutting. Determine the proper tool style for the work. Select an insert with adequate cutting-edge length. Choose the largest shank possible.

When selecting inserts for CNC machining, whether utility or precision, keep the following in mind: Utility inserts have both top and bottom ground for rough machining. Precision inserts have all surfaces ground for general rough and finish machining. Inserts with preformed chip-control grooves can be used for general rough and finish turning, particularly for ductile materials.

The following cutting tool shapes are available:

- Square inserts have a strong structural shape (90° point angle). They are used in lead and chamfering tools.
- Triangular inserts (60° point angle) are used for cutting to a square shoulder, for profiling, for chamfering, or plunge turning.
- Round inserts produce shallow feed marks using high feedrates on finishing passes. They are particularly well suited for cutting cast iron because they decrease the incidence of edge breakout.
- Diamond inserts (80° nose angle) are used for combination turning and facing tools.
- Inserts with a 55° nose angle are used for profiling tools.

Toolholder Identification System

The identification systems shown in Figures 10.44 and 10.45 have been developed by the American Standards Association and are generally adopted by the carbide tool industry. These charts make identification of toolholders and inserts fast and accurate.

GRADES of CARBIDE INSERTS

Different grades of carbide inserts are available, corresponding to the machining conditions of the work. In the industry-standard Kennametal system, three general-purpose grades can machine about 90% of the CNC Machining work in most shops. See Figures 10.46(a) and 10.46(b).

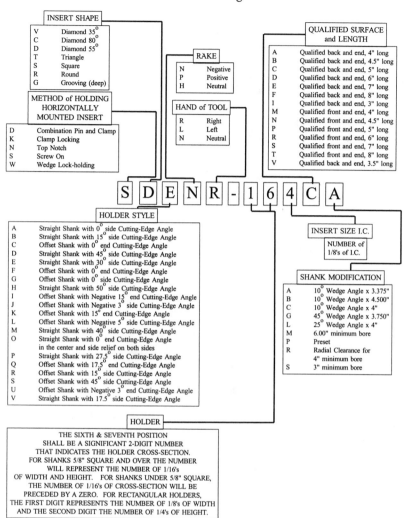

Figure 10.44 *CNC Toolholder Identification System*

CNC MACHINING TIPS WHEN USING CARBIDE INSERTS

- Tools must be kept sharp at all times.
- Tools should be lightly honed.
- Tool overhang should be kept to a minimum.
- Avoid excessive tool wear to minimize cutting forces.
- Use positive rake tools whenever possible.
- Use negative rake tools only where necessary and when surface speeds can be kept in the higher ranges.

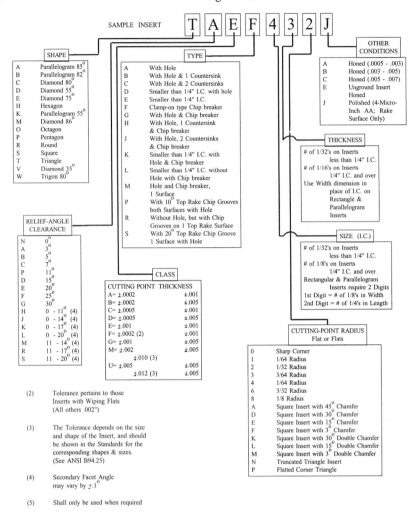

Figure 10.45 *CNC Insert Identification System*

- Machine tools must be kept rigid.
- Workpiece must be well clamped and well supported to avoid flexing.
- Depth of cut should be deep enough to avoid glazing.
- Feed should be positive to avoid dwelling and work-hardening.
- Minimum chip discoloration is desirable. See Figure 10.47.

COMPLETE CNC TOOLHOLDING SYSTEMS

Many new multiaxis Turning centers that have milling capabilities are fitted with complete CNC Tooling Systems to accommodate a full range of turning

CNC INSERT GRADES and corresponding MACHINING APPLICATIONS

COATED CARBIDE GRADES	TYPICAL MACHINING OPERATIONS	COATING TYPE
KC950	Productive over a wide range, from Medium Roughing to Finishing Cast Irons, High-temperature Alloys, and Stainless, Low-Carbon and Alloy Steels. Can handle up to 50 to 60% of a typical manufacturer's machining operations. Designed with strength to withstand Interrupted Cuts at Ceramic-coated Insert Speeds.	Multilayered Titanium Nitride, Aluminum Oxide, Titanium Carbide
KC910	High-speed Finishing to Light Roughing applications. May be used in machining Carbon or Alloy Steels, Cast Irons, some High-Temperature Alloys, and Stainless Steels. Maximum edge wear and heat resistance for very Abrasive or Hot Machining cuts.	Aluminum Oxide Coated
KC850	Finishing to Heavy Roughing applications ideally suited to conditions that demand Maximum Edge Strength and Wear Resistance. May be used in machining Carbon or Alloy Steels, most Cast Irons, and High-temperature and Stainless Steel Alloys. Superior Thermal and Mechanical Shock resistance make this an excellent Heavy Roughing grade for milling and turning of all types of steel.	Multiphase TiN coated
KC810	General-purpose grade for Finishing to Roughing applications in Steels, Cast Irons, and Stainless Steel Alloys at conventional coated carbide speeds.	Multiphase TiN coated
KC250	Semifinishing to Heavy Roughing applications in Cast Irons and Stainless Steel Alloys. Ideally suited to conditions that demand High Edge Strength and Wear Resistance such as roughing cuts on Stainless Steel Castings. Also suitable for machining some High-Temperature Alloys and Steels at moderate speeds. Superior Mechanical Shock Resistance.	Multiphase TiN coated
KC210	Finishing to Light Roughing applications on Cast Irons, Stainless Steel Alloys, High-Temperature Alloys, and Heat-Treated Steels. Excellent Wear in very Abrasive cuts.	Multiphase TiN coated

UNCOATED	HARDNESS HRA	TYPICAL MACHINING APPLICATIONS
K7H	93.5	Precision Finishing of Steels and Alloyed Cast Irons at high speeds & low to moderate chip loads. Frequently applied in Single-point Threading of Steels heat treated to a high hardness.
K45	92.5	May be used in Finishing and light Roughing of all Steels. Excellent Crater, Edge Wear, and Thermal Shock Resistance. Frequently used in Grooving where maximum Edge Wear Resistance is required.
K4H	92.0	Excellent Threading and Form Tool grade for Steels and Cast Irons. May also be used for semifinishing to light roughing of Steels and Cast Irons at moderate speeds and chip loads.
K2884	92.0	General-purpose Steel Milling grade that may be used in moderate to heavy chip loads. Excellent Edge Wear and Mechanical Shock Resistance.
K420	91.3	Heavy to moderate Steel Machining grade. Superior Edge Strength and Thermal Shock Resistance. Used in Steel Milling or Turning through severe Interruptions at high chip loads.
K21	91.0	For light to heavy roughing of Steels at moderate speeds and chip loads. Excellent Mechanical and Thermal Shock Resistance.
K11	93.0	Primarily used for the precision finishing of Cast Irons, Nonferrous Alloys, Nonmetals at high speeds, and light chip loads. K11 may also be used in finishing Hard Steels at moderate speeds and light chip loads. Excellent Edge Wear Resistance.
K68	92.5	General-purpose Turning, Milling, and Threading grade for light roughing to Finishing of Cast Irons, Nonferrous Alloys, and Nonmetals at moderate to high speeds and light chip loads. Excellent Edge Wear Resistance for machining all Nonferrous Alloys and most High-Temperature Alloys.
K6	92.0	Moderate Roughing grade for Cast Irons, Nonferrous Alloys, Nonmetals, and most High-Temperature Alloys. High Edge Strength and good Edge Wear Resistance.
K8735	92.0	Excellent Milling and Broaching grade for Gray, Malleable, & Nodular Cast Irons at high speeds and light chip loads. Also superior resistance to edge buildup when machining all Stainless Steels and Aluminum Alloys.
K1	90.0	Excellent Mechanical Shock Resistance for Roughing with Heavy Interruptions, machining Stainless Steels, most High-temperature Alloys, Cast Irons, and cast Nonferrous Alloys. Machining speeds will be low to moderate in most applications.

Figure 10.46(a)   *CNC Insert Machining Applications*

KYON & CERAMIC Grades	HARDNESS HRA	TYPICAL MACHINING APPLICATIONS
KYON 2000		A new cutting material designed for High-Velocity machining of Cast Irons & Nickel-based Alloys with heavier chip loads than solid ceramics or ceramic-coated carbides. Offers excellent Thermal Shock & Impact Resistance for use with coolants and milling applications.
K090	94 - 94.5	A black, hot-pressed ceramic for machining Cast Irons over 235 Bhn and to 66 HRC, also for steels over 34 HRC to 66 HRC. Excellent Edge Wear Resistance and Hot Hardness for machining most high-temperature Alloys.
K060	93 - 94	A white, cold-pressed ceramic for machining Cast Irons below 235 Bhn and Steels under 34 HRC. Superior Edge Wear Resistance in machining most Cast Irons below 235 Bhn.

MACHINING RECOMMENDATIONS for HIGH-TEMPERATURE ALLOYS

IRON-BASED ALLOYS	ROUGHING	GENERAL	FINISHING
SPEED FEED DEPTH of CUT GRADE	30-100 ft/min. (9-30 m/min.) .010-.040 in. (.25-1.00 mm.) .125-.375 in. (3.0-9.5 mm.) K21-K42	50-125 ft/min. (15-38 m/min.) .008-.020 in. (.20-.50 mm.) .0625-.250 in. (1.5-6.5 mm.) K42-K6	75-200 ft/min. (23-60 m/min.) .003-.010 in. (.08-.25 mm.) .031-.093 in. (.8-2.4 mm.) K68-K8
NICKEL-BASED ALLOYS	ROUGHING	GENERAL	FINISHING
SPEED FEED DEPTH of CUT GRADE	30-90 ft/min. (9-27 m/min) .010-.035 in (.25-.90 mm) .125-.250 in. (3.0-6.5 mm) K21-K42	50-100 ft/min. (15-30 m/min) .008-.020 in. (.20-.50 mm) .0625-.1875 in (1.5-4.8 mm) K42-K6	70-175 ft/min. (21-53 m/min.) .003-.010 in. (.08-2.4 mm.) .031-.093 in. (.8-2.4 mm.) K68-K8
COBALT-BASED ALLOYS	ROUGHING	GENERAL	FINISHING
SPEED FEED DEPTH of CUT GRADE	25-75 ft/min. (8-23 m/min.) .010-.030 in. (.25-.75 mm.) .0625-.1875 in. (1.5-4.8 mm.) K21-K42	40-90 ft/min. (12-27 m/min.) .008-.020 in. (.8-3.0 mm.) .031-.125 in. (.8-3.0 mm.) K42-K45	60-125 ft/min. (18-38 m/min.) .003-.01 in. (.08-2.4 mm.) .031-.093 in. (.8-2.4 mm.) K45-K68

Figure 10.46(b)   *CNC Insert Machining Applications*

tools and standard milling cutters as well. Drills and Endmills can be held securely in solid holders for nominal sizes and collet systems for off-nominal sizes. Multiblock Holders can be bolted directly onto the turret stations with the versatility built in to quick-change tool blocks. See Figure 10.48.

CNC TOOLING for GRINDING

Workholding

Much of the workholding Tooling used on Turning machines is identical to Tooling for CNC Grinding machines: Live Centers, Face Plates, 3- and 4-Jaw Chucks, and Collet Systems. Some areas do vary dramatically from turning tooling. Workholding Chucks are one type of tooling that is unique to CNC Grinding systems.

Magnetic Chucks

Permanent-Magnet Chucks are ideal for metallic workpieces with ferrous content that require flatness operations to be performed. Their ability to be

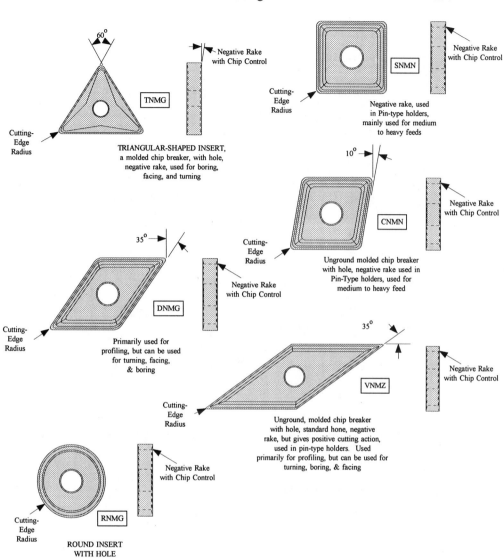

Figure 10.47 *CNC Insert Shapes and Applications*

flat-ground in place, with a fine finish, enables the full accuracy to be attained from precision-grinding machines.

Permanent-Magnet Chucks come in several different types. The standard Loop-Pole Chuck contains four to eight oblong loop magnets spaced symmetrically across the chuck face. The Radial-Pole Chuck arranges magnets in a radial pattern with a central intersection. The Micropitch Pole Chuck typically arranges linear bands with fine spacing across four to six circular bands. The resulting micropitch leaves little surface area unmagnetized.

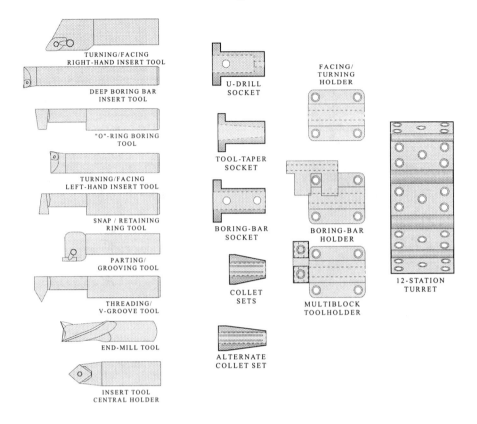

Figure 10.48 *Versatile CNC Tooling System for Turning Centers*

Air-Diaphragm Chucks

Precision Air-Diaphragm Chucks use a flat surface mounted on the responsive plate of an air diaphragm. On the flat surface, three or four soft jaws are flush-mounted. Nests can be precision-ground to hold delicate or nonferrous work-pieces with very little part distortion. See Figure 10.49.

CNC Grinding Dressers: Diamonds

Standard wheel-dressing diamonds come in a variety of sizes. Typically available and the most commonly used for CNC Grinding machines are the Single-Point Standard Diamond Dresser. For common radii, the Coned Radius Dresser is typically used, coming in a full range of angular selections. Thread-Grinding Diamond Tools normally are supplied in 60° and 38° configurations.

Toolroom Diamond Grinding-Wheel Dressers commonly are available in three types: Norton, Cincinnati, and Landis. See Figure 10.50.

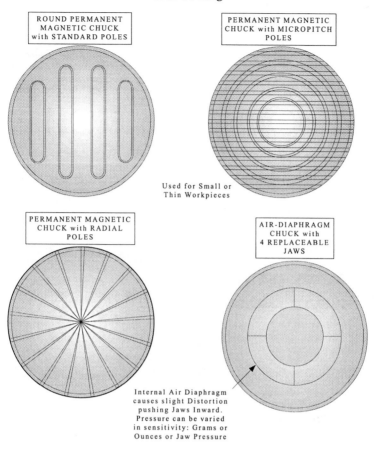

Figure 10.49 *Workholding Chucks for CNC Grinding*

CNC Grinding Wheels

Precision CNC Grinding includes such operations as cylindrical grinding (between centers or centerless), internal grinding, surface grinding, and tool and cutter grinding. The only differences in these are in the methods for grinding and tooling specialized for each type of machine.

A basic relationship exists between the different grades of grinding wheels, the grits, and the material they can cut. On hard materials, the increased number of cutting points on the face of a moderately fine-grit wheel will remove stock faster than the fewer cutting points of the coarser wheel. The larger abrasive grains of a coarse wheel cannot penetrate as deeply into the hard material without burning it. On soft, ductile metals, the larger grains of a coarse wheel penetrate easily and provide the necessary chip clearance to minimize wheel loading.

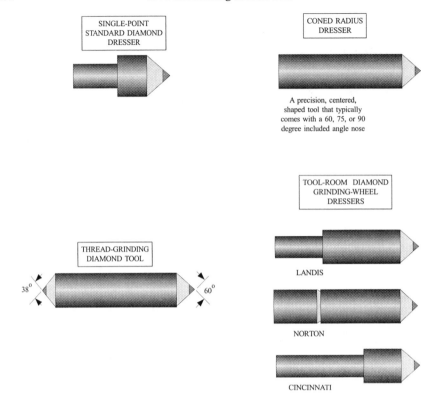

Figure 10.50 *Dressing Diamonds for CNC Grinders*

Abrasive Grits and Grains

On a grinding-wheel surface, the cutting tool is actually the abrasive grit or grains. For CNC Grinding, the essential requirements of the perfect grain are the ones that maintain resistance to point dulling and the ability of the grain to fracture under normal grinding pressures before serious dulling occurs. During a grain fracture, new, sharp cutting points are exposed.

There are two general categories into which abrasive grains fall: natural and manufactured. Emery, sandstone, corundum, quartz, and diamond are all natural grains.

Conventional electric-furnace abrasives or the manufactured abrasives are classified in two categories. The first includes aluminum oxide, aluminum oxide/zirconium alloy, and silicone carbide. The second includes diamond and cubic boron nitrite. Aluminum oxide is manufactured by alloying aluminum oxide and zirconium oxide. Silicon carbide is produced from silica sand and carbon in the form of coke.

For high-tensile-strength material, carbon and alloy steels, malleable cast

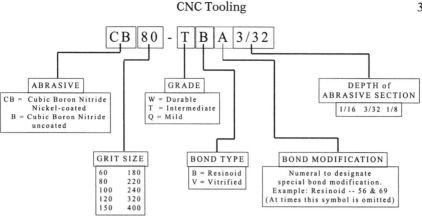

Figure 10.51 *CBN-Wheel Identification System*

iron, and wrought iron, Aluminum oxide wheels are used. Alundum abrasives are widely used for heavy-duty work on a wide range of steels. Zirconia alumina abrasive alloys are very well suited for high-pressure, high-speed grinding of cast and rolled steels.

A black silicon carbide wheel is used for cast iron, brass, soft bronze, aluminum, copper, and nonmetallic materials. A special green-colored silicon carbide wheel is used for sharpening carbide-tipped tools. Silicon carbide is extremely brittle and is used for low-tensile-strength materials.

For grinding cemented tungsten carbide in both wet and dry applications, diamond abrasives, natural or man-made, are used. The type of diamond abrasive selected depends on how much steel is to be ground along with the carbide, or if brazing materials are contacted. Also, whether the grinding operation is wet or dry is another significant factor.

For grinding hard and tough alloy steels and all tool steels of Rockwell C50 hardness or better, cubic boron nitride (CBN), a material manufactured by a process similar to that used to make synthetic diamond abrasive is recommended. See Figure 10.51.

CNC GRINDING-WHEEL COMPONENTS

Regardless of the application, a critical part of any grinding machine is the grinding wheel. The productivity and efficiency of any grinding operation, as with any other machine tool cutter, depend on the selection of the proper wheel for the work at hand. Every grinding wheel has two separate and distinct components, the abrasive grits that do the actual cutting and the bond that supports and hold the grains together.

Grit Specifications

Grits or grains are classified by their individual measurements, as small gems would be. They are sorted according to overall dimensions by using various sizes of screen to sift them and sort them out. The number designating grits size represents the approximate number of openings (per linear inch) in the final screen used to size the grain (e.g., 30 grits size is one in which the grains pass through a screen with 27 openings per linear inch and are held on a screen with 33 openings per inch). Grit sizes commonly used are 10, 12, 14, 16, 20, 24, 30, 36, 46, 54, 60, 70, 80, 90, 100, 120, 150, 180, and 220. Typically, the most commonly used sizes fall into the rage of 24 to 80 grits. Less-commonly used sizes are 240, 280, 320, 400, 500, and 600 grits. Coarse-grain wheels are sized from 10 to 24; medium-grain wheels range from 30 to 60; fine-grain wheels range from 70 to 180; and very fine-grain wheels range from 220 to 600.

Bond Specifications

The abrasive grits are held together by a material called a bond. The basic types of bond are Vitrified, Resinoid, Rubber, Shellac, and Metal. Seven of ten CNC Grinding wheels used are manufactured using a Vitrified bond. Vitrified Bond is an extremely hard, glasslike bond that is not affected by water, acid, oils, or ordinary temperature variations.

For high-speed wheels in foundries and for grinding wheels used in cutoff and thread-grinding operations, a Resinoid bond is used. For common center-less-feed wheels, precision ball-race grinding wheels, portable grinders where finish is important (stainless welds), and cutoff wheels of less than 1/32" thick, a Rubber bond is used. For producing high finishes on cam shafts and on steel and large mill rolls, centerless-ground, a Shellac bond is very well suited.

A Metal bond is used on diamond wheels for grinding carbides. The toughness and high strength of the Metal bond helps retain costly diamond abrasives firmly throughout their entire useful life. Diamond wheels for grinding carbides use Metal bonds. They are also used either with diamond or aluminum-oxide abrasive. Metal bonds are used for electrical discharge grinding and electro-chemical grinding when an electrically conductive wheel is needed.

Grades of CNC Grinding Wheels

The strength (relative holding power) of the bond that holds the abrasive grains in place is indicated by the Wheel Grade. Normally, it is the amount of bond that determines the hardness with any given bond. To grade the wheels, letters of the alphabet are used, "A" being the softest wheel and "Z" the hardest. The "pores," or open spaces, between the grains are necessary for chip clearance or residual chip storage, application of coolant, and heat dissipation.

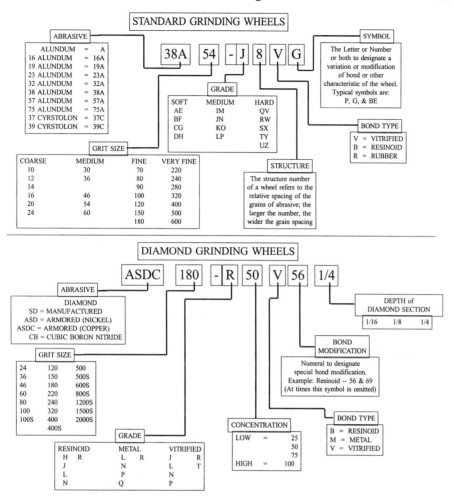

Figure 10.52 *CNC Grinding-Wheel Identification System*

Grinding-Wheel Structure

The relative spacing of the abrasive grains in the wheel is indicated by the Wheel Structure. Despite the fact that structure numbers are not always shown in the standard marking system, the scale used is 0, 1, 2, 3, 4, 5, 6, 7, 8, 9, 10, 11, 12, with 0 the denser structure and 12 the more open structure. See Figure 10.52.

Factors in the Selection of a CNC Grinding Wheel

• The hardness of the material to be ground affects the selection of the abrasive, the grit size, and the grade of the wheel. For steel and steel alloys, and silicon carbide for cast iron, nonferrous materials, and nonmetallic materials, the abrasive should be aluminum oxide. For hard, brittle materials, a fine grit should be selected; for soft ductile materials, a coarse grit. For soft materials, a hard grade of wheel should be used; for hard materials, a soft grade.

- The selection of grit size and the type of bond is determined by the amount of stock to be removed and the finish required. For rapid stock removal and for rough grinding, a coarse grit size should be selected. A fine grit size produces a high finish. A vitrified bond should be chosen for fast cutting. For the highest finish, choose a resinoid, rubber, or shellac bond.
- The selection of grade or hardness of a wheel is affected by whether the operation is wet or dry. Wet grinding typically allows the use of wheels one grade harder than for dry grinding, without the danger of burning the work.
- Remember that the actual surface speed of a grinding wheel is determined by its diameter. Larger wheels running at the same RPMs as smaller worn wheels have a much higher surface feet per minute (SFM) rate. And the speed of the wheel determines the bond chosen. Standard vitrified wheels can be used with speeds up to (but not over) 66,000 SFM (1950 m/min.). Resinoid, rubber, and shellac bonds can be used for most applications in the range of 6500 to 16,000 SFM (1950 to 4800 m/min.). Wheel-speed ratings should never be exceeded.
- The actual area of grinding contact (the area of the wheel in contact with the work) determines grade and grit size. For a large area of contact, a coarse grit is well suited. A fine grit is best for a smaller area of contact. If there is a very small area of contact, a harder grade of the wheel should be used.
- For grinding steel and steel alloys under severe conditions, a tough abrasive like 76A or ZS should be chosen. For grinding all kinds of tool steels, including tough Vanadium alloy steels, a milder abrasive like 32A or 38A is excellent. For work of average severity, medium abrasives such as 23A or 57A are well suited.

Variable Conditions

When CNC Grinding workpieces that include very close tolerances on particular dimensions, special considerations should be made. If an extremely accurate ground finish is required, particularly if the material is of hard temper, the workpiece should be removed from the grinding setup after the next-to-last cut or grind. If at all possible, set the parts aside for a full day or two. This heat-treatment relief period gives sufficient time for the workpieces to adjust to any residual stresses present, possibly resulting in a slight distortion. After flexing has taken place, close-tolerance dimensions may be then finish-ground without danger of further distortion.

To produce a moderate rate of metal removal, CNC wheels should be of a soft grade. Abrasive grains are quite likely to be embedded in the material surfaces if Hard wheels are used. Ironically, the severity of CNC Grinding conditions plays an important role through the laws of physics and their application to friction-based operations. Grinding conditions should be sufficiently severe to set in motion a continual breakdown action. If possible, a stream of soluble grinding lubricant should always flow onto the metal being ground. The oil produces a better finish, keeps the wheel from loading, significantly reduces the wheel-dressing time intervals, and allows grinding to closer dimensional limits. A good grinding oil is the best lubricant for thread and plunge/crush grinding. As a general guide, surface speeds of 80–100 feet per second (25–30 m/s) are acceptable with grit density varying from 36 to 80 and grades between "I" and "Q." For information on very specific applications, the wheel manufacturer should be consulted (because of the many variables encountered in CNC Grinding).

To produce external threads, Plunge Form Grinding is normally used. An ideal grinding wheel to use is an aluminum-oxide (150-320 grit) vitrified-bonded grinding wheel (medium hard, open structure); a high grade, filtered grinding oil extends time between wheel dressing.

For operations requiring CNC Honing, using an aluminum-oxide or silicon-carbide vitrified-bonded stone of medium to soft grade has proven very successful. Speeds should be targeted in the range of 130 ft/min. (40m/min.) for roughing to 200 ft/min. (60 m/min.) for finishing with rotating hones, and 40 to 60 ft/min. (12–18 m/min.) with reciprocating hones (all should be under the application of sufficient coolant). See Figures 10.53 and 10.54.

CNC CUTTING OILS
and LUBRICANT COMPOUNDS

To perform seamless operations from workpiece feature to feature, prototype job lots to production runs, CNC Grinders are quickly becoming adapted in workpiece production worldwide. To optimize CNC operation, special cutting oils make it possible to cut metals at a higher rate of speed. Some cutting fluids form a metallic film on the metal surface. This prevents the chip from sticking to the cutting edge, a phenomenon commonly called edge buildup. The surface finish of most metals can be improved considerably by the use of the proper types of cutting fluids. Application of cutting fluids should be directed at the tool surface, if possible, so that the cutting fluid actually works between the chip and the cutting tool face.

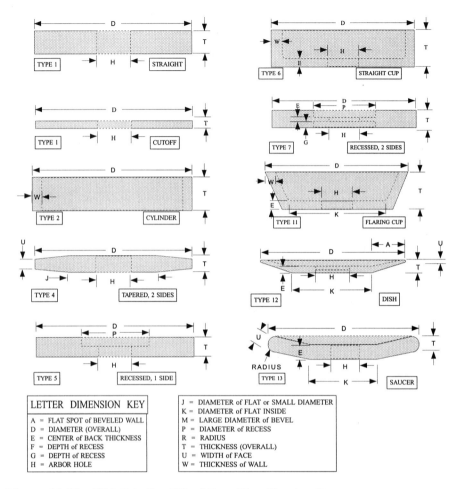

Figure 10.53 *CNC Grinding-Wheel Type Identification System*

Functions of a Cutting Fluid

CNC Grinders, operating at high machining speeds, produce high surface temperatures. A cutting fluid is used to reduce the temperature of a cutting action, to reduce the friction of chips sliding along the tool face, to prevent rust, and to flush away chips. Cutting fluids have antiseizure and antiwelding properties that inhibit the formation of edge buildup and other adhesions. Cutting fluids also have the ability to resist foaming, smoking, and misting, and possess hygienic properties (to prevent dermatitis, which is a skin rash). Water is an ideal coolant, but to avoid resting, it is mixed in various proportions with soluble or emulsifying oils, sometimes called aqueous cutting fluids. All-purpose coolants now on the market are mixed with water. Mixes of 1:5 (1 part oil to

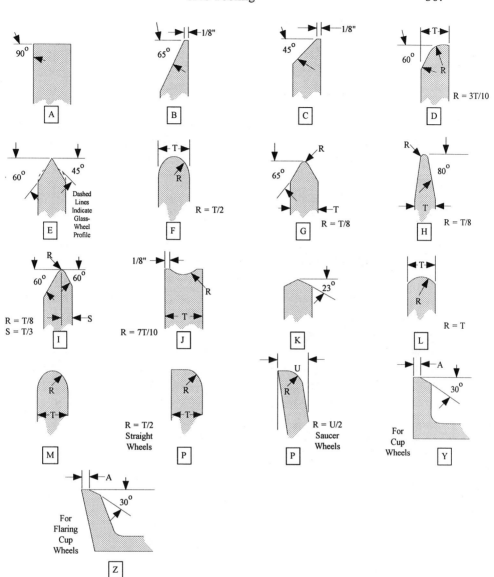

Figure 10.54 *Standard Shapes of CNC Grinding-Wheel Faces*

5 parts water) to 1:100 (1 part oil to 100 parts water) are possible. A 1:5 mix is very effective for drilling, milling, turning, and so on, and a 1:20 mix is very effective for grinding operations.

Soluble oils act mainly as coolants and have some lubricant qualities as well. In order to blend properly, it is important to always add the oil to the water, not the water to the oil. It is also preferable to use warm water above 40°F

(4.4°C), but not boiling. This ensures that proper blending takes place. Proportions of the mix should be determined by testing. To prevent corrosion when a soluble oil is used, there should be sufficient air circulation to evaporate the water from the machined surface, leaving the oil to form a protective coating. If rapid drying is prevented either by lack of air circulation or high humidity, rust is likely to occur. Virtually all types of lubricants or coolants are used in the machining of Aluminum, Magnesium, Stainless Steels, and mechanically alloyed products. In some cases, it is even possible to use no cutting fluid at all. But in most cases, a good cutting oil can increase the machining speed by about 25% over that possible with dry cutting.

Mechanically alloyed products respond well to ordinary sulfurized mineral oil. But because of their greater cooling effect, water-based coolants are preferred for use in high-speed operations such as turning, milling, and grinding. These coolants may be soluble oil or proprietary chemical mixtures.

A soluble oil at a 15:1 dilution or a straight cutting oil of the extreme-pressure (EP), heavy-duty type is suggested. Except for grinding, which depends almost entirely upon cooling and flushing, some chemical activity is desired, even in coolants, and is generally provided by chlorine, amines, or other chemicals.

For slower operations like drilling, boring, tapping and reaming, heavy lubricants and very rich mixtures of chemical coolants are desirable. The use of sulfurized oil may cause discoloration of the workpiece and is not recommended for use in CNC operations with cemented carbide tools because the heat generated at the point of the tool may cause sulfur to attack the binding agent in the carbide.

It is important to remove all lubricants from machined pieces that are subjected to high temperatures either in fabrication or in working service.

CHAPTER 11

CNC OPERATION

For clarity of understanding and for discussion purposes, the CNC Control Console is separated into two distinct panels: the Control panel, which deals specifically with the computerized functions, and the machine panel, which deals directly with machine-tool operational functions.

The Control panel is used to manipulate data through the display screen and is analogous to the keyboard of a personal computer. The machine panel is used to make the operating link to the machine tool. Figures 11.1 and 11.2, respectively, show examples of a Milling-Center Control and a Turning-Center Control.

The Control panel can be used to enter programs directly into the Control's memory or import programs through the communications port. The Control panel can be used to edit, or modify, a program once it is stored in the Control's memory. Tool Offsets are also entered and modified through the Control panel. After the programmer/operator selects the Offset mode, the display screen shows the tables of Offsets. Through the Control panel, the Offsets can be manipulated. The Control panel also accesses all functions of the display screen. Axis position, Control diagnostics and parameters, and other setting data are manipulated through the Control panel.

Machine-panel functions are used when manually jogging the axes of the machine. A joystick or a combination of push buttons can be used to make the desired Axis motion. Most CNC machines have a handwheel on the machine panel that can be used like the handwheels on a manually operated machine tool. The machine panel can be used to manually turn the spindle on and off and manipulate the speed of the spindle. The machine panel also includes many conditional switches that control how the machine functions during automatic operation. Features such as Single Block, Dry Run, and Optional Stop are among those controlled by conditional switches.

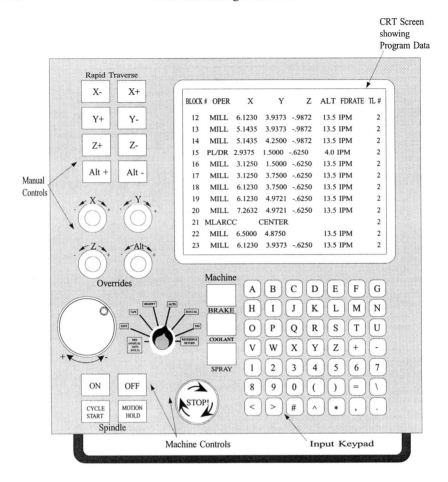

Figure 11.1 *CNC Machining-Center Control*

BUTTONS and SWITCHES
on the CONTROL PANEL

Position Button

The display-screen selector is provided to enable the programmer/operator to view the machine's current position display. The display screen shows pertinent information about where the machine is currently positioned in this mode. CNC Controls typically offer several types of position-display views. The absolute position display shows the current machine position relative to Program Zero. The relative position display allows the programmer/operator to set an Origin at any location and make measurements. The machine position display shows the distance from the machine's reference position to the current

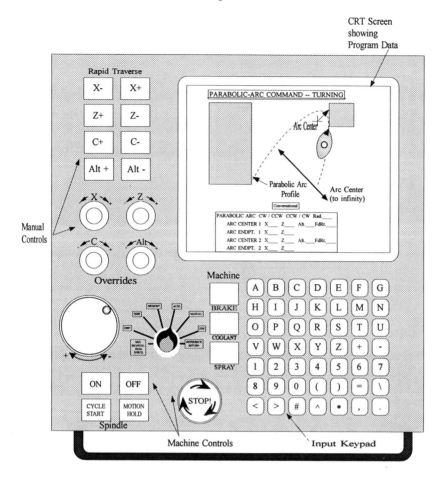

Figure 11.2 *CNC Turning-Center Control*

position. The distance-to-go position display allows the viewer to monitor the amount of movement still needed to complete an executed motion command. Position pages can be found by pressing the position button and page-up and page-down buttons.

Display-Screen Control Keys

To enable the programmer/operator to specify what the display is to show, the Display-Screen Control keys are provided. These keys select the basic modes of the display screen. They allow the programmer/operator to select the function of the display screen to be viewed.

Power Buttons

CNC machines separate the power-up procedure into stages, one for Control power and another for the power to the machine tool itself. The Control panel Power-On button must be pressed first; it powers and activates the Control screen and Control panel. Once the Control power is On, the machine panel Power-On button, usually labeled Machine Power or Machine Ready, can be pressed to complete the Power-Up procedure. To turn Off power to the machine, the steps are reversed. The power is turned Off to the machine tool and then to the Control.

Offset Button

The Offset Button is a display-screen selector button that allows the user to display and manipulate the Tool Offsets. Together with the cursor control buttons, the programmer/operator can use this button to find and change Offsets in memory.

Program Button

The Program Button is a display-screen selector button that allows the operator to monitor the active program in the Control's memory. This key is pressed when editing CNC programs and when monitoring programs in automatic operation.

Setting or Parameter Button

The Setting or Parameter Button is a display-screen selector button that enables the user to display current settings of the CNC Control. Normally, this function is required only when the machine is not reacting properly and is used at the discretion of a service engineer.

Letter Keys

Letter Keys are keypad input keys that allow alphabetical character entry. Various CNC Control panels provide only those alpha keys (N, G, X, and so on) needed for CNC programming on the keyboard. Most others provide the full character set (A through Z). Typically, these keys are positioned in the same order as on a computer keyboard. Some, however, are positioned relative to their order of common usage within a CNC program.

Alarm Button

The Alarm Button is a Control-screen selector button that can be pressed to show the Alarm condition of the Control. CNC machines automatically show the alarm on the Control screen the moment the Alarm condition is activated.

Command Key

The Command Key allows multiple usage of other keys on the Control panel on CNC Controls. This enables the Control to double the number of functions for the keyboard without increasing the number of keys required. The standard function for a key may be the Letter Q, but if the command key is used, the "command function" of the Letter Q may be the operation "Tap." When the Control utilizes the Command Key, normally the noncommanded keys are the ones most often used. That is, the Command Key is needed only for subroutine operations (as an example).

Slash Key

This is a multitasking key. If the Control allows mathematical calculations, this is the Division key. An alternate task for this key is as the Optional Block Skip code key or Scale Proportion key. If the first character of a CNC command is a slash, the Control will look to the position of the Optional Block Skip switch on the machine panel. The Control will ignore the command in which the slash code was included if the switch happens to be On already. The Control will execute the command with the slash code if the switch is Off.

Arithmetic Operator Keys

CNC Controls have the minus sign (–) available to designate a negative Axis position. Here, the minus sign is not actually performing a mathematics operation, however, it is considered an arithmetic operation key. Many CNC Controls allow actual mathematics calculations to be performed from within a program and/or through keyboard entry. The Control panel allows entry of the necessary arithmetic operators. The addition sign (+), the subtraction sign (–), multiplication sign (*), division sign (/), and equal sign (=) are the basic arithmetic operators available on some CNC Controls. Advanced Controls have full scientific-calculator functions internalized.

Number Keys

Number Keys enable numeric entry. CNC Controls have these keys positioned close to the Letter keypad.

Decimal-Point Key

The Decimal-Point Key allows numeric entry with a decimal point. Setting Offsets and entering CNC programs are typical uses of this key.

Input Key

The Input Key is used to enter data. This key is pressed when entering Offsets and Parameter settings.

Cursor Control Keys

The CNC Control display screen sometimes shows a prompt cursor that indicates the current entry position. The highly visible prompt cursor appears as a blinking square or underline character in the entry position. It is at the current position of the cursor that data is entered. The programmer/operator positions the cursor to the desired location to enter data in the correct program areas. The Control panel has at least two keys to accomplish this. These keys allow movement of the cursor forward and backward throughout the entry positions until the correct position is reached.

The cursor is moved when editing a CNC program, executing a CNC program from the beginning of a specific tool, and entering setting data and parameters. The Control manufacturers mark the cursor control keys using varied methods. A common method is to designate one key with an arrow down and the other with an arrow up. When pressed once, the arrow-down key moves the cursor forward one position within the entry data. The arrow-up key moves the cursor backward one position within the entry data. CNC Controls usually give a fast way of moving the cursor over long distances, instead of only one position at a time. One common way is to incorporate a page-up and page-down function. When pressed, the page-down key causes the cursor to jump forward one full page on the display. The page-up key causes the cursor to jump backward one full page on the display. These functions are basically hybrids of text-handling capabilities that word processors incorporate.

Program Editing Keys

Often a program that is stored in the Control's memory must be changed or modified. Especially during a program's verification, the operator will be required to make alterations to the program being executed. Program editing keys allow program entry and verification. The precise procedures used to make these modifications vary from Control to Control.

Insert Key

The Insert Key is a program editing key that allows new information to be entered into a program. Most CNC Controls insert the entered program data after the current position of the cursor. This has a separate and distinct functional purpose from the Input Key.

Alter Key

The Alter Key is a program editing key enabling data in the program to be altered. After positioning the cursor to the incorrect word in the CNC program, the programmer/operator can enter the new word and press the Alter Key. This causes the current data in the program to be changed to the entered data. This cannot be done to running programs (programs currently active).

Delete Key

The Delete Key allows program data to be deleted. CNC Controls allow a word, a command, a series of commands, or even an entire program to be deleted with this key. Many Controls enable whole pages or sections of a program to be highlighted with the cursor keys, and then the Delete Key is pressed to erase the highlighted section.

Reset Key

The Reset Key returns the program to the beginning when editing CNC programs. When the Control is executing programs, the Reset Key clears the look-ahead buffer and stops execution of the program. Care must be taken, however, when using the Reset Key when an active program is loaded in the Control's memory. "Resetting" clears the Control's look-ahead buffer. This can cause critical staging commands to be lost when a program is restarted between Blocks. When the machine is in the alarm state, this key cancels the alarm if the problem causing the alarm has been solved. Programmers/operators should be familiar with an individual Control's Reset characteristics.

Input/Output (I/O) Keys

The communication of programs, offsets, and parameters to outside devices such as computers, tape readers/punches, and telephone lines for network linkages are industry-standard features on contemporary CNC Controls. Control panels include keys needed to send and retrieve data to and from these devices. Typically, a combination of keys sends data and others receive data. The send keys may be labeled as output, communication ports, or punch. The receive keys may be labeled as Input, Load, or Read.

Graphic Keys

Graphic keys are usually labeled as a series of Control panel keys related to the Control's graphic functions (scaling, plane display, rotation, and so on). These can be available in a wide variety of formats, from individual CNC Control manufacturers' products to CAD/CAM systems linked to a company's main computer system.

Soft Keys

In order to minimize the number of buttons and switches required on the Control panel, most CNC Controls are adopting soft keys. Soft keys are mounted close to the display screen, usually directly below and directly to the right of the Control screen. The function of these keys changes, depending on the modes of the display screen. For example, in the Program mode of the display screen, the soft keys have one meaning. In the Edit mode, the soft keys have a very different function. Their name is derived from "software," which, in effect, gives the buttons a different meaning whenever the software runs different operations. There typically are boxes close to each soft key, telling the programmer/operator the current function of the soft key. The F1 through F8 keys directly under the display screen are soft keys and usually represent (F)unction 1 to (F)unction 8 in the current software program.

STANDARD MACHINE-PANEL BUTTONS and SWITCHES

Mode Switch

The Mode switch is the main selector switch for CNC machine operation. The programmer/operator must check this switch position before performing any function on the machine. The Mode switch must be positioned properly and according to the operation intended for the immediate active task. The Control will not respond to the operator's command if the Mode switch is not in the correct position. If the programmer/operator wishes to make a manual movement by jogging the machine with a handwheel, the mode switch must be positioned in the manual mode. If the mode switch is not positioned properly, no manual movement can be completed. See Figure 11.3.

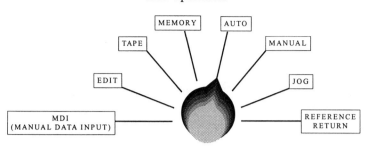

Figure 11.3 *CNC Control-Mode Switch*

Edit

The Edit mode is selected to enable the programmer/operator to enter and modify CNC programs through the keyboard and display screen in much the same way a personal computer's word processor is used. The Edit mode can be used to scan within the active program to a position at which the machining cycle is desired to be started. The programmer/operator may intend to skip to the beginning of a tool and execute the machining program from a specific Block where a workpiece feature requires recutting. The Edit mode is used to scan to the selected Block to initialize the operational sequence.

Memory or Auto

A program can be executed from the Auto or Memory mode. In this switch position, the automatic cycle can be started by the programmer/operator, executing the active program from within the Control's memory. Many Controls also allow full editing capabilities when in the Memory mode.

Tape

The Tape mode on CNC Controls enables a program to be executed from the Tape Reader. In this mode, the program is executed from a tape on the Tape Reader, not from within the Control's memory. Tape Readers are used less and less often to actually run the program. Computer memory (RAM), in much larger modern proportions, is used to store programs for execution once they are loaded from Tape Readers. Running very long programs that are too large to be loaded into the Control's memory is one example of a program executed from a Tape Reader in Tape mode. Also, many CNC Controls allow the selection of a mode that executes a program from the Tape Reader. At the same time, a linkage executes the program from some outside device such as a personal computer that can be connected through the communications port. This allows a program to be transferred from the computer to the Control. The programmer/operator executes the program in the Tape mode, but the program is actually run from the computer. With this arrangement, the Control can run programs much longer than would fit into the Control's memory. This platform of operation for a CNC system is called Direct Numerical Control (DNC). DNC is especially well suited for very complex three-dimensional contouring.

Manual Data Input (MDI)

The Manual Data Input mode-switch position enables the programmer/operator to enter and execute commands manually. The keyboard and display screen of the CNC Control are used to provide a way to make CNC commands manually in the Manual Data Input mode. An MDI command can be given in order to make manual tool changes involving the T-word and M06. Anything that can be commanded in a CNC program is possible in the MDI mode.

In the MDI mode, however, commands are single-execution only. Unlike a CNC program in the Control's memory, once an MDI command has been executed, it is no longer in memory. If the command must be repeated, it must be entered again. Critical geometry and trigonometric functions can be cross-checked using this method.

Manual or Jog

In the Manual or Jog mode-switch position, the CNC machine reacts as a manual machine tool. This mode empowers many of the machine panel's buttons and switches wired to machine functions. Many CNC machines use some type of handwheel to manually move each Axis. CNC machines also have a Jog function, allowing Axis motion to be initiated by a joystick or push button, and have push buttons to turn the spindle On and Off, as well as a variable-speed switch to control spindle speed.

Reference Return

Modern CNC machines have a manual method of returning each Axis to its Reference Zero or Origin Point. The Reference Return mode (also called Zero Return, Home Position, or Grid Zero) must be selected. This can be accomplished by selecting the Reference Return mode and pressing a single key on some Controls. Other CNC machines require that the programmer/operator jog each Axis to its reference point Axis by Axis until the process is complete.

Cycle Start

The Cycle Start button is typically used to activate the active program in the Control's memory. The machine goes into the automatic cycle. In addition, CNC

Controls use the Cycle Start button to activate Manual Data Input commands that are independently entered.

Motion Hold or Feed Hold

The Motion Hold or Feed Hold enables the operator to halt Axis motion temporarily when a program or MDI is being executed. The cycle start button can again be used to reactivate the cycle. Note that all Axis motion freezes, but all other functions of the machine (coolant, spindle, and so on) continue to operate. During verification of a program, the Motion Hold button serves as a panic button. If a problem is found during execution, the program is taken out of cycle (by pressing the Reset Key). The Emergency Stop button should not be considered the "panic button." The Emergency Stop button actually turns off the power to the machine tool, causing additional problems during some circumstances. When the machine power is turned off, the axis of the machine drifts until Axis locks can hold them in position. Axes bearing a great deal of weight move the most. The amount of drift is usually quite small, under .008" in most cases. But if a cutting tool is actually machining a workpiece when the Emergency Stop button is pressed, the drift could cause damage to the tool and workpiece. Or if the drift is against a setup, the entire fixture could be moved. Jobs can be scrapped as a result of this.

Feedrate Override

The Feedrate Override is a multiposition switch that enables the programmer/operator to increase or decrease the programmed feedrate during cutting commands (G01, G02, G03, and so on). This switch has no control over Rapid Traverse motions. The Feedrate Override switch is usually segmented in 10% increments and usually range from 0 to 200% This means the programmer/operator can slow down programmed feedrates to nothing, stopping motion, or increase the feedrate to double its programmed value of 100%.

During the verification of a new program, this override is invaluable. When the first workpiece is being machined, the programmed feedrate can be adjusted under actual cutting conditions. Typically, it is very difficult to predict feedrates of a specific surface cut because of many variables. If the Feedrate Override switch is set at its lowest value, the machine will not move. With the command activated, the programmer/operator can slowly increase the Feedrate Override switch position, watching and feeling what the cutting tool is doing. If everything else appears to be alright, each command can continue to be monitored. This procedure must be repeated for every tool in the program. A Feedrate Override setting of 100% is the target for every tool. Once a program is verified, all tools should run properly at 100% to allow automatic operation. If problems are found during program verification with the programmed feedrates, the feedrates in the actual program Blocks should be edited.

Rapid Traverse Override

The Rapid Traverse Override is used to modify the Rapid Motion rate. One version of this switch is a simple On/Off switch. Switched On, all rapid motion is slowed to 25% of the normal rapid rate, which is still fairly fast. It is advised that during program verification, this switch should be used to assure that the machine will not be allowed to move at its maximum Rapid Traverse rate. Another version of Rapid Override is a four-position switch that can be adjusted to 5, 25, 50, and 100% of the normal Rapid Traverse rate. It is imperative that Rapid Override be used during program verification to monitor that rapid movements toward the workpiece setup are set at the correct feedrate.

Emergency Stop

This button will turn Power Off to the machine tool. Normally, power to the Control remains on to save programs, rewind tapes, load disks, and so on. Emergency Stop shuts off all systems of machine control, however. It also stops coolants, applies spindle brakes, and axis brakes immediately.

Conditional Switches

Conditional Switches are On/Off switches on the machine panel that determine how the machine reacts during automatic and manual operation. They could be toggle switches, locking push buttons, membrane switches, or screen-sensitive switches set through the display screen and keyboard.

Dry Run

Dry Run is a conditional switch typically used with programs during the verification process. With this switch On, the operator controls the motion rate at which the machine will move; this is especially valuable during rapid traverse motions. The rapid rate of current CNC machines is very fast, ranging from 100 to 800 IPM. At these extremely fast rates, the programmer/operator will not be able to stop the machine before danger strikes. The programmer/operator does not know if some motion mistake has been unintentionally typed into the program. By turning On the Dry Run switch, the programmer/operator can control the machine's motion rate. Dry Run works in conjunction with other multiposition switches such as Feedrate Override or Jog Feedrate. This multiposition switch enables a change of rate at which the machine axes move. By decreasing the multiposition switch setting, the motion rate is slowed. By turning up the multiposition switch, the motion rate is increased. The lowest settings of the multiposition switch cause CNC machines to creep along, allowing even rapid motions to be checked carefully.

Single Block

Single Block is used when executing a program. As a conditional switch, it can force the Control to execute one command of the program at a time. Turned On, the Control stops when each command is completed. To reactivate the cycle (execute the next command), the programmer/operator must push the Cycle Start button. Single Block is helpful during program verification. New programs mandate that each motion the machine makes is carefully checked one at a time. With Single Block in the On condition, the programmer/operator can be certain that the machine stops at the end of each motion, while visually monitoring the motion previously completed.

Machine Lock

When Machine Lock is turned On, this conditional switch keeps all axes of the machine from moving. Other functions of the machine continue to operate: the automatic tool changer still changes tools, the spindle still runs, coolant still comes on, and so on. However, all axis motion freezes. Machine Lock is effective at all times, even during automatic operation and manual operation. This conditional switch is commonly used during program verification. The very first time a new program is executed, Machine Lock and Dry Run are turned On. The Control quickly scans the program for errors in basic program format. During this verification procedure, the operator/programmer is assured that the axes of the machine will not move. The Control advances through the program as if running a workpiece, but no axis motion occurs. If a format mistake is found by the Control, it generates an alarm. The kinds of mistakes that can be found during a Machine Lock–Dry Run include syntax mistakes. For example, if the programmer intended to program the command:

G01

a mistake was made while typing the G01 word. Suppose the typographical error

G10

was entered. Typically, in CNC Controls, there is no such command as a G10. And even if there were, its format would probably not be that of G01. In this case, when the Control came across G10, it would generate an alarm. After correcting the mistake, the program would be executed again with Machine

Lock On and continue to do so until the entire program can be run without the alarm being generated.

If the Control finishes executing the program without generating an alarm, the operator would know that at least the Control can interpret all commands in the program. Motion errors could still exist, therefore, the operator must still be cautious even after doing a Machine Lock–Dry Run.

Optional Block Skip

Optional Block Skip is a conditional switch that works in combination with slash codes (/) in the program. If the Control were to read a slash code at the beginning of any CNC command in the program, it will scan to the position of the Optional Block Skip switch, also called Block Delete. Switched On, the Control ignores the command in which the slash code is included. Switched Off, the Control executes the command. The Optional Block Skip switch isolates specific feature-related operations that could be optional in some job lots.

Optional Stop

The Optional Stop is a conditional switch that works in combination with an M01 code in the program. If the Control reads an M01, it scans to the position of the Optional Stop switch. If switched On, the Control will immediately stop the execution of the program. The programmer/operator must press the Cycle Start button to start the program. If switched Off, the Control will ignore the M01 and continue executing the program. The M01 is commonly used in the program at the completion of each tool. During the program's verification, these M01 commands give the ability to stop after each tool and check the workpiece features for accuracy and to make program adjustments.

Manual Axis Motion

CNC machines use several methods to allow manual axis motion from the Control panel. One method uses a handwheel that is very similar to the handwheels on a manual machine tool. The desired axis to be moved and the direction to move are chosen and moved accordingly. Another incorporates a joystick or a series of push buttons used to jog the axis at a rate selected by the Feedrate Override. See Figure 11.4.

The handwheel of a CNC machine can be used to move any of the machine's axes, one at a time. Even though the CNC machine may have up to five axes, only one handwheel is used. This is accomplished by a switch, usually right on or close to the handwheel, that is used to select the axis to be moved (X, Y, Z, and so on). There is another switch related to the handwheel used to select the rate at which the motion will occur. This switch usually has three positions. In

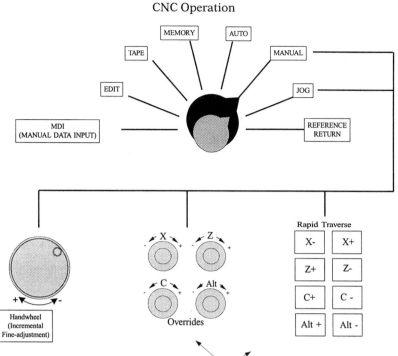

Figure 11.4 *CNC Control—Manual Function: Switch Position*

the × 1 (times 1) positions, each increment of the handwheel is .0001" (or 0.001 mm). In the × 10 (times 10) mode, each increment is .001" (or .010 mm). In the × 100 (times 100) position, each increment is .010" (or .100 mm). The handwheel can be used any time the programmer/operator wishes to make manual axis motion. This includes making measurements on the machine during setup and actually machining a part manually.

Controls for Jogging

There are two common techniques used by CNC machine tool builders that allow axes to be jogged. One involves a joystick that is very similar to the joystick used with computer games. The normal methods to jog CNC machine axes are through the use of a joystick, and the other involves an axis selector switch and a series of push buttons. With both methods, there is also a multiposition switch called Jog Feed Rate that controls the rate at which the jog motion will occur. Normally, this switch is marked with inches-per-minute values as well as millimeters-per-minute values. The range of motion usually runs from .25 IPM all the way up to the machine's rapid rate, so that the programmer/operator has complete control of the desired rate. Before making the jog motion, the Jog Feedrate switch must be set to the desired position. The joystick technique is usually applied to two-axis machines, such as Turning Centers. The switch is marked with the axis directions the joystick causes. These directions match the basic layout of the machine's axis motion.

For Turning Center applications, Up on the joystick is X minus. Right on the joystick is Z plus. Each direction of the joystick matches the actual direction of motion the machine makes. For machines with more than two axes, most machine tool builders will use two push buttons to allow the direction of motion (plus or minus) along with an Axis Selector Switch to designate in which axis the manual motion is to occur. For example, a programmer/operator who wishes manual motion along the X-Axis in the minus direction at 40 IPM first sets the Jog Feedrate selector switch to the 40 IPM position. The Axis-selector switch is then set to the X position. Last, the minus push button is pressed.

Because the motion rate is consistent in the jog mode, this makes a better choice for actually machining a workpiece manually than the handwheel. But, most CNC machines that utilize a reference position (grid zero, home, or zero return) require the operator to use jogging techniques to manually send each Axis to its Reference Zero or Origin.

Controls for Tool Changing

CNC machines that use automatic tool-changing devices also allow manual changing of tools by actuating specific Control panel switches. These multiposition switches with which the programmer/operator can select the desired tool station and push a button that activates a tool change are typically locked out of operation when the machine is in Auto operation.

Spindle Control

CNC machines with rotating spindles always provide a manual method of turning the spindle On and Off. Typically, push buttons are used, one for spindle On and another for spindle Off. There will also be a variable-rate switch that can be used to adjust the spindle speed in revolutions per minute. The spindle RPM may also be commanded by the manual data input mode.

Spindle-Horsepower Meter

Most CNC machines have meters that show the programmer/operator key information about the spindle. One meter is the RPM meter, which shows how fast the spindle is rotating. Some machines show this information through the display screen instead of by an actual meter. Another spindle-related meter is a Load Meter, which monitors how much stress the spindle is under during machining operations. This meter typically shows a percentage of load, ranging from 0 to 150% of the normal load. It is therefore easy to tell to what extent the machining operation being performed is taxing the spindle motor of the machine.

Axis-Drive Horsepower Meter

The Axis-Drive Horsepower Meter monitors how much horsepower is being drawn by any of the machine axis drive motors. Usually, there is only one meter, and the axis is selectable (X, Y, Z, and so on), depending on the operations being performed.

Reference Position Indicator Lights

Reference Position Indicator Lights on CNC machine Controls are a set of indicator lights that come On if an axis is currently at its Reference Zero or Origin. As many Reference Position Indicator Lights exist as there are individual axes on the machine. CNC positioning systems are designed to be calibrated from their reference point. The programmer/operator can easily see if the machine is in its proper starting position by checking these lights being on.

Optional Stop Indicator Light

Many CNC machines use indicator lights close to the optional stop switch. Once the machine is frozen by an optional stop (M01), this indicator light comes on to show the programmer/operator why the machine has stopped its program execution.

CNC MACHINE OPERATIONAL MODES

Manual Data Input Mode

The Manual Data Input (MDI) mode uses multiple positions on the mode switch—the Edit position and the Manual Data Input position. In either position, data are entered through the keyboard on the Control panel and display screen. The two switch modes provide manual capability through automated methods. By using the Edit mode switch position, CNC programs can be entered into the Control's memory. The program can also be loaded from some outside device, such as a computer or tape reader. CNC commands are entered through the keyboard and display screen manually using the

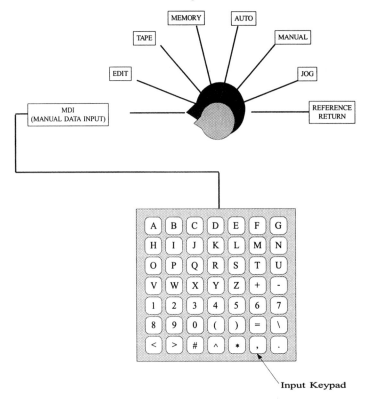

Input Keypad

Figure 11.5 *Control MDI Function: Manual Data Input Keys*

MDI code. These are executable only a single time. If the same command is included in a program format, it is executable over and over without having to reenter it. By using the MDI position of the mode switch, CNC commands are entered and executed. By using the Edit position of the mode switch, a program is entered or modified. Therefore, both mode switch positions involve entering data through the keyboard. See Figure 11.5.

Mode Switch in the Manual Data Input Position

To enter and execute CNC commands one at a time, the Manual Data Input position of the mode switch is used. The CNC command is erased after it has been executed. The MDI mode is most often used to allow the operator to perform manual operations that are not possible by using buttons and switches. For Machining Centers, the same applies to the automatic tool changer. Many CNC machine builders provide no way of manually changing tools on a machining center. The programmer/operator is expected to use the MDI mode to execute the tool change manually through the MDI procedure.

The Manual Data Input mode switch position can also be used for machining a workpiece. Because most CNC commands are possible by MDI (including G00, G01, G02, and G03), the programmer/operator can make machining commands in the same way as in a CNC program. Often, the reason for this is to keep all the machine components in sync with the computer. Tool changers and the Control memory need to maintain constant electronic communication so that no possible error can cause future complications.

Manual Mode

The Manual Mode of a CNC Control causes the machine tool to react identically to a standard machine tool. The positions of the mode switch that are included in the manual modes include Manual or Jog, Handwheel, and Reference Return. In the Manual Mode position, the programmer/operator of a CNC machine is allowed to press buttons, turn handwheels, and activate switches in order to attain the desired machine response as if it were a standard manual machine. The activation of each button or switch in the Manual Mode has an immediate response. When the correct button is pressed, the spindle starts rotating. Switched On, the coolant comes on. A joystick held in one direction or another causes the corresponding machine Axis to move. CNC machines can vary considerably with regard to what a programmer/operator can perform "manually." See the Operators Manuals for the exact functions of individual CNC Controls.

DETERMINING the MEASUREMENT from PART ORIGIN or PROGRAM ZERO to the MACHINE's REFERENCE POSITION

The location of Program Zero in dimensional relationship to the machine's Reference Point is normally an essential setup stage of most CNC Machining Centers. It typically involves making measurements in each individual axis. The Control must "know" the location of the Part Origin point in order to make specific axis motions during the program. The Manual Mode is used to make the measurements for Program Zero. A complete understanding of the Axis position page on the display-screen function is very important. There is a digital readout on the position page of the display screen showing the current position for each axis (X, Y, Z, and so on). It is essentially the same as a digital readout on a manual machine tool. The position display for each Axis changes as an Axis moves and indicates the current Axis position. The position display for each Axis can be preset to any number, including zero, during the procedure.

PROGRAM MODIFICATION of a
PREVIOUSLY ENTERED PROGRAM

After a program has been entered into the CNC Control's memory, verification is the next important step. Insert, Alter, and Delete are editing keys that enable the programmer to change anything within the program. To modify words in the program, the programmer/operator moves the cursor to the position in the program to be modified, enters the modification through the keypad, and presses the Alter Key. When adding information to the program, the programmer/operator positions the cursor to the word just before the addition, types in the additional words, and presses the Insert Key. To delete words from the program, the cursor is positioned to the word to be deleted and the Delete Key is pressed. These techniques may vary from Control to Control in perhaps the sequence of keys that are pressed. The programmer/operator of a CNC Control is allowed to edit the program from within the Control's memory. But, if changes are made at the Control and if the company wishes to back up the program after any modification, the program should be sent from the Control to an outside device (computer, tape backup) for permanent storage. Many CNC Controls have a key switch called Memory Protect that is in place to prevent unintended or unauthorized modification to the program. A key is used that can be removed from the CNC machine once Memory Protect has been turned On. After program verification and actual production is being run, there is no need for further program modification. The Memory Protect switch can be turned Off after verification and the key removed, preventing further program modification. Many companies require this to prevent unauthorized "adjustments" to a program. This is not only for sabotage protection. Many times continued adjustments are made without consideration that mechanical failures, fixture movements, or tool wear actually causes workpiece inaccuracies.

PROGRAM OPERATION MODE

This is a mode of operation that involves actual program execution. The mode switch positions are Memory or Auto and Tape. The Control, in these modes, is actually executing programs. The programmer/operator uses this mode to verify programs and run production. The Cycle Start button is used in both mode switch positions to activate the program with the feed hold button being used to stop axis motion temporarily at any time during the cycle. Several conditional switches can effect machine reaction in the program operation mode. The Dry Run conditional switch enables the programmer/operator to change the motion rate. Single Block forces the Control to execute only one command at a time. Optional Stop (if On) causes the Control to halt the program when an M01 word is read. Optional Block Skip (if On) causes the machine to skip commands beginning with a Slash code (/). Machine Lock causes the machine to execute the program, but stops all axis motion.

During the program operation mode, most CNC Controls "look ahead" several commands into the program to prepare for tool-geometry relationships between the present command being executed and upcoming commands. This necessary feature keeps the machine from pausing between commands and is also required for compensation-based decisions. This look-ahead buffer is constantly updated during program execution. The buffer is emptied when the Reset Key is pressed. Care should be taken to avoid pressing this button during active program execution.

SWITCH POSITION for TAPE MODE

The main purpose for the use of Tape Readers in most cases is to load programs into the Control's memory. CNC Controls allow programs to be executed from the tape mode, but usually there are only two occasions when this is the norm. When programs are too long to fit into the Control's memory, a tape can be run from the Tape Reader. The Tape Reader has a limitation, however, related to the length of the program. If programs are extremely long, too long to be run from the Tape Reader, CNC Controls allow programs to be run from an outside device such as a personal computer. Very long programs can be executed using this method. The programmer/operator, using this method however, is allowed to see only one or two commands of the program being executed on the display screen. In contrast, in the memory position of the mode switch, the programmer/operator can monitor a whole page of the program. Another drawback of the tape mode is that modification of the program is not possible from within the CNC Control. This means the program must be perfected before it can be executed. If changes need to be made, they must be made at the computer. Today's CNC Controls are rapidly advancing in the area of increased memory. More RAM memory capabilities have alleviated this problem and allow large programs to be loaded in CNC Control memory.

MODE SWITCH POSITION for MEMORY or AUTO

The most frequently used mode switch position to execute programs is the Memory or Auto mode switch position. The Memory or Auto position of the mode switch should be used when the Control's memory is large enough to hold the CNC program.

The Control executes the active program from within the Control's memory in this mode switch position. There could be several programs stored in the Control's memory, but only one is active. The program that runs when the Cycle

Start button is pushed is the active program. To choose the active program on most Controls, the Edit mode is used. When a program is being executed from the memory of most CNC Controls, the programmer/operator is able to see one full page of the program on the Control's display screen. During program execution, the cursor advances through the program, allowing commands to be seen that follow the command currently being executed. If a pause or stop is required during execution, Motion Hold may be used until decisions are made.

CNC MACHINE OPERATIONAL PROCEDURE

All CNC machining procedures involve the use of Operational Sequences that are repeated over and over. Operational Sequences include Powering Up, Powering Down, Loading Tools, Setting Offsets, and Editing Programs. These procedures can be encapsulated into sequences with which the programmer/operator should become familiar. In this book, the series of procedures given present quick-and-easy reference material about operating CNC machines. The basic sequences are divided into logical categories such as the following:

1. Manual Operation procedure
2. MDI procedure
3. Data-Loading and Data-Saving procedure
4. Program Editing and Display-Related procedure
5. Setup procedure
6. Program Operational procedure

MACHINING CENTER OPERATIONAL PROCEDURE

The following list of Operational Sequences works for typical CNC Controls coupled to Machining Centers. Even though some specific details may vary from Control to Control, the basic sequences are the same. The Operational Sequence checklists have been designed to lead the user through important machine sequences, complete with check boxes for completed steps.

Manual Procedure

Sequence to do the following:

☐ Start machine operation
☐ Initiate Manual Reference Return

☐ Start Spindle—Manually
☐ Jog Axes—Manually
☐ Axis Movement via Handwheel operation
☐ Loading Tools into Spindle—Manually
☐ Loading Tools into Magazine—Manually
☐ Turn/Off Coolant—Manually
☐ Cause Axis Displays to read Zero or any Number
☐ Enter Tool-Offset Lengths and Radii
☐ Activate Mirror Image
☐ Switch to Inch or Metric Mode

Manual Data Input (MDI) Procedure

Sequence to use MDI to do the following:

☐ Change Tools
☐ Turn ON/Off Spindle
☐ Initiate a Reference Return
☐ Move Axes

Data-Loading and Data-Saving Procedure

Sequence to do the following:

☐ Load Programs into Memory through a Keyboard
☐ Load Programs into Memory by Tape
☐ Load Punch Programs from Memory to Tape Punch or Computer
☐ Load Programs into Memory by a Communications Port

Program Editing and Display-Related Procedure

Sequence to do the following:

☐ Display a Directory of the Programs in Memory
☐ Delete Words and Commands in a Program
☐ Insert Words and Commands in a Program
☐ Delete an Entire Program from Memory
☐ Search other Programs in Memory
☐ Search Words inside a Program
☐ Alter Words in a Program

Setup Procedure

Sequence to do the following:

☐ Measure Program Zero Positions in X, Y, and Z
☐ Measure Tool Lengths

Program Operational Procedure

Sequences to do the following:

☐ Verify Programs
☐ Run from the Beginning of any Tool
☐ Run Verified Programs in Production

Procedure to Start Machine

A standard power-up sequence used by CNC Controls does the following:

☐ Turn On the main breaker, usually located in the back of the machine
☐ Press Control Power ON button
☐ Press Machine On or Hydraulic ON button
☐ Follow sequences to do a Reference Return
☐ Machine is started

Procedure to Begin Axis Travel to Machine Zero, Table Zero, or Reference Return Position

The Reference Return Sequence is very important. CNC Machining Centers require that the machine reach the reference return position before executing a program. See Figure 11.6.

☐ Turn Mode switch to Machine Zero or Reference Return
☐ Using the Axis select switch, first select X-Axis
☐ Using the minus direction joystick or push button, move the machine several inches in the minus direction
☐ Using the plus direction joystick or push button, travel in plus until the Reference Return origin indicator light for the X-Axis comes on
☐ Repeat steps for all other axes (Y, Z, and C/B axis if the machine has a fourth axis)

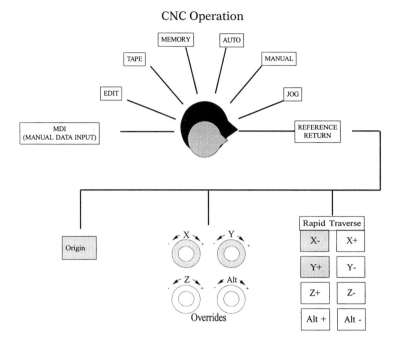

Figure 11.6 *Sequence to Send Machine to Reference Return Position*

A crash can be easily caused by activating the Cycle Start button when the machine is not where it is supposed to be.

Procedure to Manually Start the Spindle

The programmer/operator must select the RPM by the MDI mode.

☐ Set the mode switch to a manual mode (jog, manual, reference return, etc.)
☐ Adjust spindle RPM; set it to the desired position
☐ Press the Spindle On button. Spindle comes on at the RPM set or last programmed RPM
☐ To Stop Spindle, press the Spindle Stop button

Most machines also let you select the desired spindle direction by entering a plus or minus before the RPM.

Procedure to Manually Jog Axes

Sequence to do the following:

☐ Set the mode switch to jog or manual
☐ Set Axis select switch to desired Axis (X, Y, Z, or C/B)

☐ Set the jog feedrate switch to the desired position to select the feedrate amount

☐ Using plus or minus joystick or push buttons, jog the axis in the desired direction and amount

Procedure to Use the Handwheel

Sequence to do the following:

☐ Set mode switch to handwheel
☐ Set Axis select switch to desired Axis (X, Y, Z, or B/C)
☐ Set handwheel rate switch to desired position ($\times$ 1, $\times$ 10, or $\times$ 100)
☐ By using handwheel, rotate plus or minus to cause desired motion

($\times$ 1 = .0001" per increment of the handwheel; $\times$ 10 = .001"; and $\times$ 100 = .010")

Procedure to Manually Load Tools into the Spindle

Sequence to do the following:

☐ Set the mode switch to manual or jog
☐ If a tool is in the spindle, hold the tool and press the unclamp button; the tool will drop out of the spindle and the spindle will be left unclamped
☐ To load a tool into the spindle, place the tool into the spindle with one hand and press the clamp button with the other

Some machines require that the keys be aligned.

Procedure to Load Tools into the Tool-Changer Magazine

Sequence to do the following:

☐ Set the mode switch to jog or manual
☐ Rotate the tool changer to the desired position
☐ Load the tool into the desired position by unclamping a lever or by snapping it into position
☐ Rotate Tool magazine and load tools for all tools needed

Always align the keys properly on the tool-changer magazine. Always load a tool into the magazine so that the key is the same way.

Procedure to Manually Turn On the Coolant

A simple toggle switch is used to activate the coolant manually.

☐ Set the mode switch to jog or manual
☐ Set the coolant toggle switch to On; coolant turns On
☐ To turn coolant Off, turn Off the toggle switch

Many machines also have an auto position for the coolant switch. If the switch is in this position, the coolant will come on only when an M08 is commanded from the Control during program execution.

Procedure to Make the Axis Displays
Read Zero or Any Number

It is very important to understand the function of tool offsets for tool-length compensation and tool-radius compensation as presented in the programming section of this book before attempting this procedure.

☐ Set the mode switch in any position
☐ Press the soft key until Offset appears at the bottom of the screen
☐ Press the soft key under Offset
☐ Using the arrow keys, position the cursor to the Offset to enter
☐ Enter the value of the Offset
☐ Press the soft key under Input (or the hard Input Key)

Procedure to Manually Turn On and Off the Mirror Image

Sequence to do the following:

☐ Set the mode switch to MDI
☐ Press the soft key until Setting appears at the bottom of the screen
☐ Press the soft key under Setting
☐ Using cursor arrow key, move the cursor to the selected position of X or
   Y mirror image
☐ To turn On mirror image, enter 1 and press Input
☐ To turn Off mirror image, enter 0 and press Input

Procedure to Manually Select Inch or Metric Mode

Sequence to do the following:

☐ Set the mode switch to MDI
☐ Press the soft key until Setting appears at the bottom of the screen

☐ Press the soft key under Setting
☐ Using cursor control arrow keys, move the cursor to the desired inch/metric position
☐ Enter 1 and press Input to select Inch mode or enter 0 and press Input to choose the Metric mode

Procedure to Use MDI to Change Tools

It is very important to understand how the tool changer is programmed. The "T" word selects the tool to be placed in the waiting position and the M06 word makes the tool exchange.

☐ Set the mode switch to MDI
☐ Press the soft key until Program appears at the bottom of the screen
☐ Press the soft key under Program until MDI appears at the top of the screen
☐ Enter T and the number of the tool you wish to load into the spindle
☐ Press the End-of-Block key and press the soft key under Insert
☐ Press the Start Key or Cycle Start button (tool changer rotates into waiting position)
☐ Enter M06
☐ Press the End-of-Block key and press the soft key under Insert
☐ Press the Start Key or Cycle Start button (tool change is executed)

Procedure to Use MDI to Turn On and Off the Spindle

Sequence to do the following:

☐ Set the mode switch to MDI
☐ Press the soft key until Program appears at the bottom of the screen
☐ Enter S and the desired RPM (i.e., S1200 = 1200 RPM)
☐ Press the End-of-Block key and press the soft key under Insert
☐ Enter M03 for Clockwise or M04 for Counterclockwise
☐ Press the End-of-Block key and press the soft key under Insert
☐ Press Start Key or Cycle Start button (Spindle starts)
☐ To stop spindle, enter M05, press the End-of-Block key, press the soft key under Insert, and then press Start Key or Cycle Start button

The last programmed RPM is also the selected RPM for the manual mode when the spindle starts rotation.

Procedure to Use MDI to Do a Reference Return

Sequence to do the following:

☐ Set mode switch to MDI
☐ Press the soft key until Program appears at the bottom of the screen
☐ Press the soft key under Program until MDI appears at the top of the screen
☐ Check that the machine can reach Reference Return with no interference in all axes
☐ Enter: G91 G28 X0 Y0 Z0; then press the End-of-Block key and Press the soft key under Insert
☐ Press Start key or Cycle Start button

Procedure to Use MDI to Move Axis

Sequence to do the following:

☐ Set mode switch to MDI
☐ Press the soft key until Program appears at the bottom of screen
☐ Press the soft key under Program until MDI appears at the top of screen
☐ Enter the mode of motion: G90 = absolute, G91 = incremental
☐ Press the End-of-Block key and press the soft key under Insert
☐ Enter the kind of motion: G00 = rapid, G01 = linear
☐ Press the End-of-Block key and press the soft key under Insert
☐ Enter X, Y, or Z, and the value to be commanded
☐ Press the End-of-Block key and press the soft key under Insert
☐ Press the Start Key or Cycle Start button (motion is executed)

Procedure to Load Programs into Memory from the Tape Reader

Sequence to do the following:

☐ Set the mode switch to Edit
☐ Press the soft key until Program appears at the bottom of the screen
☐ Press the soft key under Program until a program appears on the screen
☐ Set the tape on the Tape Reader. The Tape goes from right to left and the leader holes are facing front
☐ Set the toggle switch to Auto
☐ Enter the letter O and enter the Program Number of the program to be loaded
☐ Press the soft key until Read appears at the bottom of the screen
☐ Press the soft key under Read

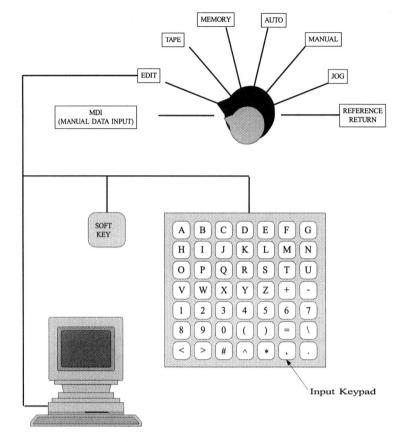

Figure 11.7 *Sequence to Load a Program into Memory via Communications Port*

Procedure to Load Programs into Memory through the Communications Port

See Figure 11.7. Sequence to do the following:

☐ Set the mode switch to Edit
☐ Press the soft key until Program appears at the bottom of the screen
☐ Press the soft key under Program until a program appears on the screen
☐ Connect the outside device to the machine
☐ Enter the letter O and the Program Number to be loaded
☐ Press the soft key until Read appears at the bottom of the screen
☐ Press the soft key under Read
☐ Send the program from the computer or Tape Reader

Procedure to Load Programs into Memory through the Keyboard

Sequence to do the following:

☐ Set the mode switch to Edit
☐ Press the soft key until Program appears at the bottom of the screen
☐ Press the soft key under Program until a program appears on the screen
☐ Enter the letter O and the Program Number of the program to be loaded
☐ Press the soft key under Insert
☐ Enter one command at a time and press the soft key under insert after each command. Enter the rest of the program until completed

Procedure to Punch Programs from Memory to a Tape Punch or Computer

Sequence to do the following:

☐ Set the mode switch to Edit
☐ Press the soft key until Program appears at the bottom of the screen
☐ Press the soft key under Program until a program appears on the screen
☐ Connect an outside device and prepare it to receive a program
☐ Enter the letter O and the Program Number of the program to be sent
☐ Press the soft key until Punch appears at the bottom of the screen
☐ Press the soft key under Punch

Procedure to Display a Directory of Programs in Memory

Sequence to do the following:

☐ Set the mode switch to Edit
☐ Press the soft key until Program appears at the bottom of the screen
☐ Press the soft key under Program until a program appears on the screen
☐ Press the soft key under Program again

The programmer/operator must record details of the programs in memory. When it is time to delete programs from memory, the programs to be kept in memory are easily identifiable.

Procedure to Delete an Entire Program from Memory

Sequence to do the following:

☐ Set the mode switch to Edit
☐ Press the soft key until Program appears at the bottom of the screen

☐ Press the soft key under Program until a program appears on the screen
☐ Enter the letter O and the Program Number to be Deleted
☐ Press the soft key under Delete

Caution must be used to avoid Deleting a program intended to be saved for future reference.

Procedure to Search Programs in Memory

Sequence to do the following:

☐ Set mode switch to Edit
☐ Press soft key until Program appears on the screen
☐ Press soft key under Program until a program appears on the screen
☐ Enter the letter O and the Program to be Searched
☐ Press the soft key until FW SRCH appears at the bottom of the screen
☐ Press the soft key under FW SRCH

Procedure to Search Words in Memory

Sequence to do the following:

☐ Set the mode switch to Edit
☐ Press the soft key until Program appears at the bottom of the screen
☐ Press the soft key under Program until a program appears on the screen
☐ Press the Reset key to return the program to the beginning
☐ Enter the Word to be searched
☐ Press the soft key until FW SRCH appears at the bottom of the screen
☐ Press the soft key under FW SRCH

To search for the first occurrence of any Letter Address Word, enter the Letter address of the Word and press the down arrow key. Once the words appear with a first Letter occurrence, advance until the desired Word is reached.

Procedure to Alter Words in a Program

Sequence to do the following:

☐ Set the mode switch to Edit
☐ Press the soft key until Program appears at the bottom of the screen
☐ Press the soft key under Program until a program appears on the screen
☐ Search to the Word to be altered
☐ Enter the new Word
☐ Press the soft key under Alter

Procedure to Delete Words in Memory

Sequence to do the following:

☐ Set the mode switch to Edit
☐ Press the soft key until Program appears at the bottom of the screen
☐ Press the soft key under Program until a program appears on the screen
☐ Search to the Word to be Deleted
☐ Press the soft key under Delete Word

Procedure to Insert Words in a Program

Sequence to do the following:

☐ Set the mode switch to Edit
☐ Press the soft key until Program appears at the bottom of the screen
☐ Press the soft key under Program until a program appears on the screen
☐ Search to the Word just before the Word to Insert
☐ Enter the Word to Insert
☐ Press the soft key under Insert

Procedure to Determine the Distance to the Program Zero Position

Sequence to do the following:

☐ Secure a workpiece accurately in its fixturing
☐ Hold an edgefinder of known diameter in the machine spindle
☐ Rotate the spindle at a previously set RPM
☐ Using manual buttons and the handwheel, "pick up" the X side of the workpiece surface to be designated Program Zero
☐ "Zero out" the Axis display so that it reads "Zero" for the X-Axis
☐ Move away with the Z-Axis; motion the center of the edgefinder over Program Zero
☐ "Zero out" the X-Axis display again
☐ Repeat steps for the Y-Axis
☐ Send the machine to its Table Zero or Reference Return in X and Y. The axis readout dimensions indicate the G92 dimensions to be used in the G92 command in X and Y

To find Zero Position for the Z-Axis:

☐ Release and remove any tools from the spindle taper
☐ Position the nose of the spindle using the handwheel so that it reaches the Program Zero point in Z

☐ "Zero out" the Z-Axis display
☐ Send the machine to its Z-Zero or Reference Return position in the Z-Axis. The Z-Axis display will read the G92 Z dimension to be used as the dimension for Z-Axis calibration purposes

Procedure to Measure Tool Lengths

Sequence to do the following:

☐ Set a gage feeler-block on the subplate or machine table
☐ Touch the nose of the spindle to the workpiece
☐ "Zero out" the Z-Axis display
☐ Retract the Z-Axis to load the tool to be measured
☐ Load the tool to be measured into the spindle
☐ Manually move the tip of the tool to the workpiece
☐ The Z-Axis display will be indicating the tool's length

Sequence for measuring the distance from the tip of the tool down to Z-Zero:

☐ Send the machine to Reference Return position, the Z-Axis
☐ "Zero out" the Z-axis display zero
☐ Touch the tip of the tool to the Program Zero point in Z
☐ The Z-Axis display will indicate the distance from the tip of the tool at the Reference point to Program Zero in Z

Procedure for Program Verification

Sequence to do the following:

☐ Send the machine to its starting point, usually Table Zero or Reference Return
☐ Set the mode switch to Edit
☐ Press the soft key until Program appears on the screen
☐ Press the soft key under Program until the program appears on the screen
☐ Press the Reset Key; check the Program Number
☐ Turn on the Machine Lock toggle switch
☐ Set the mode switch to Memory or Auto
☐ Press the Cycle Start button. Machine executes the program cycle without moving the axes. Spindle, tool changer, pallet changer, and so on, function as normal

Free-Flowing Dry Run

All motions that the machine will make during the program with Jog feedrate and Feed Hold will be operational during this sequence. If the machine appears to be doing something wrong, use Feed Hold to stop the cycle.

☐ Check that no part is in the fixture
☐ Send the machine to its starting point, usually Table Zero or Reference Return
☐ Set the mode switch to Edit
☐ Press the soft key until Program appears at the bottom of the screen
☐ Press the soft key under Program until program appears at the bottom of the screen
☐ Press the Reset Key; check program number
☐ Switch On the Dry-Run toggle switch
☐ Switch Off the Machine Lock toggle switch
☐ Set the mode switch to Memory or Auto
☐ Press the Cycle Start button. The machine executes cycle; the Jog feedrate controls the rate of motion previously set

Air-Cutting Normal Run Cycle

When using a Free-Flowing Dry Run, there is little difference between a rapid command and a cutting command. The following sequence enables the programmer/operator to see where the rapid commands exist. The machine performs as if it is actually machining a part, but no workpiece will be in the workholding fixture.

☐ Check that no part is in the fixture
☐ Send the machine to its starting position, Table Zero or Reference Return
☐ Set the mode switch to Edit
☐ Press the soft key until Program appears at the bottom of the screen
☐ Press the soft key under Program until the program appears on the screen
☐ Press the Reset Key; check the Program Number
☐ Switch Off the Dry-Run toggle switch
☐ Set the mode switch to Memory or Auto
☐ Set the Feedrate Override switch to 100%
☐ Press the Cycle Start button. The machine executes the program cycle as if it is machining a workpiece. The programmer/operator visually checks where the rapid and cutting commands are located

Running the First Workpiece

When running the first workpiece, carefully observe the machine motions toward the workpiece. Each tool's approach to the part with Dry Run and Single Block should be watched closely.

☐ Secure the first workpiece into the workholding fixture
☐ Send the machine to its starting point, Table Zero or Reference Return

☐ Set the mode switch to Edit

☐ Press the soft key until Program appears at the bottom of the screen

☐ Press the soft key under Program until the program appears on the screen

☐ Press the Reset Key; check the Program Number

☐ Switch On the Dry-Run toggle switch

☐ Switch On the Single-Block toggle switch

☐ Set the mode switch to Memory or Auto

☐ Set the Feedrate Override switch to 100%

☐ Press the Cycle Start button continuously until the spindle eventually starts and the axis motion occurs. Approaching the part, use the manual feedrate to control the motion rate

☐ Switch Off the Dry-Run toggle switch

☐ Continue pressing Cycle Start as many times as necessary until this tool is finished

☐ Repeat steps for every tool in the program, checking after each tool

Procedure to Execute Verified Programs from the Beginning

After program verification, this procedure is used to run parts in production phases:

☐ Secure the workpiece in the workholding fixture

☐ Send the machine to its starting point, Table Zero or Reference Return

☐ Set the mode switch to Edit

☐ Press the soft key until Program appears at the bottom of the screen

☐ Press the soft key under Program until the program appears on the screen

☐ Press the Reset Key; check the Program Number

☐ Check the position of all conditional switches, Dry Run, and so on

☐ Set the mode switch to Memory or Auto

☐ Set the Feedrate Override switch to 100%

☐ Press the Cycle Start button

Procedure to Execute Programs from the Starting Point of a Specific Tool

Often, surfaces need to be remachined; the same Program Blocks are reexecuted. Follow the procedure to run programs from the beginning of the specific tool that needs rerunning. This procedure enables the execution from the beginning of any tool in the program.

☐ Indicate the tool station of the tool to be rerun

☐ Send the machine to its starting point, Table Zero or Reference Return

☐ Set the mode switch to Edit

☐ Press the soft key until Program appears at the bottom of the screen
☐ Press the soft key under Program until the program appears on the screen
☐ Press the Reset Key; check the Program Number
☐ Enter T and the Tool Station Number of the tool you wish to rerun
☐ Press the soft key under FW SRCH. The Control scans to the first occurrence of the T word
☐ Enter T and the Tool Station Number of the tool you wish to rerun
☐ Press the soft key under FW SRCH
☐ Locate the cursor to the beginning of the command that starts the tool Block
☐ Set the mode switch to Memory or Auto
☐ Check the position of all conditional switches, Dry Run, and so on
☐ Set the Feedrate Override switch to 100%
☐ Press the Cycle Start button

TURNING-CENTER PROCEDURES

Despite some variations existing from Control to Control, the basic sequence of operations is procedurally identical. A programmer/operator can follow these procedures to cause the machine to perform the following operations.

Manual Procedure

Sequence to do the following:

☐ Start machine operation
☐ Initiate a Manual Reference Return
☐ Start Spindle—Manually
☐ Jog Axes—Manually
☐ Axis Movement via Handwheel operation
☐ Loading Tools onto Turret—Manually
☐ Loading Tools into Magazine—Manually
☐ Turn On/Off Coolant—Manually
☐ Cause Axis Displays to read Zero or any Number
☐ Enter Tool Offsets—Length and Radius
☐ Activate Mirror Image
☐ Switch to Inch or Metric Mode

Manual Data Input (MDI) Procedure

Sequence to use MDI to do the following:

☐ Index Turret
☐ Turn ON/Off Spindle

☐ Initiate a Reference Return
☐ Move Axes

Data-Loading and Data-Saving Procedure

Sequence to do the following:

☐ Load Programs into Memory through Keyboard
☐ Load Programs into Memory by Tape
☐ Load Punch Programs from Memory to Tape Punch or Computer
☐ Load Programs into Memory through Communications Port

Program Editing and Display-Related Procedures

Sequence to do the following:

☐ Display a Directory of the Programs in Memory
☐ Delete Words and Commands in a Program
☐ Insert Words and Commands in a Program
☐ Delete an Entire Program from Memory
☐ Search other Programs in Memory
☐ Search Words in a Program
☐ Alter Words in a Program

Setup Procedure

Sequence to do the following:

☐ Bore Chuck Soft Jaws
☐ Measure Program Zero Positions in X and Z

Program Operational Procedure

Sequences to do the following:

☐ Verify Programs
☐ Run from the beginning of any Tool
☐ Run Verified Programs in Production

GRINDING and TURNING-CENTER OPERATIONAL PROCEDURES

Procedure to Start Machine Operation

A standard power-up sequence used by CNC Controls is as follows:

☐ Turn On the main breaker, usually located in the back of the machine
☐ Press Control Power On button
☐ Press Machine On or Hydraulic On button. Check that no Emergency Stop button is locked in
☐ Follow sequences to do a Reference Return
☐ Machine is started

Procedure to Begin Machine-Axis Travel to Machine Zero or Reference Return Position

The Reference Return sequence is very important. CNC Turning and Grinding machines require that the machine axes reach the Reference Return position before executing a program.

☐ Set the mode switch to Machine Zero or Reference Return
☐ Using the joystick or Z-minus button, jog the machine Z-minus until the Turret (or carriage) moves several inches
☐ Using the joystick or X-minus push button, jog the machine X-minus until the Turret moves several inches
☐ Hold the joystick (+) in X or press the X(+) push button until the Reference Return Origin light comes on for X
☐ Hold the joystick (+) in Z or press the Z(+) push button until the Reference Return Origin light comes on for Z

A crash can be easily caused by activating the Cycle Start button to start a cycle when the machine is not where it is supposed to be.

Procedure to Manually Start the Spindle

The programmer/operator must select the RPM by the MDI mode.

☐ Set the mode switch to a manual mode (Jog, Manual, Reference Return, etc.)
☐ Adjust spindle RPM; set it to the desired position

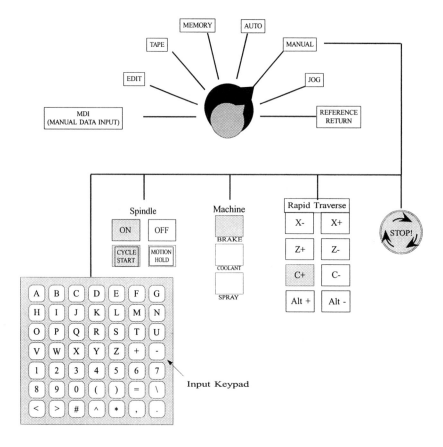

Figure 11.8 *Sequence to Start the Spindle for a Turning Center*

☐ Press the Spindle On button. Spindle comes on at the RPM set or last-pro-
grammed RPM
☐ To Stop Spindle, press the Spindle Stop button

Most machines will also let you select the desired spindle direction by entering
a plus or minus before the RPM. See Figure 11.8.

Procedure to Manually Jog Axes

☐ Set the mode switch to Jog or Manual
☐ Set the feedrate using Feedrate Override or Jog Feedrate
☐ Using the X-Z push buttons or the Joystick, jog the machine in the desired
direction and amount

Procedure to Use the Handwheel

☐ Set mode switch to Handwheel
☐ Set Axis select switch to desired position (X or Z)
☐ Set Handwheel rate switch to desired position (× 1, × 10, or × 100)
☐ By using Handwheel, rotate plus or minus to cause desired motion

(× 1 = .0001" per increment of the handwheel; × 10 = .001"; and × 100 = .010")

Procedure to Manually Turn On the Coolant

To activate the coolant manually, a toggle switch is used.

☐ Set the mode switch to Jog or Manual
☐ Set the Coolant toggle switch to On; Coolant turns On
☐ To turn Coolant Off, turn Off the toggle switch

Many machines also have an auto position for the coolant switch; if the switch is in this position, the coolant will come on only when an M08 is commanded from the Control during program execution.

Procedure to Make the Axis Displays Read Zero or Any Number

Method to cause the Axis display to read Zero:

☐ The mode switch can be set to any position
☐ Press the soft key until Position appears at the bottom of the screen
☐ Press the soft key under Position
☐ Enter the Letter Address of the Axis you wish to make Zero (X or Z)
☐ Press the soft key under Origin
☐ Enter the value of the Offset

Method to cause the Axis display to read any number:

☐ The mode switch can be set to any position
☐ Press the soft key until Position appears at the bottom of the screen
☐ Press the soft key under Position
☐ Enter the Letter Address for the Axis to set
☐ Enter the value
☐ Press the soft key under preset; the Value and Axis to be set will be displayed on the position page

Procedure to Enter and Change Tool Offsets

An understanding of each Tool-Offset function for Dimensional Tool Offsets and Tool-Nose-Radius Compensation is required for this sequence.

☐ The mode switch can be in any position
☐ Press the soft key until Offset appears at the bottom of the screen
☐ Press the soft key under Offset
☐ Use the arrow keys to move the cursor to the Offset needed. The cursor must be located at the actual offset position (X, Z, R, or T)
☐ Enter the value of the desired offset
☐ Press the soft key under Input or Plus Input

If the soft key under Input is pressed, the actual Value entered will be designated as the new Offset. If the soft key under Plus Input is pressed, the value entered will be added to or subtracted from the current Value of the Offset.

Procedure to Toggle between Inch and Metric Modes

Sequence to do the following:

☐ Set the mode switch to MDI
☐ Press the soft key until Setting appears at the bottom of the screen
☐ Press the soft key under Setting
☐ Position the cursor to the desired inch/metric position
☐ Enter 1 and press Input to set Inch mode or enter 0 and press Input to set the Metric Mode

Procedure to Use MDI to Index the Turret

The "T" word sets the Tool Station # to be indexed and the Tool-Offset Number to be used.

☐ Set the mode switch to MDI
☐ Press the soft key until Program appears at the bottom of the screen
☐ Press the soft key under Program until MDI appears at the top of the screen
☐ Enter "T," the Tool Station #, and the Tool-Offset Number chosen (T0100 indexes the Turret to station number 1 and calls up no Offset)
☐ Press the End-of-Block key and press the soft key under insert
☐ Press the Start Key or Cycle Start button

The Tool will index to desired station. If a Tool Offset is called up, the Turret will move the offset amount. A crash can occur if the Turret is left out of position and the next machine cycle starts.

Procedure to Use MDI to Turn the Spindle On and Off

Sequence to do the following:

☐ Set the mode switch to MDI
☐ Press the soft key until Program appears at the bottom of the screen
☐ Press the soft key under Program until MDI appears at the top of the screen
☐ Enter S and the desired RPM (G96 = SFM, G97 = RPM)
☐ Press the End-of-Block key and press the soft key under Insert
☐ Enter the desired Spindle Range (M41 equals low range, M42 equals high range)
☐ Press the End-of-Block key and press the soft key under Insert
☐ Press Start Key or Cycle Start button
☐ Enter S and the chosen Spindle Speed (S1400 means 1400 SFM or 1400 RPM)
☐ Press the End-of-Block key and press the soft key under Insert
☐ Enter M03 for Clockwise or M04 for Counterclockwise
☐ Press the End-of-Block key and press the soft key under Insert
☐ Press Start key or Cycle Start button. The Spindle will start
☐ To Stop spindle, type M05, press the End-of-Block key, and press the soft key under Insert
☐ Press Start key or Cycle Start button

The last programmed RPM will be the starting speed for the manual mode when the spindle is turned On. Check the M41 and M42 codes for Spindle Range using this sequence. If only one spindle range exists, omit the spindle range selection step.

Procedure to Use MDI to Perform a Reference Return

Sequence to do the following:

☐ Set the mode switch to MDI
☐ Press the soft key until Program appears at the bottom of the screen
☐ Press the soft key under program until MDI appears at the top of the screen
☐ Be sure that all Axes can reach Reference Zero
☐ Enter: G28 U0 W0
☐ Press the End-of-Block key and press the soft key under Insert
☐ Press Start Key or Cycle Start button

Procedure to Use MDI to Move Axis

Sequence to do the following:

☐ Set the mode switch to MDI
☐ Press the soft key until Program appears at the bottom of screen
☐ Press the soft key under Program until MDI appears at the top of screen
☐ Enter the mode of motion (G00 = absolute, G01 = linear)
☐ Press the End-of-Block key and press the soft key under Insert
☐ Type "X" or "Z" and the Value to be commanded
☐ Press the End-of-Block key and press the soft key under Insert
☐ Press the Start Key or Cycle Start button. Axes will move

Procedure to Load Programs into Memory from the Tape Reader

Sequence to do the following:

☐ Place the mode switch to Edit
☐ Press the soft key until Program appears at the bottom of the screen
☐ Press the soft key under Program until a program appears on the screen
☐ Set the tape in place on the Tape Reader. Tape is oriented from right to left and the leader holes are facing front
☐ Set the toggle switch to Auto
☐ Enter the letter O and enter the Program Number of the program to be loaded
☐ Press the soft key until Read appears at the bottom of the screen
☐ Press the soft key under Read

Procedure to Load Programs into Memory through the Communications Port

Sequence to do the following:

☐ Place the mode switch to Edit
☐ Press the soft key until Program appears at the bottom of the screen
☐ Press the soft key under Program until a program appears on the screen
☐ Connect the outside device to the machine
☐ Enter the letter O and the Program Number to be loaded
☐ Press the soft key until Read appears at the bottom of the screen
☐ Press the soft key under Read
☐ Send the program from the computer or Tape Reader

Procedure to Load Programs into Memory through the Keyboard

Sequence to do the following:

☐ Set the mode switch to Edit
☐ Press the soft key until Program appears at the bottom of the screen
☐ Press the soft key under Program until a program appears on the screen
☐ Enter the letter O and the Program Number of the program to be loaded
☐ Press the soft key under Insert
☐ Enter one command at a time and press the soft key under Insert after each command. Enter the remainder of the program until completed

Procedure to Punch Programs from Memory to a Tape Punch or Computer

Sequence to do the following:

☐ Set the mode switch to Edit
☐ Press the soft key until Program appears at the bottom of the screen
☐ Press the soft key under Program until a program appears on the screen
☐ Connect an outside device and prepare it to receive a program
☐ Enter the letter O and the Program Number of the program to be sent
☐ Press the soft key until Punch appears at the bottom of the screen
☐ Press the soft key under Punch

Procedure to Display a Directory of Programs in Memory

Sequence to do the following:

☐ Set the mode switch to Edit
☐ Press the soft key until Program appears at the bottom of the screen
☐ Press the soft key under Program until a program appears on the screen
☐ Press the soft key under Program again

The programmer/operator must record details of the programs in memory. When it is time to delete programs from memory, the programs to be kept in memory are easily identifiable.

Procedure to Delete an Entire Program from Memory

Sequence to do the following:

☐ Set mode switch to Edit
☐ Press the soft key until Program appears at the bottom of the screen

☐ Press the soft key under Program until a program appears on the screen
☐ Type the letter O and the Program Number to be Deleted
☐ Press the soft key under Delete

Caution must be used to avoid Deleting a program intended to be saved for future reference.

Procedure to Search Programs in Memory

Sequence to do the following:

☐ Set mode switch to Edit
☐ Press soft key until Program appears on the screen
☐ Press soft key under Program until a program appears on the screen
☐ Enter the letter O and the Program to be Searched
☐ Press the soft key until FW SRCH appears at the bottom of the screen
☐ Press the soft key under FW SRCH

Procedure to Search Words in Memory

Sequence to do the following:

☐ Set the mode switch to Edit
☐ Press the soft key until Program appears at the bottom of the screen
☐ Press the soft key under Program until a program appears on the screen
☐ Press the Reset Key to return the program to the beginning
☐ Enter the Word to be searched
☐ Press the soft key until FW SRCH appears at the bottom of the screen
☐ Press the soft key under FW SRCH

To search for the first occurrence of any Letter Address Word, enter the Letter Address of the Word and press the down arrow key. Once the Words appear with a first Letter occurrence, advance until the desired Word is reached.

Procedure to Alter Words in a Program

Sequence to do the following:

☐ Set the mode switch to Edit
☐ Press the soft key until Program appears at the bottom of the screen
☐ Press the soft key under Program until a Program appears on the screen
☐ Search to the Word to be altered
☐ Enter the new Word
☐ Press the soft key under Alter

Procedure to Delete Words in Memory

Sequence to do the following:

☐ Set the mode switch to Edit
☐ Press the soft key until Program appears at the bottom of the screen
☐ Press the soft key under Program until a program appears on the screen
☐ Search to the Word to be deleted
☐ Press the soft key under Delete Word

Procedure to Insert Words in a Program

Sequence to do the following:

☐ Set the mode switch to Edit
☐ Press the soft key until Program appears at the bottom of the screen
☐ Press the soft key under Program until a program appears on the screen
☐ Search to the Word before the Word to Insert
☐ Enter the Word to Insert
☐ Press the soft key under Insert

Procedure to Determine the Distance to the Program Zero Position

Sequence to do the following:

☐ Secure a workpiece in a Turning spindle workholding device
☐ Index the Turret to the desired tool
☐ Manually move the tool close to the workpiece
☐ Start spindle rotation through MDI or manually at the chosen RPM
☐ Using the handwheel, skim-cut a diameter
☐ Keeping the X-Axis in the same position, motion the Turret away from the workpiece in Z
☐ Measure the machined diameter
☐ "Zero out" the X-Axis display to read the diameter machined
☐ Send the machine to its Machine Zero or Reference Return position in X. The X-Axis display will now indicate the G50 X value

To find Zero Position for the Z-Axis:

☐ Secure a workpiece in a Turning Spindle workholding device
☐ Index the Turret to the intended tool
☐ Manually motion the tool near to the workpiece

☐ Start spindle rotation at the required RPM for the workpiece operation
☐ Using the handwheel, machine the face of the workpiece to Z-Zero position
☐ Keeping the Z-Axis stationary, motion the tool away from the part using the X-Axis
☐ "Zero out" the Z-Axis display
☐ Send the machine to its Z Zero or Reference Return position in the Z-Axis. The Z-Axis display will then indicate the G50 Z value

Procedure to Manually Bore Soft Jaws

The programmer/operator must always be sure that the Jaws are gripping something while being bored. See Figure 11.9.

The diameter of the tool tip of the boring bar should be measured at the machine's Reference Return position. The programmer/operator can cause the X-Axis display to read the diameter of the tool tip at the Reference Return position. This enables monitoring of the X-Axis display to determine the exact diameter that the boring bar is cutting any one time. To determine this diameter for the boring bar, the following sequence can be used to measure the Program Zero X position.

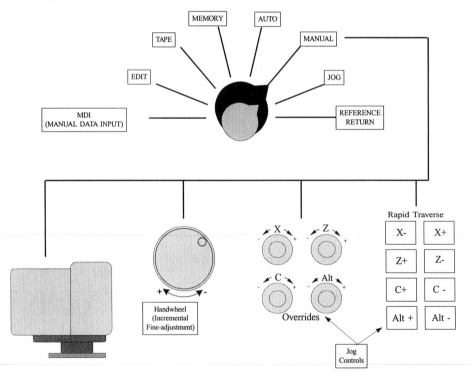

Figure 11.9 *Sequence to Manually Bore Soft Chuck Jaws*

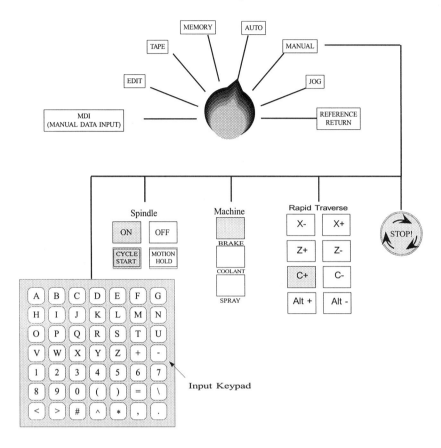

Figure 11.10 *Sequence for Program Verification*

☐ Mount the soft jaws on the master jaws of the chuck. Match-mount the
   serration of each master jaw with the soft jaw serrations
☐ Hold a practice workpiece or chucking ring firmly
☐ Using the handwheel or manual motion, bore the jaws to the diameter
   and depth required

By "zeroing out" the tip of the boring bar to the front surface of the jaws
and causing the Z-Axis to read Zero at that point, the programmer/operator
can determine the depth to which the jaws are being bored.

Procedure for Program Verification

See Figure 11.10. Sequence to do the following:

☐ Send the machine to its starting point, usually Machine Zero or Reference
   Return

☐ Set the mode switch to Edit
☐ Press the soft key until Program appears on the screen
☐ Press the soft key under Program until the program appears on the screen
☐ Press the Reset Key; check the Program Number
☐ Turn on the Machine Lock toggle switch
☐ Set the mode switch to Memory or Auto
☐ Press the Cycle Start button. Machine executes the program cycle without moving the axes. Spindle, tool turret, and so on, function as normal

Free-Flowing Dry Run

All motions that the machine would typically make during program execution are monitored by the programmer/operator manipulating the Jog feedrate and Feed Hold. Jog feedrate acts as a variable-speed controller; Feed Hold can be used as the panic button if the machine appears to be doing something wrong.

☐ Check that no part is in the chuck
☐ Send the machine to its starting point, usually Machine Zero or Reference Return
☐ Set the mode switch to Edit
☐ Press the soft key until Program appears at the bottom of the screen
☐ Press the soft key under Program until program appears at the bottom of the screen
☐ Press the Reset Key; check Program Number
☐ Switch On the Dry-Run toggle switch
☐ Switch Off the Machine Lock toggle switch
☐ Set the mode switch to Memory or Auto
☐ Press the Cycle Start button. The machine executes cycle; Jog feedrate controls the rate of motion previously set

Air-Cutting Normal Run Cycle

When using a Free-Flowing Dry Run, there is little difference between a rapid command and a cutting command. The following sequence enables the programmer/operator to see where the rapid commands exist. The machine performs as if it is actually machining a part, but no workpiece will be in the spindle.

☐ Check that there is no workpiece in the chuck
☐ Send the machine to its starting position, Machine Zero or Reference Return
☐ Set the mode switch to Edit
☐ Press the soft key until Program appears at the bottom of the screen

☐ Press the soft key under Program until the program appears on the screen
☐ Press the Reset Key; check the Program Number
☐ Switch Off the Dry-Run toggle switch
☐ Set the mode switch to Memory or Auto
☐ Set the Feedrate Override switch to 100%
☐ Press the Cycle Start button

The machine executes the program cycle as if it is machining a workpiece. The programmer/operator visually checks where the rapid and cutting commands are located.

Running the First Workpiece

When running the first workpiece, carefully observe the machine motions toward the workpiece. Each tool's approach to the part with Dry Run and Single Block should be watched closely.

☐ Secure the first workpiece into the workholding fixture
☐ Send the machine to its starting point, Machine Zero or Reference Return
☐ Set the mode switch to Edit
☐ Press the soft key until Program appears at the bottom of the screen
☐ Press the soft key under Program until the program appears on the screen
☐ Press the Reset Key; check the Program Number
☐ Switch On the Dry-Run toggle switch
☐ Switch On the Single-Block toggle switch
☐ Switch On the Optional-Stop toggle switch
☐ Set the mode switch to Memory or Auto
☐ Set the Feedrate Override switch to 100%
☐ Press the Cycle Start button continuously until the spindle eventually starts and the axis motion occurs. Approaching the part, use the manual feedrate to control the motion rate
☐ Switch Off the Dry-Run toggle switch
☐ Continue pressing Cycle Start as many times as necessary until this tool is finished
☐ Repeat steps for every tool in the program, checking after each tool

Procedure to Execute Verified Programs from the Beginning

After program verification, this procedure is used to run parts in production phases:

☐ Secure the workpiece into the workholding fixture
☐ Send the machine to its starting point, Machine Zero or Reference Return
☐ Set the mode switch to Edit
☐ Press the soft key until Program appears at the bottom of the screen

☐ Press the soft key under Program until the program appears on the screen
☐ Press the Reset Key; check the Program Number
☐ Check the position of all conditional switches, Dry Run, and so on
☐ Set the mode switch to Memory or Auto
☐ Set the Feedrate Override switch to 100%
☐ Press the Cycle Start button

Procedure to Execute Programs from the Starting Point of a Specific Tool

Often, surfaces need to be remachined; the same Program Blocks are re-executed. Follow the procedure to run programs from the beginning of the specific tool that needs rerunning. This procedure enables the execution from the beginning of any tool in the program.

☐ Indicate the Turret Station Number of the tool to be rerun
☐ Set the machine to its starting point, Table Zero or Reference Return
☐ Set the mode switch to Edit
☐ Press the soft key until Program appears at the bottom of the screen
☐ Press the soft key under Program until the program appears on the screen
☐ Press the Reset Key; check the Program Number
☐ Enter "N" and the Sequence Number of the beginning Block of the tool you wish to rerun. Typically, it is the G50 command for that tool
☐ Press the soft key under FW SRCH. The Control scans to that Sequence Number
☐ Set the mode switch to Memory or Auto
☐ Turn ON the Optional Stop (M01)
☐ Check the position of all conditional switches, Dry Run, and so on
☐ Set the Feedrate Override switch to 100%
☐ Press the Cycle Start button

PROGRAM VERIFICATION

CNC Controls obey commands dictated to them. The CNC Program can instruct the machine to produce the ultraprecision masterpiece or can instruct the machine to self-destruct. Without the programmer/operator standing by to verify programs between workpieces or machining operations, the CNC Control never actually "knows" a program is executing a routine that produces a perfect workpiece. Or, the tool could be cutting into the fixture instead.

Program formatting errors, syntax errors, machining environment interference, and tool-length discrepancies are all "mistakes" today's CNC Controls can detect and "warn" the user about. Producing a workpiece .010 undersize on two dimensions or executing a program with mirroring an Axis in the wrong quadrant are not signal flags that CNC Controls can "see."

Newer CAM-generated programs do a very thorough job of screening for program errors. There are still stages where the programmer must give the "go-ahead nod" to computer-generated toolpaths and part profiles on the CRT. CAM-generated programs tend to be more correct than manually generated programs, however, problems could still exist with cutting conditions (feeds, speeds, workholding, depth of cut, and so on). Conversationally generated CNC programs should be treated with the same respect as CAM-generated CNC programs.

Syntax Errors

Syntax errors are the easiest to find and correct. Most syntax errors prevent commands from ever being executed.

Motion Errors

Motion errors can be much more difficult to diagnose, mainly because they are caused by misinforming the Control of the dimensional coordinates to achieve. In this case, the Control follows the program's instructions without generating an alarm. Additional mistakes of this type include forgetting to in-state or cancel tool offsets, reversing clockwise or counterclockwise commands, and improper mode selection for incremental vs. absolute. This category of mistake can be very serious if not found. In many cases, this kind of mistake means the program is telling the Control to crash the tool into the workpiece, workholding device, or machine slides.

Setup Errors

If mistakes are made during setup procedures, even the most carefully checked program can react undesireably. Some dimensional measurements have to be made by the programmer/operator. The Fixture Offset Numbers, Program Zero, and Workpiece Zero need to be measured and recorded. For machining centers, a tool-length offset must be entered for every tool and a tool-radius offset must be entered for tools using cutter-radius compensation. If these values are not entered, or if the values are entered incorrectly, the result could be very serious machining errors.

Program-Verification Procedures

Throughout verification procedures, the programmer/operator must become familiarized with the CNC machine's Feed Hold button. If an unexpected Rapid

Motion takes place, Feed Hold will save the expensive CNC equipment from serious damage.

Machine Dry-Lock Run

Machine Dry-Lock Run enables the Control to search the program for Formatting and Syntax errors. The programmer/operator can switch On the Machine Lock and Dry-Run switch after all the program-related information has been entered (Program Zero, Tool Offsets, and so on). The program will move quickly through the machining blocks if the Feedrate Overrides are set at their highest switch positions.

The Machine Dry-Lock Run Verification cycle has the following capabilities: The cycle is activated; the Control quickly scans the program for syntax mistakes. During the program's execution, the spindle comes on, the tools change, and the Control simulates actual running of the program. However, the Axes (X, Y, Z , and so on) will not move. The cycle enables the programmer/operator to be assured that the Control can execute the program. After confirming that no Axis motion is occurring (machine lock is really on), the programmer/operator can rest easy until one of two things happens. Either the Control will generate an alarm or it will complete the program without generating an alarm. If the Control finds a syntax mistake in the program and generates an alarm, the operator must diagnose the alarm, fix the problem, and execute the program again. Editing must be repeated until the entire program can be executed without generating alarms.

Upon completion of the entire program (without generating an alarm), confirmation that the Control can accept the program has been established. Motion mistakes within the program could still exist, but the program can be executed from the beginning to end without generating an alarm after completing this sequence.

Free-Flowing Dry Run

Once the Machine-Lock Dry-Run cycle is satisfactorily completed, the programmer/operator is ready to execute the program in full Axis motion. There could still be mistakes in the program. Therefore, the purpose of performing a Free-Flowing Dry Run is to screen for motion problems. The workholding setup should be finalized with no workpiece in the machining position.

To execute the Free-Flowing Dry Run, switch Off the Machine Lock switch, turn down the Dry-Run motion rate switch (usually, either Feedrate Override or Jog feedrate) to its lowest position, and set the rapid override switch to its slowest motion rate. The cycle is then activated. The programmer/operator must be ready to press the Feed Hold button. Feed Hold will be the Emergency Stop button in case anything seems wrong and the cycle needs to be stopped. With the Dry-Run motion-controlling switch set to its lowest position, the Axes will move along very slowly. The programmer/operator can increase the setting of this switch by rotating it clockwise; the axes will then move at a faster rate.

The Dry-Run motion rate can be turned down as each tool comes close to the workholding device. If the programmer/operator is concerned about a specific workpiece feature, the Feed Hold button can be pressed to temporarily stop the cycle. The Cycle Start button can be pressed for the machine to move again. If the cycle must be canceled because of a motion mistake in the program, after pressing Feed Hold, the Emergency Stop or Reset Key can be pressed. The machine can be sent back to its Machine Zero or Reference Point.

The Free-Flowing Dry Run can cause the machine to go into an alarm state even though a Machine-Lock Dry Run has been successfully completed. Axis overtravels and problems related to offsets and other forms of compensation are some of the things that can generate alarms during a Free-Flowing Dry Run that are not observed during a Machine-Lock Dry Run.

Execution of an Air-Cutting Cycle

The programmer/operator should always execute a cycle one more times with the Dry Run switch turned Off and without a workpiece in position. This enables the programmer/operator to scan for something that could not be seen during a Free-Flowing Dry Run. The Free-Flowing Dry Run enables the programmer/operator to monitor all motion rates with the Dry Run motion rate switch. If the Dry Run is switched On, the user will not be able to differentiate between rapid motions and cutting motions. All motions appear the same from the programmer/operator's standpoint. The mistake-revealing Air-Cutting cycle is most effective in observing the machine Axes traveling through full program execution, following all commands at their full movements and feedrates. This capability allows confirmation that rapid feedrates occur when they should and machining feedrates are set approximately at the correct motion rates.

For extremely long cycles, the programmer/operator can toggle the Dry-Run switch On and Off. Once the current command is determined to be a cutting command, instead of enduring the entire time period, the Dry-Run switch can be activated to enable the rest of the command to be completed quickly. After completion, Dry Run can be switched Off. Using this method allows advancement through a lengthy program quickly, confirming the cutting commands are where they were intended.

Running the First Workpiece

Every tool in a program executes at least one motion command that could be dangerous for the programmer/operator. Many CNC programmers rapid traverse all tools very near to the workpiece surface before machining. During verification procedures, caution must be taken with each tool's first approach to the workpiece surface. This is why Rapid Traverse should be turned down to a minimal feedrate so that motion mistakes can be prevented. Turn On Dry Run and Single Block during each tool's approach to the workpiece and during rapid motions to new machining surfaces. With Dry Run and Single Block On, the motion rate can be monitored during each tool's approach. As the tool nears the surface to be machined, the rate can be slowed. If Single Block is On, the programmer/operator is confident that all motions will stop at the end of every command. With the motion stopped, the clearance approach amount can be checked. The Dry-Run switch is turned Off and the Single Block is left On. At the end of each command, the motion stops and the programmer/operator presses the Cycle Start button and continues to the next command. If an upcoming command is a Rapid Traverse command to another surface-clearance position, the operator can switch On Dry Run to monitor the motion rate again. Every tool in the program should pass this test.

OPERATIONAL PROCEDURES

There is a fine balance between being as safety conscious as possible and producing as many high-quality parts as possible. A primary concern is always safety. Operator safety and machine tool safety are one and the same. Always run a well-organized, consistent routine of checking tools, tightening fixtures, tooling, and double checking where and whenever the thought arises.

There are also ways to prevent scrapping workpieces early in job lots. If the programmer/operator considers what each tool is going to be doing during its machining operation, Tool Offsets can be adjusted in a way that causes the tool to leave excess stock on the surface being machined. After machining with the trial Offset, the machined surface can be measured so precisely how much material left to be machined can be determined. The Offset can be adjusted accordingly, and the tool can be rerun. This time the tool machines exactly on size. This procedure can be repeated for every tool in the program to bring the first part within print dimensions.

First workpiece factors to consider are as follows:

☐ Consider what material the tool will be machining.
☐ Machine the workpiece with one tool at a time.
☐ Adjust the Tool Offsets in the direction of leaving excess stock.
☐ Measure what each tool has machined.
☐ Adjust the Offsets to machine to dimensional requirements.
☐ Rerun the tool.
☐ Always make one tool machine to size before going on to the next tool.

OPTIMIZING and FULL PRODUCTION

After the inspection department is satisfied with the dimensional requirements of the first workpiece, and the programmer/operator has been given the "go-ahead nod" for full production, it may be wise to keep the machine from rapid-traverse movement for the first few workpieces, using rapid override until the user is comfortable with the cycle. If many workpieces are in the job lot, it is worthwhile to closely monitor the first few parts run. Many times there are areas of the program that can be improved to minimize cycle time. Also, cutting conditions (feeds and speeds) can be adjusted to improve cycle time or lengthen tool life. Remember, however, that if major revisions are edited into the program during the optimizing process, program verification is recommended again.

CNC machines are, out of necessity, very powerful. To cut tough materials, machine tools in general have the power to cut themselves into pieces. Despite the great amount of work verification procedures seem to involve, scrapping expensive parts, rebuilding fixturing, and crashing expensive CNC equipment are not attractive alternatives. It is a fact of life in the CNC world that program verification is a requirement.

CHAPTER 12

CNC FORMS AND WORKSHEETS

This up-to-date, compact reference *Handbook* is an invaluable, comprehensive guide for working professionals, programmers, engineers, operators, and management personnel who use CNC machine tools. This text has been prepared so that it can be readily referenced when planning, writing, and entering data in programs, or operating the machining centers themselves.

CNC Programming Forms and Operational Sequence Sheets have been prepared as worksheets that can be photocopied from the text for use and distribution to in-house CNC users. These Programming Forms have been developed and revised over the years. The Operational Sequence checklists have been designed to lead the user through important machine sequences, complete with boxes to check after steps are completed.

ABSOLUTE DIMENSION SHEETS

Absolute Dimension Sheets are perhaps the most useful of all CNC Worksheets. They are the very first sheets made up using dimensions gleaned directly from the working blueprints. All dimensional rotations originate from a single Datum Zero or Origin for each Axis of machine travel. Every computational effort should be made to dimension each surface from a single Origin.

After a rough outline or profile of a single face of a workpiece is sketched, care should be taken to include every possible surface machinable from that face. On or close to the surface outline, write in the Absolute Dimension to that surface from the Datum Zero in that specific Axis direction of movement. In turn, dimension all the surface outlines from the outer Axis in the same view.

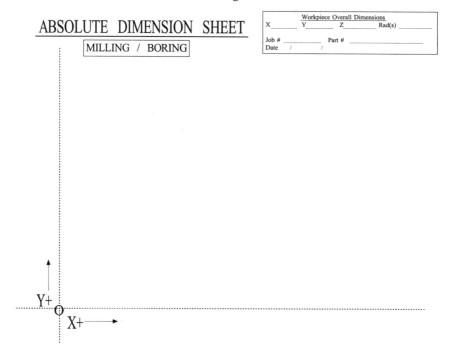

Figure 12.1 *Absolute Dimension Sheet: Milling/Boring*

One Absolute Dimension Sheet should be made up for each complete work-piece face that is to be machined. In the Legend Box on each sheet, the overall dimensions of the workpiece, Job #, Part #, and the Date that the Absolute Dimension Sheet was written are recorded for easy file management. Some newer CAD/CAM software programs contain similar hard copies that can be printed for filing along with other worksheets.

Sequential Tool-Radius Sheets, Program Sheets, and CNC Inspection Sheets subsequently use the dimensions that originate from the Absolute Dimension Sheets. It is very important to calculate and note all dimensions very carefully when compiling Absolute Dimensions. Once they are complete and correct, the time invested will be beneficially reflected right through workpiece inspection stages.

The Absolute Dimension Sheet for Milling and Boring has a single Datum in the lower left-hand corner. All dimensions computed from this Origin, therefore, will be in the (+) positive directions of machine movement. See Figure 12.1.

The Absolute Dimension Sheet for Turning and Grinding has unnamed axes labeled with the cross-axis originating at the workpiece Center Line. The longitudinal Axis originates on the left near the Turning/Grinding spindle. See Figure 12.2.

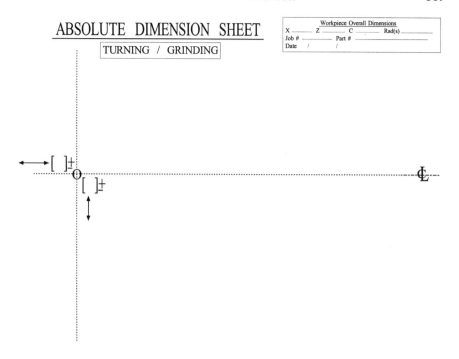

Figure 12.2 *Absolute Dimension Sheet: Turning/Grinding*

OPERATIONAL SEQUENCE SHEET

The Operational Sequence Sheet is a strategic planning guide to complete after the initial Absolute Dimension Sheets are finished. The individual operations labeled by their machining sequence are numbered in the required order. After Absolute Dimensions are calculated, an extensive view of surface depths, spans, and relationships clearly unfolds. Close-tolerance dimensions are noted and labeled; excessive stock removal in certain areas can be recognized.

Roughing sequences can be planned over the entire workpiece before any finishing operations are performed, if that requirement is crucial. All milling could be completed on all surfaces before any hole operations are started. All turning could be finished before critical grooving is dimensioned from finished diameters.

On the Operational Sequence Sheets, ample room is provided after the operation name and sequence # to note the tooling used, machines, feeds, speeds, cutting lubricant, and so on. Operational data specific to material finishing are noted across the bottom of the sheets: Stress Relief, Heat Treatment, Deburring, and Finishing. In the Legend Box, notations are made for file management purposes: Job #, Part #, Overall Dimensions, Date, and so on. See Figures 12.3 and 12.4.

OPERATIONAL SEQUENCE SHEET				Workpiece Overall Dimensions
			X _____ Z_____ C _____ Rad(s) _____	
TURNING / GRINDING			Job # _____ Part # _____	
			Date / /	

Phase	Phase	Phase	Phase	Notes
1				
2				
3				
4				
5				
6				
7				
8				
9				
10				
11				
12				
13				
14				
15				
16				
footnotes				
STRESS RELIEF		DEBURRING		
HEAT TREATMENT		FINISHING		

Figure 12.3 *Operational Sequence Sheet: Turning/Grinding*

TOOL-RADIUS SHEETS

Tool-Radius Sheets are used to plot out detailed and complex areas of workpiece geometry. The center of each sheet is divided by Axis quadrant lines.

The quadrant lines do not have to represent the Datum Zeros or Origins in this case. They may be designated as Arc Center Lines or Center-Lines of workpiece-feature profiles. Designate them as each geometry warrants.

The Axis labels for Tool-Radius Sheets are left blank to fit any profile configuration from any Axis orientation. For Turning and Grinding, the Center Lines may be chosen as an Axis designation. For Milling and Boring, the Center Lines could represent Part Zero or be assigned a new dimension coordinate.

Dimensions can be entered directly onto the Tool-Radius Sheets from the Absolute Dimension Sheets for surfaces and geometry features involved in this particular area being plotted. In the Legend Box on each sheet, the workpiece

OPERATIONAL SEQUENCE SHEET

MILLING / BORING

Workpiece Overall Dimensions
X_____ Y_____ Z _____ Rad(s) _____

Job # _____ Part # _____
Date / /

Phase	Phase	Phase	Phase	Notes
1				
2				
3				
4				
5				
6				
7				
8				
9				
10				
11				
12				
13				
14				
15				
16				

footnotes

STRESS RELIEF	DEBURRING
HEAT TREATMENT	FINISHING

Figure 12.4 *Operational Sequence Sheet: Milling/Boring*

Overall Dimensions, Tool Radii, Job #, Part #, and entry Date are typically entered for file management purposes. See Figures 12.5 and 12.6.

PROGRAM SHEETS

After all dimensions of a workpiece are calculated and plotted on Absolute Dimension Sheets and Tool-Radius Sheets, and all operations are listed on the Operational Sequence Sheets, the Program can be written on Program Sheets. Program Sheets contain the actual program data the CNC machine uses to command Axis movement and execute the operations intended. See Figures 12.7 and 12.8.

Block #'s are entered; the numbering sequence can follow the basic numerical

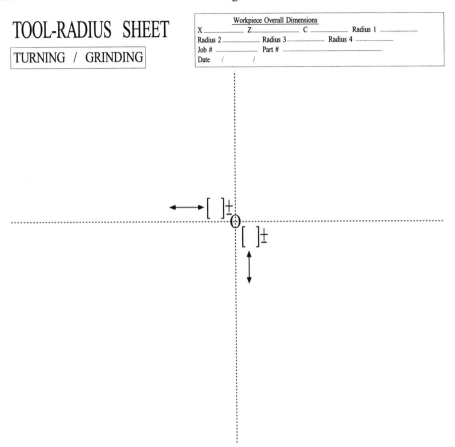

Figure 12.5   *Tool-Radius Sheet: Turning/Grinding*

pattern, 1, 2, 3, and so on, or be entered in the space provided as individual
Controls require, 001, 002, 003, and so on. Block Insertion can be added, 6.1,
6.2, 6.3, and so on, if desired.

   The next data column contains the Operation the Control is to execute, is to
continue, or is to end. Drill, Mill, Tap, Turn, Face, Bore, Arc CW, Arc End Point,
and so on, and Subroutines can be commanded at this data location. Starting
or Ending Subroutines or sequences of Subroutines can be nested within each
other. Sequential Blocks of this type could contain the required subroutine data
to execute hundreds or thousands of machine movements while the program
functions wholly within these same blocks.

   The next three or four columns of data contain the actual Axis coordinates
to which incremental units the machine is to move. A sign is required in most
Controls only when the movement is in a (–) negative direction. Decimal places

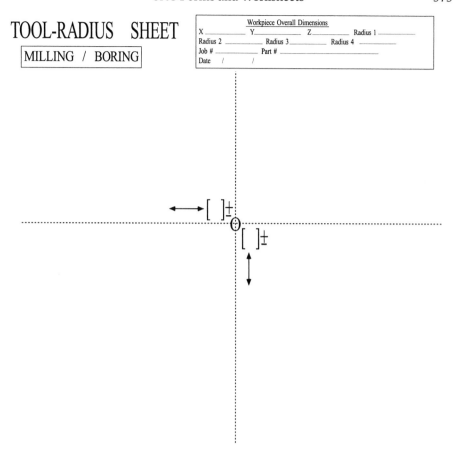

TOOL-RADIUS SHEET

MILLING / BORING

Workpiece Overall Dimensions

X _____ Y_____ Z_____ Radius 1 _____
Radius 2 _____ Radius 3_____ Radius 4 _____
Job # _____ Part # _____
Date   /   /

Figure 12.6 *Tool-Radius Sheet: Milling/Boring*

are contextual to individual Controls, and resolutions exist to five or six places on ultraprecision Axis-motion designs.

Feedrates are entered in the next data column, typically, in IPM, mm/min., IPR measurements. These rates are related to the particular Block in which they are entered. Normally, they carry over to the next Block unless a new value is entered. Accuracy to .01 of a Feedrate unit is available on most Controls.

The next column lists the Tool # the Control "thinks" is to be used for the operation. This data has several implications to the Control's function during the execution of each Block. The Tool # references directly to the Control's Tool Library in computer memory. It "knows" the Tool's Diameter, Length, RPM, Geometry, and Calibration Level.

The Tool # is referenced during Tool Compensation to keep the cutting edge away from a dimension a set distance corresponding to the Tool Radius, Ge-

	Block #	OPER	X Axis	Z Axis	C Axis	Alt Axis	Fd Rate	Tool #	Notes
1									
2									
3									
4									
5									
6									
7									
8									
9									
10									
11									
12									
13									
14									
15									
16									

PROGRAM SHEET

TURNING / GRINDING

Workpiece Overall Dimensions
X———— Z———— C———— Rad(s) ————
Job # ———— Part # ————
Date / /

footnotes

STRESS RELIEF   DEBURRING

HEAT TREATMENT   FINISHING

Figure 12.7 *Program Sheet: Turning/Grinding*

ometry, and so on. Tool Compensation keeps the tool's length a "known" distance from machine environmental interference and prevents crashes during rapid traverse and other Axis movements. Tool #'s search and reference Tool-Calibration levels, which tell the tool where to cut in relation to Part Zero and Machine Zero.

Tool #'s in the data reference cause the computer to read ahead or "look ahead" at dimensional data, making sure the Tool's geometry "fit" into intended workpiece profiles.

Tool #'s in the data column advance tool changers in a readiness state for tool carousel sequencing, tool station sensing, and tool sensing executions on more advanced Controls.

The Notes column farthest to the right of a Program Sheet provides for Block

PROGRAM SHEET	Workpiece Overall Dimensions
MILLING / BORING	X_____ Y_____ Z_____ Rad(s) _____
	Job # _____ Part # _____
	Date / /

Block #	OPER	X Axis	Y Axis	Z Axis	Radius	Z Up	Z Down	Fd Rate	Tool #	Notes
1										
2										
3										
4										
5										
6										
7										
8										
9										
10										
11										
12										
13										
14										
15										
16										

footnotes

| STRESS RELIEF | DEBURRING |
| HEAT TREATMENT | FINISHING |

Figure 12.8 *Program Sheet: Milling/Boring*

or operation notes particular to this specific program area, tooling detail, Part Zero locations, and so on.

The Legend Box provides a place for workpiece Overall Dimensions, Job #, Part #, Date of the Program Sheet's compilation, and Programmer's Signature to be entered.

The lower Footnotes Boxes detail specific workpiece data and status of in-process procedures such as Stress Relief, Heat Treatment, Deburring, and Finishing.

TOOL-OFFSET SHEETS

The Offset Sheets are essential to Program File Management. Listed are all the parameters specific to individual Tools, categorized by Tool #, Sizes, Offset

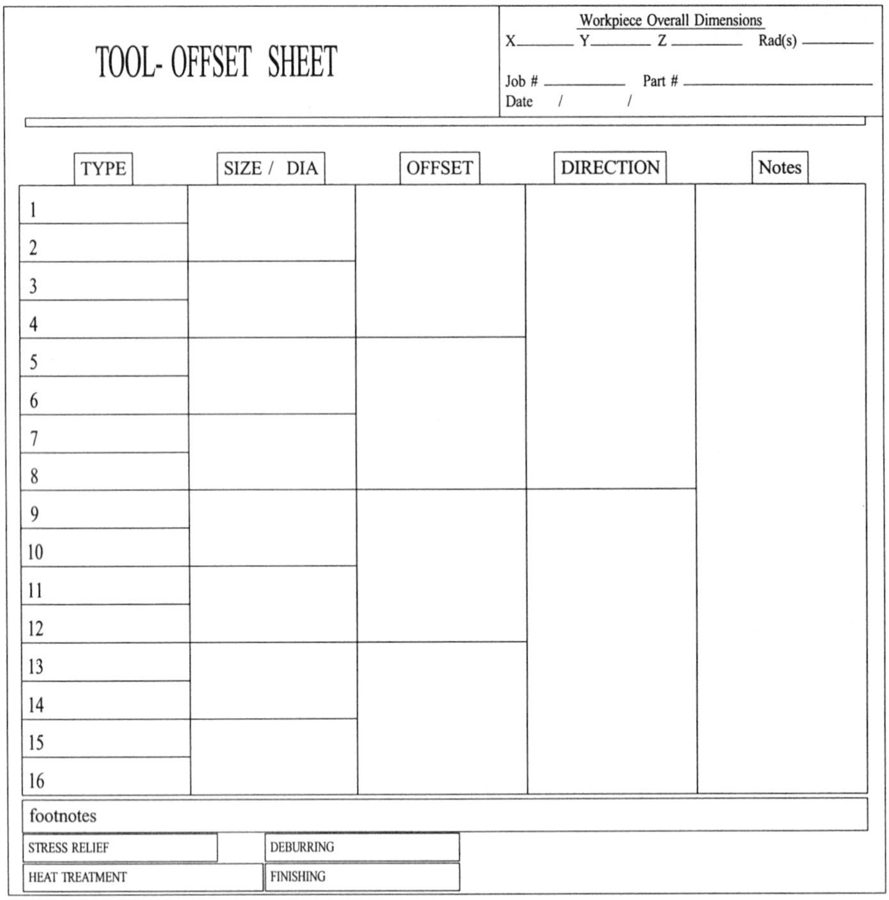

TOOL- OFFSET SHEET	Workpiece Overall Dimensions
	X_____ Y_____ Z _____ Rad(s) _____
	Job # _____ Part # _____
	Date / /

	TYPE	SIZE / DIA	OFFSET	DIRECTION	Notes
1					
2					
3					
4					
5					
6					
7					
8					
9					
10					
11					
12					
13					
14					
15					
16					

footnotes	
STRESS RELIEF	DEBURRING
HEAT TREATMENT	FINISHING

Figure 12.9 *Tool-Offset Sheet*

Measurements, Direction of Offset, and Notes concerning the Offsets. See Figure 12.9.

Tools may be numbered by the numeric sequence they are used in the Program Blocks. They also may be numbered by the Tool Station, Magazine, or Carousel slots in Automatic Tool Changers. Tool #'s can be designated more than once for the same tool, in effect calibrating a set of different Offsets for the same tool.

Size measurements can be entered as Diameters, Radii, and Length. Normally, these values are recorded in the Control's memory using the Soft Keys. Diameters and Radii are measured to four-place decimal values. Diameters and Radii parameters are also crucial entries and tie in directly with Cutter Compensation. Compensation uses these Diameter/Radius values for every calculated geometry for profiles, contours, or any toolpath programmed.

Trigonometric formulas are completed in the Control's computer using the Diameter/Radius values. By changing the value, the machine Axes compensate positively or negatively (roughing and finishing).

The Offset column designates the actual measurement to which the tool is calibrated from Datum Zero. By entering an Offset value, the Tool Length, reach, or depth will correspond accordingly. Critical dimensions can be precisely adjusted in very precision measurements by manipulating this electronic fine-tuning value.

Direction of Offset should be noted by machine directional language along with axis notation (i.e., Z+). Along with the sign notation, ample space is provided to sketch surface outlines to help illustrate calibration directions.

Legend Box, Notes Column, and Footnotes areas are provided to allow notation of all pertinent material concerning Tool Offsets.

FIXTURE-OFFSET SHEETS

Fixture Offset Sheets are essential in Program File Management to provide references to Offsets for individual or groups of Machining Fixtures related to the workpiece. See Figure 12.10.

A Fixture # Column lists tooling by simple numerical order, 1, 2, 3, and so on, or by Fixture Serial #'s in the space provided. Typically, a numbering pattern is adhered to specific to Control type. Some manufacturers require the numbering pattern to begin in the lower left-hand corner of a milling center table, for example, continuing in a clockwise direction. Turning and Grinding machines may record chucks by #, Collet systems by another Offset #. Fixtures with consistent locations by means of alignment keys and pins can be numbered and located effectively using this reference sheet.

Axis notations designate the actual location of the fixture in each individual axis direction. Most Controls define locations to four or five decimal places.

A Notation Grid is provided at the right along with the Center Lines and blank Axis labels. When specific fixture sketches are required to show the precise fixture numbering scheme, rotation, orientation, and order of fixtures, the grid enables machine Axes to be sketched and relative fixture locations plotted.

Legend Box, Footnotes area, and workpiece status data are recorded in their respective data boxes on each Fixture-Offset Sheet.

SETUP SHEETS

A Fixture # column lists tooling by simple numerical order, 1, 2, 3, and so on, or by Fixture Serial #'s in the space provided. Typically, a numbering pattern is specific to Control type. Some manufacturers require the numbering pattern to begin in the lower left-hand corner of a milling center table, for example, continuing in a clockwise direction. Turning and Grinding machines may record

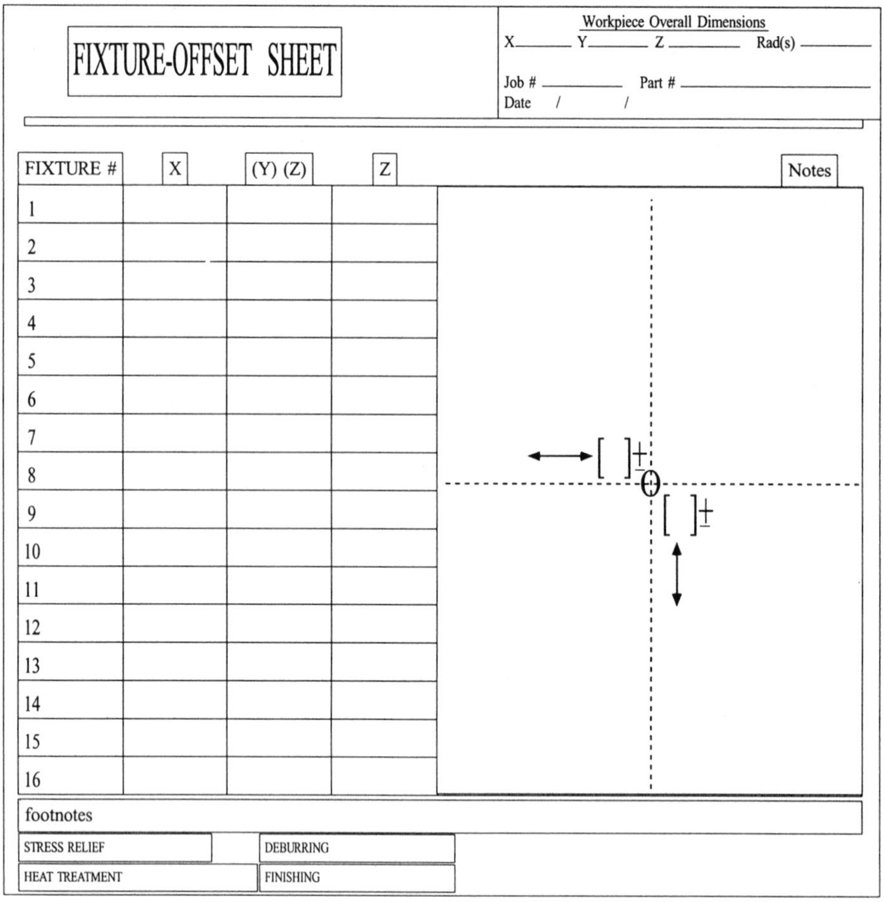

FIXTURE-OFFSET SHEET

Workpiece Overall Dimensions

X____ Y____ Z____ Rad(s) ____

Job # ____ Part # ____

Date / /

FIXTURE #	X	(Y) (Z)	Z
1			
2			
3			
4			
5			
6			
7			
8			
9			
10			
11			
12			
13			
14			
15			
16			

Notes

footnotes

STRESS RELIEF	DEBURRING
HEAT TREATMENT	FINISHING

Figure 12.10 *Fixture-Offset Sheet*

chucks by #, Collet systems by another Offset #. Fixtures having consistent locations by means of alignment keys and pins can be numbered and located effectively using this reference sheet.

Gage #'s are recorded to accompany setups and fixture #'s. Gages may be referenced from inspection department requirements to correspond with specific setup fixture spacings, alignments, and squareness specifications. Precision gages can be serialized to correlate with Fixture #'s on Fixture-Offset Sheets.

Location #'s are noted in their respective columns to designate where specific fixtures are located within the machining environment. Modular tooling can be used effectively by recording fixed fixture-setup locations for alignment pin holes and keyways. Combinations of Fixture #'s can be recorded for the same fixture moved to different locations.

A Notation Grid is provided at the right along with the Center Lines and

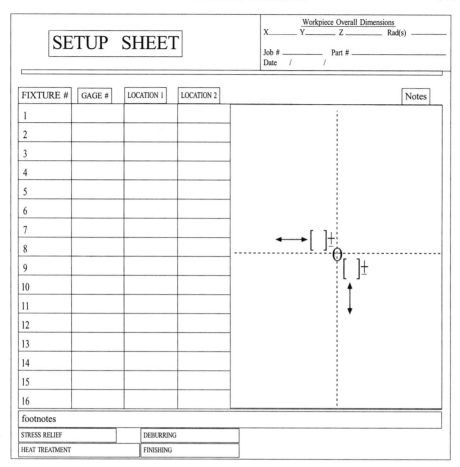

Figure 12.11 *Setup Sheet*

blank Axis labels. When specific fixture sketches are required to show the precise fixture numbering scheme, rotation, orientation and order of fixtures, the grid enables machine Axes to be sketched and relative fixture locations plotted.

Legend Box, Footnotes area, and workpiece status data are individually recorded in their respective data boxes on each Fixture-Offset Sheet. See Figure 12.11.

ADVANCED CNC CONTROL FEATURES

Format Managers

Format Managers allow the development of CNC Programs in virtually any CNC format using a variety of methods. Simple, on-screen, fill-in-the-blank forms are used to develop linear, circular, and helical motions. Other functions are selected and programmed using simple pull-down menus. Program code can be inserted using a text statement and edited using a single line-tab editor. The entire program is developed or edited using the Format Manager's menu-driven word processor, including Block Move, Copy, Find and Replace, and so on. These methods are combined to provide the most convenient and powerful CNC Format development and editing system ever.

English-Language Translation

With a single key stroke, the CNC Program can be changed from "M" and "G" codes to a simple English-language translation. Even the most experienced CNC Programmers find this feature very helpful to check and verify new programs. Typing and input errors are found almost instantly. The entire system format toggles to the English translation with a single switch.

Test Running CNC Program Codes

It is no longer necessary to go into the machining center memory, interrupting production to load programs to find simple errors. Instead, the Format Manager is configured for the machine (both mechanical and program format) and the new program test runs can be done in the programming office. In addition to testing the validity of the data, the program can be run in real time, providing accurate cycle times in advance.

Full Graphical Interface of the Program

With a simple key stroke, a full three-Axis representation of the program relative to the operating limits of the machine is viewable on CRT. The Center Line of the cutter is displayed in one color and the resulting part in another color based on the tooling radius to be used. Errors are found quickly and easily with full zoom and pan capabilities, allowing detailed examination of the machining environment.

Full-Program Format Conversion

The Format Feature Manager provides a simple positive way to convert a CNC Program from one data format to another. Programs are easily moved from one machine to another. It is also possible to run the program cycle in real time and in several formats to test which machine is best from a variety of CNC machines.